Black Prison Movements USA

The NOBO Journal of AfricanAmerican Dialogue

Volume II Number I
ISSN: 1056-683X

Africa World Press, Inc.
P. O. Box 1892
Trenton, New Jersey 08607

Africa World Press, Inc.
P.O. Box 1892
Trenton, New Jersey 08607

First Printing 1995

Cover and Book design by Lisa Babb

ISSN: 1056-683X

ISBN: 0-86543-494-8 Cloth
0-86543-495-6 Paper

We would like to thank Alphonso Pinckney, Jill Nelson, Glenn Thompson and Diane Gaines for their persistence, critical support and ideas.

We would also like to thank Brother Sam Anderson Sr. for his generous financial contribution.

The Black Pledge of Allegiance

I pledge allegiance to my people - the Black Race,
the Original Man and Woman of the Earth,
and Founders of Civilization -
and to the Struggle which I must fight to help bring
my beloved brothers and sisters
to total and uncompromising freedom;
and I pledge to study and discipline myself,
mentally and physically, so that I may grow into a soldier for justice
because my people need strong and intelligent warriors;
and I pledge to live
my life standing tall, for a person on his knees is not respected;
and if I am challenged, I must say I will not surrender my position
nor my dignity
but instead endure until victory is won.

Editorial Staff

Senior Editors	
Contemporary Issues	***Muntu Matsimela***
Cultural Issues	***S. E. Anderson***
	Joel Washington
Managing Editor	***Aton Archer***
Graphic Designer	***Lisa M. Babb***
Art Consultant	***Ademola Olugebefola***
Photography Editors	***Chris Burns***
	Eric Prideaux
Womens' Issues Editors	***Safiya Bandele***
	Joyce C. Duncan
National Editor	***Segundo Modibo***
Copy Editors	***S. V. Sparks***
Poetry Editor	***Tony Medina***
Business Manager	***Sandra Rivers***
Senior Editorial Assistants	***Walter Knox***
	Daaiya Samusi

Table of Contents

We're back!!
and we're Black!!

It has been nearly three years since some of you have seen NOBO. During that time, we have struggled to build a secure base of operation for the Network Of Black Organizers and its journal: NOBO. But most of you are holding this journal for the first time. We welcome you to the NOBO Family dedicated to the liberation of peoples of African descent everywhere... especially here in the United States.

We have expanded the Editorial Collective and physically transformed the journal from magazine styled to a "bookazine" format. The Editorial Collective reflects our legacy of activism and critical insight that has been the cornerstone of progressive Africanamerican journalistic and literary tradition. We have young sisters & brothers working with veteran activists and writers bringing new insights and energy to our liberation struggle. The Editorial Collective recognizes the need to address the reality that we have no journal for the perspective of independent progressive Black political analysis and cultural critique. We saw that in the United States we had no journal that opens its pages for genuine Black *progressive* dialogue about our liberation movement and also be a forum for the tremendous wealth and beauty of our cultural creativity. We also saw that we had no journal that reflected that *international* nature of our struggle. International not only because we are historically and culturally linked to Africa and the rest of the Diaspora, but also because of the international nature of our oppressor's political economy: capitalism and imperialism.

Our reconstructed Editorial Collective now includes a Women's Editorial staff. This was a political decision based on the real needs to struggle with male chauvinism among our brothers and its acceptance among our sisters as well as looking at health, economic, political , spiritual and cultural issues that sisters shape or are affected. NOBO also recognizes and accepts the historical reality that sisters often play a leading role in our struggles for Human and Civil Rights. In fact, we wish to have an ongoing dialog in every issue that will help bring Brothers & Sisters closer together as equals in our fight for liberation.

After a lot of discussions with various African & Africanamerican editors and publishers– but especially with Brother Glen Thompson of Writers & Readers– we decided to redesign the journal into a *bookazine*.

Distribution of a magazine format periodical is extremely costly: the distributor usually asks for 70% of the price! And then, because of racism, we get displayed as an afterthought. In addition to this, as a quarterly we would only have a 30 to 45 day shelf life. The book-look will give us a wider distribution and longer shelf life... and it will make it easier for you to carry!

We were able to secure our desktop publishing system through a generous *loan* from one of our senior brothers (see acknowledgements). Hence, we have the capabilities of accepting your written works or artworks on any disc you send us. We encourage you to send us a disc. But for those who can't, clean copy on white paper, double-spaced (except, of course, poetry) or artwork either on paper or a color photo will do fine. All photo-essays will be in black and white.

It is most fortunate that we are being published and distributed by one of the most prestigious Black publishers– **Africa World Press**. This means that you will find us in all major Africanamerican bookstores, bookstores in the Diaspora, and many major bookstores, universities and colleges throughout the world.

Sisters and Brothers, we are looking to your subscriptions (see the subscription form on last page) *and* submission of articles summing up your local struggles; political, economic, cultural, spiritual, historical, psychological analyses are also welcomed. We are looking forward to your poetry, short stories, works-in-progress, youthworks, review essays of important books, plays, movies, music, videos, software and TV programs.

NOBO will have a thematic approach to each issue. However, this does not mean that you must submit articles or artwork addressing the theme. We will feature full color works by Black Artists on the cover of each issue. They will represent some of the more powerful works of creativity-for-struggle that one can find. The artists will be comprised of young progressive Brothers & Sisters and veteran artists... living or deceased.

The Editorial Collective of NOBO is committed to presenting you with a written forum for dialog around all aspects of our struggles to end oppression and exploitation. We are interested in presenting uncompromising works which inspire the reader to either engage or intensify their Freedom work.

One final point. We are looking for advertisements. We are accepting ads reflecting positive Black cultural expressions that help us cope and struggle politically, culturally, economically and spiritually. Send all ads to our Marketing Department at 402 W. 145th St. Harlem, NY 10031. Write to us for ad rates.

Brothers & Sisters, you will look forward to receiving our quarterly and sharing it with your family and friends. For 1994 and 1995 we have the following themes to dialog around:

The Politics of Blacks In Prison
Malcolm X and Black Activists Today
On Being Po'– Black Political Economy Today
Which Way Forward For The Black Liberation Movement?
Sistafire! Black Women in Struggle
Creating Black Culture for Liberation
Struggle to Learn to Learn to Struggle: **Black Youth & Education**
The Sickness of Black Health: Rx for Change

Members of the Editorial Collective Working Group are available for lectures, literary presentations, forums, classroom discussions, community meetings and consultations on a wide range of topics within the Black Liberation Movement nationally and internationally.

NOBO's Bird

Folk often ask us why we have the bird as our logo. Well, we're following a very long African tradition that predates even (Egyptian) civilization which sees the bird as symbolizing the concepts of Freedom, Wisdom, Ancestors... Cunning Intelligence. When we look at any of the hundreds of African societies, past and present, on the Continent or in the Diaspora we see a bird image representing at least one of these concepts. Just like the drum and its polyrythmic beats are an integral part of our societies, so is the bird. We see them in the fading tradition of how we decorate our graves and yards– now only sporadically found in the rural south. The "hawk" in its cunningness plays a serious role in esoterically delivering super cold weather when we least expect it or need it. The bird-symbol is more noticeable within the African religious and cultural forms found among our brothers & sisters in the African Diaspora of the Caribbean and the Americas, the areas which had direct retention from the Motherland.

In essence, NOBOjournal of Africanamerican Dialogue aspires to embody the spirit of our *fighting* ancestors, our revolutionary wisdom linked to our esteemed cunning intelligence in our battle for freedom. Our bird-symbol, our *Nonyana* (Lesotho), *Nsusu Mpembe* (Congo), *Bennu* (ancient Egypt) is thus a traditional spiritual and fighting symbol guiding us to new levels of victory.

-Sam Anderson

NOBO EDITORIAL

ON PRISONS

African Americans and other people concerned with freedom and justice in this country have long asked how can the U.S. criminal justice system truly represent a system of principle and justice for those who have become victims of criminal acts when it has never rendered justice to the millions of Africans and their descendants for committing against them the most horrendous crime in modern human history: the kidnapping, enslavement, murder and rape of millions, torture, maiming, dehumanization and the systematic destruction of our history, culture, languages, religions and family structure? For the captive African the entire society was a prison where any attempt at escape or rebellion against this system meant severe punishment... often a death sentence. It was the fear whites had of rebellion and retribution against this inhuman system of organized applied terror and violence which became their central motivation for the legislation of repressive and dehumanizing slave laws as well as the motive for those racist and repressive laws legislated after slavery was abolished.

Although context has changed from an antebellum slave system and post-slavery apartheid, exploitation, dehumanization, repression, rebellion and punishment are still fundamental features of the U.S. criminal justice system within the current desperate reality of the advanced capitalist society. The U.S. through its manipulation and control of what is taught about its history has promoted the concept that there is no relationship between its legacy of injustice and the state sanctioned terror of African people and the present society. Upon examination it can be shown that there is an unbroken chain of repression that directly links past and present conditions.

Given U.S. society has committed countless atrocities and violent acts on a captive people where laws were legislated and where its courts were used to justify and maintain a system of unfettered felonious conduct for profit, how can it establish a system of "equal justice" and "due process" against the descendants of these same peoples without first admitting their crime, making amends and paying reparations? Furthermore, how can it justify non-recognition of those who have fought against this criminal condition and were subsequently incarcerated for acts of rebellion and who were or have become political prisoners and prisoners of war?

Clearly upon any cursory analysis of the history of crime and violence committed by U.S. local, state and federal governments throughout the history of this country against people of African descent, Native americans, Asians, Caribbean and Central american peoples, you would have to conclude that the definition of what constitutes a crime is determined by who is in control and who has the Power to enforce their definition of what a crime is. This is not to say that some crimes are not universal notions and concepts. However, can any victim truly receive justice when that victim does not possess the power to enforce that justice or if those institutions established for that purpose are in control of the victimizer?

It is no wonder that this country's ruling class even in the face of its criminal and violent history has never had any serious doubt that its true nature would be exposed to all the world and that they would be forced to pay for their crimes. The perpetrators of these historical crimes and atrocities are the same people who have always been in power and control of this society and remain those who define what constitutes a crime.

We have witnessed throughout the world that the only time jails are emptied and new crimes are defined with perpetrators of these crimes held accountable, tried and punished, is when there is social transformation... fundamental change, a power shift from one force to another. Whether this change in the balance of power is backward or forward, progressive or reactionary, will determine what sector or class of people will be regarded as the new victims and the new criminals.

The struggle for reparations for the crimes committed against people of African descent is inextricably linked to and part of the struggle for power in this society. Only when there is a fundamental shift in the balance of power will there be success in our efforts to receive justice for these crimes. Just as the struggle for reparations and the struggle for power in this society are linked, social and political consciousness is also a function of the different and varying power relations. Indeed history has taught us that only upon the acquisition of power by a progressive or revolutionary movement will the prospects for those held unjustly in prisons change. For in a progressive movement the very process of building a power base must by definition entail moving the masses from one politically conscious state to another more advanced state. Obtaining specific clarity on the true nature of U.S. society and its criminal history, along with attaining the power to do something about it, is the only way people who have been unjustly imprisoned will be set free.

Our goal in this issue of NOBO is to begin to allow this journal to be utilized as a vehicle to give more exposure on the utter hypocrisy of this country's criminal justice system, the prison system in general, and the reality of political prisoners, prisoners of war and prisoners of conscience in the U.S. We have included some of the sharpest political perspectives and voices from behind prison walls who can help move our dialogue for liberation forward. As we in the Network of Black Organizers advance our efforts to create a forum on what must be done to resolve the fundamental contradictions within U.S. society and the world, we believe the dialogue and viewpoints on prisons, prisoners, crime and punishment will be a crucial contribution to the Black Liberation Movement's theory and practice.

-Muntu Matsimela

A Brief History of the New Afrikan Prison Struggle

Illustration by Eli Kince

Preface: Sundiata's Freedom Is Your Freedom
By the Sundiata Acoli Freedom Campaign
P.O. Box 5538, Manhattanville Station, Harlem, N.Y. 10027

Sundiata Acoli, the author of this article, is one of the longest held political prisoners in the United States. He is an extraordinary human being who, despite almost two decades of brutal and dehumanizing treatment at the hands of the U.S. government, remains firmly committed to the liberation of Black people in the United States. Although Sundiata is special, he is at the same time also representative of the many other Black people the United States has imprisoned for fighting for the liberation of their people. Indeed, Sundiata is one of the many Black political prisoners the U.S. has tried to bury inside its prisons; people who fought and continue to fight to transform this country and who have been made to pay a heavy price.

As the 1990s open, Sundiata Acoli is actually one of the longest held political prisoners in the *world*, having spent 18 years in prison. For eight months he endured 24 hours a day in a specially created cell in a New Jersey prison which, according to the Society for the Prevention of Cruelty to Animals, is smaller than the space requirements for a german shepherd dog. Sundiata also spent eight years locked down 23 hours a day in the worst prison in the United States, the United States Penitentiary at Marion. In fact, Sundiata, like so many other dissidents in the U.S., has been constantly brutalized in an effort to either destroy him or force him to renounce his politics. The efforts the U.S. has expended trying to destroy Sundiata is a testimony to his importance as a leader of the Black Liberation Movement.

In the last few years, we have seen the release of political prisoners in many parts of the world, from Nelson Mandela to Soviet dissidents. Yet here in the United States most people appear to be either unaware or unconcerned with our own Nelson Mandelas. We must change this situation if we ever hope to create a humane society.

The time is long past due to free Sundiata Acoli. But the only way this will happen is if there is enough of an outcry from people like you. We hope that you will commit some time and energy in this direction for two reasons. First, because the injustice of this 18-year imprisonment demands redress. And second, because his release will enable him to even more fully contribute to the struggle for the liberation of Black people.

Historical Background

Sundiata Acoli was born in 1937 in Vernon Texas, a small town below the Panhandle, where he grew up, went to Booker T. Washington High School, did agricultural work, hunted, fished, played sports, and did all the other things kids do while growing up. Upon graduation he went to Prairie View A & M College at Prairie View, Texas. He graduated in 1956 with a B.S. in Mathematics. After unsuccessfully looking for work in New York City, he took a job as a Mathematician/Computer Programmer for NASA at Edwards Air Force base in California. Three years later Sundiata returned to New York where he worked with computers for the next 13 years.

The 1960s were a time of intense ferment and change, particularly among Black people. The civil rights movement, and later the movement for Black liberation and power, instilled a sense of new possibilities and transformation, as Black people *en masse* challenged the power structure.

Sundiata was an integral part of that process. He first became politically active in the summer of 1964, doing voter registration work in Mississippi with the Student Nonviolent Coordinating Committee. He was not a member of SNCC or any other organization. He was simply a computer programmer in New York City who read about the murder of three civil rights workers. The article implied that the murders would deter volunteers from going south to register voters and it listed the Conference of Federated Organizations (COFO) in New York City as the coordinator of the volunteer project. Sundiata called COFO and volunteered. They said yes, if he paid his own fare to Mississippi. Sundiata bought an airline ticket and flew down. In the fall, he returned to his Mathematician/ Computer career but felt that:

I couldn't be proud of survival under the system in America, because too many of my brothers and sisters hadn't survived...I was aware of the subtle pressures working to force upon me the acceptance of white values, to give up more and more of being Black...I loved being Black–the Black mentality, mores, habits and associations. I looked around for an organization that was dedicated to alleviating the suffering of Black people.

In 1968, Sundiata joined the Black Panther Party (BPP) chapter in Harlem. The BPP was one of the most important political organizations of the 1960s. It particularly captured the imagination and energy of young Black people and mushroomed into chapters in many cities. The BPP supported community programs such as community control of schools, tenant control of slum housing, free breakfast programs for school children, free health care, day care, and legal clinics, political education classes for the community, and publication of a weekly national newspaper. Perhaps most notably, the BPP also fought against rampant police brutality in the Black community and was committed to armed self-defense.

Counter Intelligence Program

The Black Panther Party's enormous popularity was matched by an enormous hatred of the BPP by the United States government, which launched a major political/military offensive to destroy it. The ultimate goal was to destroy the Black Liberation Movement. To this end, the FBI along with local police departments, unleashed what was later revealed to be the Counter Intelligence Program, otherwise know as **COINTELPRO**. Panther headquarters around the country were militarily assaulted by local and federal police forces. False rumors and divisions were propagated that caused internal squabbling in the Black movement. **COINTELPRO** also left scores of Black revolutionaries dead and many others imprisoned. For example, in 1969 alone, 28 Panthers, including Fred Hampton and Mark Clark, were murdered and 749 others were arrested and/ or imprisoned.

Sundiata was one of those arrested. As he has written:

On April 2, 1969, I was arrested to stand trial in the Panther 21 case. Twenty-one of us were accused of conspiring to carry out a ridiculous plot to blow up a number of New York department stores and the New York Botanical Gardens. Although the legal process took two years and the trial lasted eight months – the longest criminal prosecution in New York history – the jurors took only 56 minutes to acquit all the defendants of every charge. Police agents appearing at the Panther 21 trial had also attended some group political education classes held at my apartment.

Although an ad hoc organization of my fellow workers named "Computer People for Peace" had raised and posted bail for me during the Panther 21 trial, and although several other defendants had been released on bail, the judge refused to let me out on bail. I had to do the entire two years on trial in jail until released on acquittal. I endured 2 years of political internment.

After Sundiata was released, he was constantly followed and harassed by the F.B.I. and local police forces. He finally decided that he could not be effective in the pursuit of Black Liberation under these conditions, and so he went underground. On May 2, 1973, Sundiata, Assata Shakur and Zayd Malik Shakur were ambushed by state troopers on the New Jersey Turnpike. The incident that ensued resulted in the murder of Zayd as well as the serious wounding of Assata. Trooper Werner Foerster was also killed. Sundiata managed somehow to elude arrest on that day. However, police launched a two-day massive search of the surrounding area: "When I was arrested, police immediately cut my pants off me so that I only wore shorts. Whooping and hollering, a gang of New Jersey state troopers dragged me through the woods, through water puddles, and hit me over the head with the barrel of their shot gun. They only cooled out somewhat when they noticed that all the commotion had caused a crowd to gather at the edge of the road, observing their actions."

Sundiata was tried in an environment of mass hysteria and convicted, although there was no credible evidence he killed the trooper or even been involved in the shooting. At sentencing the judge stated that Sundiata was an avowed revolutionary and sentenced him to life and to 30 more years, to be served consecutively!

Incarceration

Since his incarceration, Sundiata has been subjected to all the worst that U.S. prisons have to offer and that is saying a lot. During his pre-trial detention he was denied all medical care, was kept in isolation the entire time, was permitted *NO* visits from family, friends, or anyone except his attorney; and was not permitted to receive or read any newspapers. A light was kept on in his cell 24 hours per day, he was fed very sparse meals, and state troopers were allowed to come into the jail and threaten him.

After sentencing he was transferred to Trenton State Prison (TSP), in New Jersey, which was built before the civil war in 1835, and had been condemned for years as uninhabitable. Shortly after his arrival the warden visited San Quentin Prison in California to study its maximum security wing called MCU (Management Control Unit) or "O" Wing. He returned to Trenton and copied the exact setup, including the name MCU, and instituted it at Trenton State Prison. Overnight they rounded up 250 prisoners and put them in this instantly erected MCU. Sundiata was the first prisoner they rounded up. Within a month they had released the prisoners back into population except for about 50, including Sundiata. These 50 were accused of being "politically oriented."

After many stays in the "doghouse", contracting tuberculosis, and constant battling with prison officials, Sundiata was transferred to the United States Penitentiary at Marion. Marion, considered to be the worst prison in the U.S., has been condemned by Amnesty International for violating the United Nations' Standard Minimum Rules for the Treatment of Prisoners. Marion is located over a thousand miles from Sundiata's home and is supposedly reserved for prisoners who commit violent acts while in prison.

(Sundiata had no such charges pending while at Trenton.) Most prisoners at Marion are locked down for 22-23 hours per day, subjected to many degrading practices such as anal finger probes and being shackled spreadeagle to their bed blocks. Drinking water at Marion Penitentiary is drawn from a federally-designated emergency toxic waste dump clean-up site, and many prisoners suffer unexplained skin rashes and benign tumors.

At Marion, Sundiata was immediately put on controlled visit status (restricted to non-contact visits where prisoners spoke over the telephone while sitting in a small booth) as punishment for being the co-defendant of Assata Shakur, who had just escaped (in 1979) from the Clinton, New Jersey Women's Prison. Sundiata remained on control visit status during his entire eight years at Marion, and was usually the only prisoner classified as such.

Sundiata writes: *I was permitted visits with immediate family and attorneys only, with no friends or associates allowed. Because of the great distance and costs, these visits were possible only every one to three years. Prison officials constantly berated my children and threatened to cut off their visiting privilege for playing (i.e., not sitting still in the visiting booth). They once declared a baby blanket a non-permitted item, and took it from under my daughter's infant sister who was sleeping on the floor, causing the child and mother to cry. Only 24 total hours of visiting were permitted each month. Once my mother travelled 2000 miles to visit me, unaware that I had already 16 visiting hours that month. Prison officials rudely cut off her visit after only 8 hours, causing my mother to cry. In another instance, legal aide Anne Else traveled 550 miles to visit me. The FBI and Marion staff eavesdropped on our meeting until they were inadvertently discovered in the act by another prisoner, Leonard Peltier. The FBI then interrupted my visit and called Anne Else to the front office, where they attempted to interrogate, terrorize and intimidate her into not filing a lawsuit against them.*

In still one more instance of harassment, Scott Anderson, editor of the Milwaukee Courier newspaper, traveled over 500 miles to interview me. He was allowed one hour to conduct a tape-recorded interview over a phone in the visiting booth. At the end of the hour he discovered that Marion officials cut off the line to the tape recorder's telephone soon after the interview began. The officials refused to let him redo the interview. At Marion I was also not permitted to telephone my lawyer unless I could prove it was less than five days before he was to appear in court on my behalf, otherwise all communications to my lawyer had to be written.

After eight years, in large part due to demonstrations at Marion and substantial national pressure to end the lockdown, Sundiata was transferred to Leavenworth, where he remains today.

Assata Shakur was one of the key targets of **COINTELPRO.** She was called the "soul of the Black Liberation Army" by the government. After spending 6 years in prison, Assata Shakur escaped in 1979. In her autobiography, written from her new home in Cuba, Assata describes Sundiata's Character:

There is something about Sundiata that exudes calm. From every part of his being you can sense the presence of revolutionary spirit and fervor. And his love for Black people is so intense that you can almost touch it and hold it in your hand.

Sundiata is a true hero. He has been an unceasing fighter for the liberation of Black people and for this he has spent the last 18 years of his life in prison. And if we do not do something about it, the U.S. government will be only too pleased to watch Sundiata die in his cell. Join us in our campaign to ensure Sundiata's freedom.

For More Information

about the efforts to free Sundiata or to added to the mailing list, please write to: Sundiata Acoli Freedom Campaign, P.O. Box 5538, Manhattanville Station, Harlem, New York 10027. If you would like to order more of these articles, please send requests to Sundiata Acoli Freedom Campaign, P.O. Box 579154, Chicago, Illinois 60657-9154. Price is $3 plus $1 for postage and handling.

Write to Sundiata: Sundiata Acoli
#39794-066
P.O. Box 1000
Leavenworth, KS 66048.

This article was first written at the request of the New Afrikan Peoples Organization (NAPO). Its original title was "The Rise and Development of the New Afrikan Liberation Struggle Behind the Walls." The New Afrikan liberation struggle behind the walls refers to the struggle of Black prisoners, "behind the walls" of U.S. penal institutions, to gain liberation for ourselves, our people, and all oppressed people. We of the New Afrikan Independence Movement spell "Afrikan" with a "k" because Afrikan linguists originally used "k" to indicate "c" sound in the English language. We use the term "New Afrikan", instead of Black, to define ourselves as an Afrikan people who have been forcibly transplanted to a new land and formed into a "new Afrikan nation" in North America. But our struggle behind the walls did not begin in America.

The 16th Century–*Through The Civil War*

The Afrikan prison struggle began on the shores of Afrika behind the walls of medieval pens that held captives for ships bound west into slavery. It continues today behind the walls of modern U.S. penitentiaries where all prisoners are held as legal slaves – a blatant violation of international law.

The conception of prison ideology began to take form as far back as the reign of Louie XIV of France (1643-1715) when the Benedictine monk Mabillon wrote that: "... penitents might be secluded in cells like those of Carthusian monks, and there being employed in various sorts of labor." In 1790, on April 5th, the Pennsylvania Quakers actualized this concept as the capstone of their 14-year struggle to reform Philadelphia's Walnut Street jail. No longer would corporal punishment be administered. Henceforth prisoners would be locked away in their cells with a Bible and forced to do *penitence* in order to rehabilitate themselves. Thus was born the penitentiary.

In 1850, approximately 6,700 people were found in the nation's newly emerging prison system. Almost none of the prisoners were Black. They were more valuable economically outside the prison system because there were other means of radical control. During this time most New Afrikan (Black) men, women, and children were already imprisoned for life on plantations as chattel slaves. Accordingly, the Afrikan struggle behind the walls was carried on primarily behind the walls of slave quarters through conspiracies, revolts, insurrections, arson, sabotage, work slow downs, poisoning of the slavemaster, self-maimings, and runaways. If struggle behind the walls of the local jails, many of which were first built to hold captured runaways. Later they were also used for local citizens.

Shortly after 1850, the imprisonment rate increased, then remained fairly stable with a rate of between 75 and 125 prisoners per 100,000 population. The Afrikan struggle continued primarily behind the slave quarter's walls down through the issuance of the Emancipation Proclamation. This was a declaration issued by President Lincoln on January 1, 1863, during the height of the Civil War. It declared the slaves free *only* in those states still in rebellion and had little actual liberating effect on the slaves in question. Their slavemasters, still engaged in war against the Union, simply ignored the declaration and continued to hold their slaves in bondage. Some slavemasters kept the declaration a secret after the war ended following Lee's surrender on April 9, 1865. This date, called "Juneteenth," is celebrated annually by New Afrikans in Texas and outlying states as "Black Independence Day."

Post-Civil War *To The 20th Century*

Immediately after the Civil War and at the end of slavery, vast numbers of Black males were imprisoned for everything from not signing slave-like labor contracts with plantation owners to looking the "wrong" way at some White person, or for some similar "petty crime." Any "transgression" perceived by Whites to be of a more serious nature was normally dealt with on the spot with a gun or rope...provided the Black was outnumbered and outarmed. "Black-on-Black" crime was then, as now, considered to be "petty crime" by the U.S. justice system. But petty or not, upon arrest most New Afrikans were given long, harsh sentences at hard labor.

Within five years after the end of the Civil War, the Black percentages of the prison population went from close to zero to 33 percent. Many of these prisoners were hired out to Whites at less than slave wages. Overnight, prisons became the new slave quarters for many New Afrikans. Likewise the Afrikan prison struggle changed from a struggle behind the walls of slave quarters to a struggle behind the walls of county workhouses, chain gang camps, and the plantations and factories that used prisoners as slave laborers.

The 20th Century *Through World War II*

From 1910 through 1950, Blacks made up 23 to 34 percent of the prisoners in the U.S. prison system. Most people, conditioned by the prison movies *The Defiant Ones* (starring Sidney Poitier, a Black, and Tony Curtis, a White), or *I Escaped From the Chain Gang* (starring Paul Muni, a White in an integrated chain gang), or *Cool Hand Luke* (starring Paul Newman, a White, in a southern chain gang) erroneously assume that earlier U.S. prison populations were basically integrated. This is not so. The U.S. was a segregated society prior to 1950, including the prisons; even the northern ones. Most New Afrikan prisoners were sent to county workhouses, Black chain gangs, and obscure negro prisons. Thus, the early populations of the more well-known or "mainline" state and federal prisons–Attica, Sing Sing, Alcatraz, and Atlanta–were predominantly White and male. Whenever New Afrikans were sent to these "mainline" prisons they found themselves grossly outnumbered, relegated to the back of the lines, to separate lines, or to no lines at all. They were often denied outright what meager amenities existed within the prisons. Racism was rampant. New Afrikans were racistly suppressed by both White prisoners and guards. All of the guards were White–there were no Black guards or prison officials at the time. The Afrikan prisoners continued to struggle behind the walls of these segregated county workhouses, chain gang camps, and state and federal prisons, yet prison conditions for them remained much the same through World War II. Inside conditions accurately reflected conditions of the larger society outside the walls, except by then the state's electric chair had mostly supplanted the lynch mob's rope.

Post-World War II *To The Civil Rights Era*

Things began to change in the wake of World War II. Four factors flowing together ushered in these changes. They were the ghetto population explosion, the drug influx, the emergence of independent Afrikan nations, and the Civil Rights Movement.

The Ghetto Population *Explosion*

Plentiful jobs during the war, coupled with a severe shortage of White workers, caused U.S. war industries to hire New Afrikans in droves. Southern New Afrikans poured north to fill these unheard-of job opportunities, and the already crowded ghetto populations mushroomed.

Drug *Influx*

New Afrikan soldiers fought during the war to preserve European democracies. They returned home eager to join the fight to make segregated America democratic too. But the U.S. had witnessed Marcus Garvey organize similar sentiments following World War I into one of the greatest Black movements in the western hemisphere. This time the U.S. was more prepared to contain the new and expected New Afrikan assertiveness. Their weapon was "King Heroin." The U.S. employed the services of the Mafia during World War II to gather intelligence in Italy to defeat Fascist Mussolini.

Before World War II, Mussolini embarked on a major campaign against the Mafia which enraged the group's leaders. Fascism was a big Mafia so it couldn't afford another Mafia to exist. Mussolini's activities turned Mafiosi into vigorous anti-Fascists, and the American Government co-operated with the Mafia both in the United States and in Sicily. In the eyes of many Sicilians, the United States helped restore the Mafia's lost power. The Americans had to win the war, so they couldn't pay much attention to these things. "They thought the Mafia could help them, and perhaps they did" said Leonard Sciascia, perhaps the best known living Sicilian novelist and student of the Mafia.

During World War II, the Office of Strategic Services (OSS), the forerunner of the Central Intelligence Agency (CIA), helped to commute

Lucky Luciano's sentence in federal prison and arrange for his repatriation to Sicily. Luciano was among the top dons in the Mafia syndicate and a leading organizer of prostitution and drug trafficking. The OSS knew that Luciano had excellent ties to the Sicilian Mafia and wanted the support of that organization for the Allied landing in Sicily in 1943.

When Luciano left the U.S., numerous politicians and Mafia dons were together at the Brooklyn docks to wave him goodbye in what was the first of many occasions that international drug dealers were recruited by the U.S. government to advance its foreign policy interests. After the war, in return for "services rendered," the U.S. looked the other way as the Mafia flooded the major U.S. ghettos with heroin. Within six years after World War II, due to the Mafia's marketing strategy, over 100,000 people were addicts, many of them Black.

The Emergence of *Independent Afrikan Nations*

Afrikans from Afrika, having fought to save European independence, returned to the Afrikan continent and began fighting for the independence of their own colonized nations. Rather than fight losing Afrikan colonial wars, most European nations opted to grant "phased" independence to their Afrikan colonies. The U.S. now faced the prospect of thousands of Afrikan diplomatic personnel, their staff, and families coming to the U.N. and wandering into a minefield of racial incidents, particularly on state visits to the rigidly segregated D.C. capital. That alone could push each newly emerging independent Afrikan nation into the socialist column. To counteract this possibility, the U.S. decided to desegregate. As a result, on May 17, 1954, the U.S. Supreme Court declared school segregation illegal.

In its landmark Brown v. Board of Education case, which heralded the beginning of the end of official segregation in the United States, the Supreme Court had been made fully aware of the relations between America's domestic policies and her foreign policy interest by the federal government's amicus curiae (i.e., friend of the court) brief, which read:

It is in the context of the present world struggle between freedom and tyranny that the problem of racial discrimination must be viewed...for discrimination against minority groups in the United States has an adverse effect upon our relations with other countries. Racial discrimination furnishes grist for the communist propaganda mills, and it raises doubts even among friendly nations as to the intensity of our devotion to the democratic faith.

Malcolm X provides similar insight into the reasoning behind the U.S. decision to desegregate. During his February 16, 1965, speech at Rochester, New York's Corn Hill Methodist Church, he said:

"From 1954 to 1964 can be easily be looked upon as the era of the emerging African state. And as the African state emerged...what effect did it have on Black America? When he saw the Black man on the [African]

continent taking a stand, it made him become filled with the desire to also take a stand...Just as [the U.S.] had to change their approach with the people on the African continent, they also began to change their approach with our people on this continent. As they used tokenism...on the African continent... they began to do the same thing with us here in the States...Tokenism... Every move they made was a token move...They came up with a Supreme Court desegregation decision that they haven't put into practice yet. Not even in Rochester, much less in Mississippi." [Applause.]

Origin of the *Civil Rights Movement*

On December 1, 1955, Ms. Rosa Parks defied Montgomery, Alabama's bus segregation laws by refusing to give her seat to a White man. Her subsequent arrest and the ensuing mass bus boycott by the Montgomery New Afrikan community kicked off the Civil Rights Movement. Martin Luther King, Jr., a young college-educated Baptist minister, was chosen to coordinate and lead this boycott primarily because he was a new arrival in town, intelligent, respected, and had not accumulated a list of grudge enemies as had the old guard. His selection for leadership catapulted him upon the stage of history. The 381-day-long boycott toppled Montgomery's bus segregation codes. A year later, in 1957, Ghana became the first string of sub-Saharan Afrikan nations to be granted independence.

As northern discrimination, bulging ghettos, and the drug influx were setting off a rise in New Afrikan numbers behind the walls. Southern segregation, the emergence of independent Afrikan nations, and the resulting Civil Rights Movement provided those increasing numbers with the general political agenda: equality and anti-discrimination.

Civil Rights Through *The Black Power Era*

Religious Struggles *in Prison*

Meanwhile, behind the walls, small segments of New Afrikans began rejecting Western Christianity; they turned to Islam as preached by Elijah Muhammad's Nation of Islam (NOI) and Noble Drew Ali's Muslim Science Temple of America (MST). The NOI preached that Islam was the true religion of Black people and that Blacks in America were a nation needing land and independence. The MST preached that the Asiatic Black people in America must proclaim their nationality as members of the ancient Moors of Northern Africa. These new religions produced significant success rates in helping New Afrikan prisoners rehabilitate themselves by instilling them with a newfound sense of pride, dignity, piety, and industriousness. Yet these religions seemed strange and thus threatening to prison officials. They moved forthwith to suppress these religions and many early Muslims were viciously persecuted, beaten, and even killed for practicing their beliefs. The Muslims fought back fiercely.

Civil Rights Struggles *in Prison*

Like American society, the prisons were rigidly segregated. New Afrikans were relegated to perform the heaviest and dirtiest jobs – farm work, laundry work, dishwashing, garbage disposal – and were restricted from jobs as clerks, straw bosses, electricians, or *any* position traditionally reserved for White prisoners. Similar discriminatory rules applied to all other areas of prison life. New Afrikans were restricted to live in certain cell blocks or tiers, eat in certain areas of the mess hall, and sit in the back of the movies, TV room, and other recreational facilities.

Influenced by the antidiscrimination aspect of the Civil Rights Movement, a growing number of New Afrikans behind the walls began stepping up their struggle against discrimination in prison. Audacious New Afrikans began violating longstanding segregation codes by sitting in the front seats at the movies, mess hall, or TV areas – and more than a few died from shanks in the back. Others gave as good as they got, and better. Additionally, New Afrikans began contesting discriminatory job and housing policies and other biased conditions. Many were set up for attack and sent to the hole for years, or worse. Those who were viewed as leaders were dealt with most harshly. Most of this violence came from prison officials and White prisoners protecting their privileged positions; some violence also came from New Afrikans and Muslims protecting their lives, taking stands and fighting back. From these silent, unheralded battles against racial and religious discrimination in prisons emerged the New Afrikan liberation struggle behind the walls during the '50s Civil Rights era. Eventually the courts influenced by the "equality/anti-discrimination" aspect of the Civil Rights Movement, would rule that prisons must recognize the Muslims' religion on an "equal" footing with other accepted religions, and that prison racial discrimination codes must be outlawed.

Black Power Through *The Black Liberation Era*

As the Civil Rights Movement advanced into the '60s, New Afrikan college students waded into the struggle with innovative lunch counter sit-ins, freedom rides, and voter registration projects. The Student Nonviolent Coordinating Committee (SNCC) was formed during this period to coordinate and instruct student volunteers in nonviolent methods of organizing voter registration projects and other Civil Rights work. These energetic young students, and the youth in general, served as the foot soldiers of the Movement. They provided indispensable services, support, and protection to local community leaders such as Mississippi's Fannie Lou Hamer, Ella Baker, and other heroines and heroes of the Civil Rights Movement. Although they met with measured success, White racist atrocities mounted daily on defenseless Civil Rights workers.

Young New Afrikans in general began to grow increasingly disenchanted with the nonviolent Philosophy of Martin Luther King. Many began to look increasingly toward Malcolm X, the fiery young minister of the NOI Temple No. 7 in Harlem, New York. He called for "self-defense, freedom by any means necessary, and land and independence." As Malcolm Little, he had been introduced to the NOI doctrine while imprisoned in Massachusetts. Upon release he traveled to Detroit to meet Elijah Muhammad, converted to Islam, and was given the surname "X" to replace his discarded slavemaster's name. The "X" symbolized his original surname lost to history when his foreparents were kidnapped from Afrika, stripped of their names, language, and identity, and enslaved in the America's. As Malcolm X he became one of Elijah Muhammad's most dedicated disciples, and rose to National Minister and spokesperson for the NOI. His keen intellect, incorruptible integrity, staunch courage, clear resonant oratory, sharp debating skills, and superb organizing abilities soon brought the NOI to a position of prominence within the Black ghetto colonies across the U.S.

In '63 he openly called the March on Washington a farce. He explained that the desire for a mass march on the nation's capital originally sprang from the Black grass roots: the average Black man/woman in the streets. It was their way of demonstrating a mass Black demand for jobs and freedom. As momentum grew for the march,President Kennedy called a meeting of the leaders of the six largest Civil Rights organizations, dubbed "The Big Six" (National Association For the Advancement of Colored People,[NAACP], Southern Christian Leadership Conference [SCLC], Congress of Racial Equality [CORE], National Urban League [NUL], Student Nonviolent Coordinating Committee [SNCC], and the NAACP Legal Defense and Education Fund) and asked them to stop the proposed march. They answered by saying that they couldn't stop it because they weren't leading it, didn't start it and that it had sprung from the masses of Black people.

If they weren't leading the march, the president decided to make them the leaders by distributing huge sums of money to each of the "Big Six," publicizing their leading roles in the mass media, and providing them with a script to follow regarding the staging of the event. The script planned the March down to the smallest detail. Malcolm explained that government officials told the "Big Six" what time to begin the March, where to March, who could speak at the March and who could not, generally what could be said and what could not, what signs to carry, where to go to the toilets (provided by the government), and what time to end the event and get out of town. The script was followed to a "T" and most of the 200,000 marchers were never the wiser. By then SNCC's membership was also criticizing the March as too moderate and decrying the violence sweeping the South. History ultimately proved Malcolm's claim of "farce" correct, through books published by participants in the planning of the

March and through exposure of government documents on the matter.

Origin of The *Five Percenter*

Clarence 13X (Smith) was expelled from Harlem's Nation of Islam Temple No. 7 in 1963 because he wouldn't conform to NOI practices. He frequently associated with the numerous street gangs that abounded in New York City at the time and felt that the NOI didn't put enough effort into recruiting these youth. After being expelled he actively recruited among these street gangs and other wayward youth, and by '64 he had established his own "movement" called "The Five Percenter." The name comes from their belief that 85 percent of Black people are like cattle, who continue to eat the poisoned animal (the pig), are blind to the truth of God, and continue to give their allegiance to people who don't have their best interests at heart, that 10 percent of Black people are bloodsuckers – the politicians, preachers, and other parasitic individuals who get rich off the labor and ignorance of the docile exploited 85 percent; and that the remaining 5 percent are the poor righteous teachers of freedom, justice, and equality who know the truth of the "Black" God and are not deceived by the practices of the bloodsucking 10 percent. The Five Percenter movement spread throughout the New York State prison system and the Black ghettos of the New York metropolitan area.

Origin of the New World *Nation of Islam*

In December 1965 Newark's Mayor Hugh Addonizio witnessed a getaway car pulling away from a bank robbery and ordered his chauffeur to follow with siren blasting. The fleeing robbers crashed into a telephone pole, sprang from their car and fired a shot through the Mayor's windshield. He screeched to a halt, and police cars racing to the scene captured Muhammad Ali Hassan, known as Albert Dickens, and James Washington. Both were regular attendees of Newark's NOI Temple No. 25, headed by Minister James 3X Shabazz. Ali Hassan and Washington were members of the New World Nation of Islam (NWI). Ali Hassan, its leader and Supreme Field commander, dates the birth of the New World Nation of Islam as February 26, 1960. He states that on that date Elijah Muhammad authorized the New World Nation of Islam under the leadership of Field Supreme Minister Fard Savior and declared that the Field Minister had authority over all the NOI Muslims. Ali Hassan and Washington were convicted for the bank robbery and sent to Trenton State Prison.

The NWI's belief in the supreme authority of Fard Savior was rejected by NOI Minister Shabazz, and thereafter an uneasy peace prevailed between the followers of Shabazz, who retained control of Newark's NOI Temple No. 25, and the followers of the NWI who sought to gain control.

Meanwhile, Ali Hassan published a book titled *Uncle Yah Yah* and ran the NWI from his prison cell. Along with the more established and influential NOI, the influence of the NWI spread throughout the New Jersey state prison system and began setting up food co-ops, barbershops, houses to teach Islam, and printing presses; and purchased land in South Carolina, all in furtherance of creating an independent Black Nation.

The Black Liberation Era

Black Panthers Usher in the *Black Liberation Movement*

Midstride the '60s, on February 21, 1965, Malcolm was assassinated but his star continued to rise and his seeds fell on fertile soil. The following year, October 1966, in Oakland, California, Huey P. Newton and a handful of armed youths founded the Black Panther Party for Self-Defense on principles that Malcolm had preached – and the Black Liberation Movement (BLM) was born.

Subsequently the name was shortened to the Black Panther Party (BPP) and a 10-point program was created which stated:

1. We want freedom. We want power to determine the destiny of our community.
2. We want full employment of our people.
3. We want an end to the robbery by the *CAPITALIST* of our Black community.
4. We want decent housing, fit for the shelter of human beings.
5. We want education for our people that exposes the true nature of this decadent American society. We want education that teaches us our true history and our role in the present day society.
6. We want all Black men to be exempt from military service.
7. We want an immediate end to *POLICE BRUTALITY* and *MURDER* of Black people.
8. We want freedom for all Black men held in federal, state, county, and city prisons and jails.
9. We want all Black people when brought to trial to be tried in court by a jury of their peer group or people from their black communities, as defined by the Constitution of the United States.
10. We want land, bread, housing, education, clothing, justice and peace. And as our major political objective, a United Nations-supervised plebiscite to be held throughout the Black colony in which only Black colonial subjects will be allowed to participate, for the purpose of determining the will of Black people as to their national destiny.

The Panthers established numerous programs to serve the Oakland ghetto – free breakfasts for children, free health care, free day-care, and free political education classes. The program that riveted the ghetto's attention was their campaign to "stop police murder and brutality of Blacks." Huey, a community college pre-law student, discovered that it was legal for citizens to openly carry arms in California. With that assurance the Black Panther Party began armed car patrols of the police cruisers that patrolled Oakland's Black colony. When a cruiser stopped to make an arrest, the Panther car stopped. They fanned out around the scene, arms at the ready, and observed, tape recorded, and recommended a lawyer to the arrest victim. It didn't take long for the police to retaliate. They confronted Huey late one night near his home. Gunfire erupted, leaving Huey critically wounded, a policeman dead and another wounded. The Panthers and the Oakland-Bay community responded with a massive campaign to save Huey from the gas chamber. The California Senate began a hearing to rescind the law permitting citizens to openly carry arms within city limits. The Panthers staged an armed demonstration during the hearing at the Sacramento Capitol to protest the Senate's action, which gained national publicity. That publicity, together with the Panther's philosophy of revolutionary nationalism, self-defense, and the "Free Huey" campaign, catapulted the BPP to nationwide prominence.

But not without cost. During August 1967 J. Edgar Hoover issued his infamous Counter Intelligence Program (COINTELPRO) memorandum which directed the FBI (and local police officials) to disrupt specified Black organizations and neutralize their leaders so as to prevent "the rise of a Black messiah."

Attacks Increase *on Revolutionaries*

The Panthers rolled eastward, establishing offices in each major northern ghetto. As they went, they set up revolutionary programs in each community that were geared to provide community control of schools, tenant control of slum housing, free breakfast for school children, free health, day care, and legal clinics, and free political education classes for the community. They also initiated campaigns to drive dope pushers and drugs from the community, and campaigns to stop police murder and brutality of Blacks. As they went about the community organizing these various programs they were frequently confronted, attacked, or arrested by the police, and some were even killed during these encounters.

Other revolutionary organizers suffered similar entrapments. The Revolutionary Action Movement's (RAM) Herman Ferguson and Max Stamford were arrested in 1967 on spurious charges of conspiring to kill Civil Rights leaders. In the same year Amiri Baraka (the poet and playwright LeRoi Jones) was arrested for transporting weapons in a van during the Newark riots and did a brief stint in Trenton State Prison until a successful appeal overturned his conviction. SNCC's Rap Brown, Stokely Carmichael, and other orators were constantly threatened or charged with "inciting to riot" as they crisscrossed the country speaking to mass audiences. Congress passed so-called "Rap Brown" laws to deter speakers from crossing state lines to address mass audiences lest a disturbance break out, leaving them vulnerable to federal charges and imprisonment. And numerous revolutionary organizers and orators were being imprisoned.

This initial flow of revolutionaries into the jails and prisons began to spread a revolutionary nationalist hue through New Afrikans behind the walls. New Afrikans prisoners were also influenced by the domestic revolutionary atmosphere and the liberation struggles in Afrika, Asia, and Latin America. Small groups began studying on their own, or in collectives, the works of Malcolm X, Huey P. Newton, The Black Panther newspaper, The Militant newspaper, contemporary national liberation struggle leaders Kwame Nkrumah, Jomo Kenyatta, Frantz Fanon, Che Guevara, Fidel Castro, Ho Chi Minh, and Mao Tse-tung, plus Marx, Lenin, and Bakunin too. Increasing numbers of New Afrikan and Third World prisoners, and decreased numbers of White prisoners, the last of the prisons' overt segregation policies fell by the wayside.

The New Afrikan *Independence Movement*

The seeds of Malcolm took further root on March 29, 1968. On that date the Provisional Government of the Republic of New Afrika (RNA) was founded at a convention held at the Blackowned Twenty Grand Motel in Detroit. Over 500 grass-root activists came together to issue a Declaration of Independence on behalf of the oppressed Black Nation inside North America and the New Afrikan Independence Movement (NAIM) was born. Since then Blacks desiring an independent Black Nation have referred to themselves and other Blacks in the U.S. as New Afrikans.

That same month, March '68, during Martin Luther King's march in Memphis, angry youths on the fringes of the march broke away and began breaking store windows, looting, and firebombing. A 16-year-old boy was killed and 50 people were injured in the ensuing violence. This left Martin profoundly shaken and questioning whether his philosophy was still able to hold the youth to a nonviolent commitment. On April 4th he returned to Memphis, seeking the answer through one more march, and found an assassin's bullet. Ghettos exploded in flames one after another across the face of America. The philosophy of Black Liberation surged to the forefront among the youth.

But not the youth alone. Following a series of police provocations in Cleveland, on July 23, 1968, New Libya Movement activists there set an ambush that killed several policemen. A "fortyish" Ahmed Evans was convicted of the killings and died in prison ten years later of "cancer."

More CIA dope surged into the ghettos from the Golden Triangle of Southeast Asia. Revolutionaries stepped up activities on both sides of the walls. Behind the walls the New Afrikan percentage steadily increased.

COINTELPRO *Attacks*

In 1969 COINTELPRO launched its main attack on the Black Liberation Movement in earnest. It began with the mass arrest of Lumumba Shakur and the New York Panther 21. It followed with a series of military raids on Black Panther Party offices in Philadelphia, Baltimore, New Haven, Jersey City, Detroit, Chicago, Denver, Omaha, Sacramento, and San Diego, and was capped off with a four-hour siege that poured thousands of rounds into the Los Angeles BPP office. Fortunately Geronimo ji-Jaga, decorated Vietnam vet, had earlier fortified the office to withstand an assault, and no Panthers were seriously injured. However, repercussions from the outcome eventually drove him underground. The widespread attacks left Panthers dead all across the country – Fred Hampton, Mark Clark, Bunchy Carter, John Huggins, John Savage, Walter Toure Pope, Bobby Hutton, Sylvester Bell, Frank "Capt. Franco" Diggs, Fred Bennett, James Carr, Larry Roberson, Spurgeon "Jake" Winters, Alex Rackley, Arthur Morris, Steve Bartholemew, Robert Lawrence, Tommy Lewis, Nathaniel Clark, Welton Armstead, Sidney Miller, Sterling Jones, Babatunde Omawali, Samuel Napier, Harold Russle, and Robert Webb among others. In the three years after J. Edger Hoover's infamous COINTELPRO memorandum, dated August 25, 1967, 31 members of the BPP were killed, nearly a thousand were arrested and key leaders were sent to jail. Others were driven underground. Still others, like BPP field marshal Donald "D.C." Cox, were driven into exile overseas.

Also in '69, Clarence 13X, founder of The Five Percenter, was mysteriously murdered in the elevator of a Harlem project building. His killer was never discovered and his adherents suspect government complicity in his death.

The RNA was similarly attacked that year. During their second annual convention in March '69, held at Reverend C.L. Franklin's New Bethel Church in Detroit, a police provocation sparked a siege that poured 800 rounds into the church. Several convention members were wounded and the entire convention, 140 people, was arrested en masse. When Reverend Franklin (father of "The Queen of Soul", singer Aretha Franklin) and Black State Representative James Del Rio were informed of the incident they called Black judge George Crockett, who proceeded to the police station where he found total legal chaos. Almost 150 people were being questioned, fingerprinted, and given nitrate tests to determine if they had fired guns, in total disregard of fundamental constitutional procedures. Hours after the roundup, there wasn't so much as a list of persons being held and no one had been formally arrested. An indignant Judge Crockett set up court right in the station house and demanded that the police either press charges or release their captives. He had handled

 about fifty cases when the Wayne County prosecutor, called in by the police, intervened. The prosecutor promised that the use of all irregular methods would be halted. Crockett adjourned the impromptu court, and by noon the following day the police had released all but a few individuals who were held on specific charges. Chaka Fuller, Rafael Vierra, and Alfred 2X Hibbits were charged with the killing. All three were subsequently tried and acquitted. Chaka Fuller was mysteriously assassinated a few months afterwards.

Revolutionaries nationwide were attacked and/or arrested – Tyari Uhuru, Maka, Askufo, and the Smyrna Brothers in Delaware, JoJo Muhammad Bowens and Fred Burton in Philadelphia, and Panthers Mondo Langa, Ed Poindexter, and Veronza Daoud Bowers, Jr., in Omaha. Police mounted an assault on the Panther office in the Desiree Projects of New Orleans which resulted in several arrests. A similar attack was made on the Peoples Party office in Houston. One of their leaders, Carl Hampton, was killed by police and another, Lee Otis Johnson, was arrested later on an unrelated charge and sentenced to 41 years in prison for alleged possession of one marijuana cigarette.

The Rise of *Prison Struggles*

Like the Panthers, most of those arrested brought their philosophies with them into the prisons. Likewise, most had outside support committees to one degree or another so that this influx of political prisoners linked the struggle behind the walls with the struggles in the outside local communities. The combination set off a beehive of political activity behind the walls, and prisoners stepped up their struggle for political, Afrikan, Islamic, and academic studies, access to political literature, community access to attorneys, adequate law libraries, relevant vocational training, contact visits, better food, health care, housing, and a myriad of other struggles. The forms of prison struggle ranged from face-to-face negotiations to mass petitioning, letter-writing and call-in campaigns, outside demonstrations, class action lawsuits, hunger strikes, work strikes, rebellions, and more drastic actions. Overall, all forms of struggle served to roll back draconian prison policies that had stood for centuries and to further the development of the New Afrikan liberation struggle behind the walls.

These struggles would not have been as successful, or would have been much more costly in terms of lives lost or brutality endured, had it not been for the links to the community and community support that political prisoners brought with them into the prisons. Although that support was not always sufficient in quantity or quality, or was sometimes nonexistent or came with hidden agendas or was marked by frequent conflicts, on the whole it was this combination of resolute prisoners, community support, and legal support which was most often successful in prison struggles.

The Changing Complexion *of Prisons*

As the '60s drew to a close, New Afrikan and Third World nationalities made up nearly 50 percent of the prison population. National liberation consciousness became the dominant influence behind the walls as the overall complexion neared the changeover from White to Black, Brown, and Red. The decade-long general decrease in prisoners, particularly Whites, brought a drop of between 16,000 and 28,000 in total prison population. The total number of White prisoners decreased between 16,000 and 23,000 while the total number of New Afrikan prisoners increased slightly or changed insignificantly over the same period. Yet the next decade would begin the period of unprecedented new prison construction, as the primary role of U.S. prisons changed from "suppression of the working classes" to "suppression of domestic Black and Third World liberation struggles inside the U.S."

Enter *The '70s*

A California guard, rated as an expert marksman, opened the decade of the '70s with the January 13th shooting at close range of W.L. Nolen, Cleveland Edwards, and Alvin "Jug" Miller in the Soledad prison yard. They were left lying where they fell until it was too late for them to be saved by medical treatment. Nolen, in particular, had been instrumental in organizing protest of guard killings of two other Black prisoners – Clarence Causey and William Powell – at Soledad in the recent past, and was consequently both a thorn in the side of prison officials and a hero to the Black prison population. When the guard was exonerated of the triple killings two weeks later by a Board of Inquiry, the prisoners retaliated by throwing a guard off the tier.

George Jackson, Fleeta Drumgo, and John Cluchette were charged with the guard's death and came to be known as the Soledad Brothers. California Black prisoners solidified around the chain of events in the Soledad Brothers case and formed the Black Guerrilla Family (BGF). The Panthers spearheaded a massive campaign to save the Soledad Brothers from the gas chamber. The nationwide coalescence of prisoners and support groups around the case converted the scattered, disparate prison struggles into a national prison movement.

On the night of March 9, 1970, a bomb exploded killing Ralph Featherstone and Che Payne in their car outside a Maryland courthouse where Rap Brown was to appear the next day on "Inciting to Riot" charges. Instead of appearing, Rap went underground, was captured a year later during the robbery of a Harlem so-called "dope bar," and was sent behind the walls. He completed his sentence and was released from prison.

On August 7, 1970, Jonathan Jackson, younger brother of George, attempted to liberate Ruchell Cinque Magee, William Christmas, and James McClain from the Marion County courthouse in California.

Jonathan, McClain, Christmas, and the trial judge were killed by SWAT teams who also wounded the prosecutor and paralyzed him for life. Miraculously, Ruchell and three wounded jurors survived the fusillade. Jonathan frequently served as Angela Davis's bodyguard. She had purchased weapons for that purpose in the breakout attempt. Immediately afterward she became the object of an international "woman hunt." On October 13, Angela was captured in New York City and was subsequently returned to California to undergo a very acrimonious trial with Magee. She was acquitted on all charges. Magee was tried separately and convicted on lesser charges. He remains imprisoned to date.

On August 21, a guard shot and killed George Jackson as he bolted from a control unit and ran for the San Quentin wall. Inside the unit lay three guards and two trustees dead. The circumstances surrounding George Jackson's legendary life and death, and the astuteness of his published writings, left a legacy that inspires and instructs the New Afrikan liberation struggle on both sides of the wall even today, and will for years to come.

September 13, 1971, became the bloodiest day in U.S. prison history when New York's Governor Nelson Rockefeller ordered the retaking of Attica Prison. The previous several years had seen a number of prison rebellions flare up across the country as prisoners protested widespread maltreatment and inhumane conditions. Most had been settled peaceably with little or no loss of human life after face-to-face negotiation between prisoners and state and prison officials. At Attica Black, Brown, White, Red, and Yellow prisoners took over one block of the prison and stood together for five days seeking to negotiate an end to their inhumane conditions. Their now-famous dictum declared "We are men, not beasts, and will not be driven as such." But Rockefeller had presidential ambitions. The rebelling prisoners' demands included a political request for asylum in a nonimperialistic country. Rockefeller's refusal to negotiate foreshadowed a macabre replay of his father John D's slaughter of striking Colorado miners and their families decades earlier. Altogether 43 people died at Attica. New York State trooper bullets killed 39 people – 29 prisoners and 10 guards – in retaking Attica and shocked the world by the naked barbarity of the U.S. prison system. Yet the Attica rebellion too remains a milestone in the development of prisoner multinational solidarity to date.

New World Clashes *With The Nation of Islam*

In 1973 the simmering struggle for control of Newark's NOI Temple No. 25 erupted into the open. Warren Marcello, a New World member, assassinated NOI Temple No. 25 Minister Shabazz. In retaliation several NWI members were attacked and killed within the confines of the New Jersey prison system, and before the year was out the bodies of Marcello and a companion were found beheaded in Newark's Weequahic Park. Ali Hassan, still in prison, was tried as one of the co-conspirators in the death of Shabazz and was found innocent.

The Black *Liberation Army*

COINTELPRO's destruction of the BPP forced many members underground and gave rise to the Black Liberation Army (BLA) – a New Afrikan guerrilla organization. The BLA continued the struggle by waging urban guerrilla war across the U.S. through highly mobile strike teams. The government's intensified search for the BLA during the early 1970s resulted in the capture of Geronimo ji-Jaga in Dallas, Dhoruba Bin-Wahad and Jamal Josephs in New York, Sha Sha Brown and Blood McCreary in St. Louis, Nuh Washington and Jalil Muntaqin in Los Angeles, Herman Bell in New Orleans, Francisco and Gabriel Torres in New York, Russel Haroum Shoats in Philadelphia, Chango Monges, Mark Holder, and Kamau Hilton in New York, Assata Shakur and Sundiata Acoli in New Jersey, Ashanti Alston, Tarik, and Walid in New Haven, Safiya Bukhari and Masai Gibson in Virginia, and others. Left dead during the government's search and destroy missions were Sandra Pratt (wife of Geronimo ji-Jaga, assassinated while visibly pregnant), Mark Essex, Woodie Changa Green, Twyman Kakuyan Olugbala Meyers, Frank "Heavy" Fields, Anthony Kimu White, Zayd Shakur, Melvin Rema Kerney, Alfred Kambui Butler, Ron Carter, Rory Hithe, and John Thomas, among others. Red Adams, left paralyzed from the neck down by police bullets, would die from the effects a few years later.

Other New Afrikan freedom fighters attacked, hounded, and captured during the same general era were Imari Obadele and the RNA-11 in Jackson, Mississippi, Don Taylor and De Mau Mau of Chicago, Hanif Shabazz, Abdul Aziz, and the VI-5 in the Virgin Islands, Mark Cook of the George Jackson Brigade (GJB) in Seattle, Ahmed Obafemi of the RNA in Florida, Atiba Shanna in Chicago, Mafundi Lake in Alabama, Sekou Kambui and Imani Harris in Alabama, Robert Aswad Duren in California, Kojo Bomani Sababu and Duaruba Cinque in Trenton, John Partee and Tommie Lee Hodge of Alkebulan in Memphis, Gary Tyler in Los Angeles, Kareem Saif Allah and the Five Percenter-BLA-Islamic Brothers in New York, Ben Chavis and the Wilmington 10 in North Carolina, Delbert Africa and MOVE members in Philadelphia, and others too numerous to name.

Political Converts *in Prison*

Not everyone was political before incarceration. John Andaliwa Clark became so, and a freedom fighter par excellence, only after being sent behind the walls. He paid the supreme sacrifice during a hail of gunfire from Trenton State Prison guards. Hugo Dahariki Pinell also became political after being sent behind the California walls in 1964. He has been in prison ever since. Joan Little took an ice pick from a White North

Carolina guard who had used it to force her to perform oral sex on him. She killed him, escaped to New York, was captured, and forced to return to the same North Carolina camp where she feared for her life. Massive public vigilance and support enabled her to complete the sentence in relative safety and obtain her release.

Dessie Woods and Cheryl Todd, hitching through Georgia, were given a ride by a White man who tried to rape them. Woods took his gun, killed him, and was sent to prison where officials drugged and brutalized her. Todd was also imprisoned and subsequently released upon completion of the sentence. Woods was denied parole several times then finally released.

Political or not, each arrest was met with highly sensationalized prejudicial publicity that continued unabated to and throughout the trail. The negative publicity blitz was designed to guarantee a conviction, smokescreen the real issues involved, and justify immediate placement in the harshest prison conditions possible. For men this usually means the federal penitentiary at Marion, Illinois. For women it has meant the control unit in the federal penitentiary at Alderson, West Virginia, or Lexington, Kentucky. In 1988 political prisoners Silvia Baraldini, Alejandrina Torres, and Susan Rosenberg won a D.C. District Court lawsuit brought by attorneys Adjoa Alyetoro, Jan Susler, and others. The legal victory temporarily halted the practice of sending prisoners to control units strictly because of their political status. The ruling was reversed by the D.C. Appellate Court a year later. Those political prisoners not sent to Marion, Alderson, or Lexington control units are sent to other control units modeled after Marion/Lexington but located within maximum security state prisons. Normally this means 23 hour-a-day lockdown in long-term units located in remote hinterlands far from family, friends, and attorneys, with heavy censorship and restrictions on communications, visits, and outside contacts, combined with constant harassment, provocation, and brutality by prison guards.

Effect of Captured Freedom *Fighters on Prisons*

The influx of so many captured freedom fighters (i.e., prisoners of war–POWs) with varying degrees of guerrilla experience added a valuable dimension to the New Afrikan liberation struggle behind the walls. In the first place it accelerated the prison struggles already in process, particularly the attack on control units. One attack was spearheaded by Michael Deutsch and Jeffrey Haas of the People's Law Office, Chicago, which challenged Marion's H-Unit boxcar cells. Another was spearheaded by Assata Shakur and the Center for Constitutional Rights which challenged her out-of-state placement in the Alderson, West Virginia, control unit.

Second, it stimulated a thoroughgoing investigation and exposure of COINTELPRO's hand in waging low intensity warfare on New Afrikan and Third World nationalities in the U.S. This was spearheaded by Geronimo ji-Jaga with Stuart Hanlon's law office in the West and by Dhoruba Bin-Wahad with attorneys Liz Fink, Robert Boyle, and Jonathan Lubell in the East. These COINTELPRO investigations resulted in the overturn of Bin-Wahad's conviction and his release from prison in March 1990 after he had been imprisoned 19 years for a crime he did not commit.

Third, it broadened the scope of the prison movement to the international arena by producing the initial presentation of the U.S. political prisoner and prisoner of war (PP/POW) issue before the UN's Human Rights Commission. This approach originated with Jalil Muntaqin, and was spearheaded by him and attorney Kathryn Burke on the West Coast and by Sundiata Acoli and attorney Lennox Hinds of the National Conference of Black Lawyers on the East Coast. This petition sought relief from human rights violations in U.S. prisons and subsequently asserted a colonized people's right to fight against alien domination and racist regimes as codified in the Geneva Convention.

Fourth, it intensified, clarified, and broke new ground on political issues and debates of particular concern to the New Afrikan community, i.e., the "National Question," spearheaded by Atiba Shanna in the Midwest.

All these struggles, plus those already in process, were carried out with the combination in one form or another of resolute prisoners, and community and legal support. Community support when present came from various sources–family, comrades, friends; political, student, religious, and prisoner rights groups; workers, professionals, and progressive newspapers and radio stations. Some of those involved over the years were or are: the National Committee for Defense of Political Prisoners, the Black Community News Service, the African Peoples Party, the Republic of New Afrika, the African Peoples Socialist Party, The East, the BlissChord Communication Network, Liberation Book Store, WDAS Radio Philadelphia, WBLS Radio New York, WBAI Radio New York, Third World Newsreel, *Libertad* (political journal of the Pueto Rican Movimiento de Liberacion Nacional [MLN], the Prairie Fire Organizing Committee, the May 19th Communist Organization, the Madame Binh Graphics Collective, *The Midnight Express*, the Northwest Iowa Socialist Party, the National Black United Front, the Nation of Islam, *Arm The Spirit, Black News,* International Class Labor Defense, the Real Dragon Project, the John Brown Anti-Klan Committee, the National Prison Project, the House of the Lord Church, the American Friends Service Committee, attorneys Chuck Jones and Harold Ferguson of Rutgers Legal Clinic, the *Jackson Advocate* newspaper, Rutgers law students, the Committee to End the Marion Lockdown, the American Indian Movement, and others.

The End *of the '70s*

 As the decade wound down the late '70s saw the demise of the NOI following the death of Elijah Muhammad and the rise of Orthodox Islam among significant segments of New Afrikans on both sides of the wall. By 1979 the prison population stood at 300,000, a whopping 100,000 increase from 100,000 to 200,000, had taken 31 years from 1927 to 1958 to reach. The initial increase to 100,000 had taken hundreds of years, since America's original colonial times. The '60s were the transition decade of White flight that saw a significant decrease in both prison population and White prisoners. And since the total Black prison population increased only slightly or changed insignificantly over the decade of the insurgent '60s through 1973, it indicates that New Afrikans are imprisoned least when they fight hardest.

The decade ended on a masterstroke by the BLA's Multinational Task Force, with the November 2, 1979, prison liberation of Assata Shakur– "Soul of the BLA" and preeminent political prisoner of the era. The Task Force then whisked her away to the safety of political asylum in Cuba where she remains to date.

The Decade *Of The '80s*

In June 1980 Ali Hassan was released after 16 years in the New Jersey state prisons. Two months later, five New World of Islam (NWI) members were arrested after a North Brunswick, New Jersey, bank robbery in a car with stolen plates. The car belonged to the recently released Ali Hassan, who had loaned it to a friend. Ali Hassan and 15 other NWI members refused to participate in the resulting mass trial which charged them in a Racketeering Influenced Corrupt Organization (RICO) indictment with conspiracy to rob banks for the purpose of financing various NWI enterprises in the furtherance of creating an independent Black Nation. All defendants were convicted and sent behind the walls.

The '80s brought another round of BLA freedom fighters behind the walls – Basheer Hameed and Abdul Majid in '80; Sekou Odinga, Kuwasi Balagoon, Chui Fergurson-El, Jamal Josephs again, Mutulu Shakur, and numerous BLA Multinational Task Force supporters in '81; and Terry Khalid Long, Leroy Ojore Bunting, and others in '82. The government's sweep left Mtyari Sundiata dead, Kuwasi Balagoon subsequently dead in prison from AIDS, and Sekou Odinga brutally tortured upon capture, torture that included pulling out his toenails and rupturing his pancreas during long sadistic beatings that left him hospitalized for six months.

But this second round of captured BLA freedom fighters brought forth, perhaps for the first time, a battery of young, politically astute New Afrikan lawyers – Chokwe Lumumba, Jill Soffiyah Elijah, Nkechi Taifa, Adjoa Aiyetoro, Ashanti Chimurenga, Michael Tarif Warren, and others. They are not only skilled in representing New Afrikan POWs but the New Afrikan Independence Movement too, all of which added to the further development of the New Afrikan liberation struggle behind the walls.

The decade also brought behind the walls Mumia Abu-Jamal, the widely respected Philadelphia radio announcer, popularly known as the "Voice of the Voiceless." He maintained a steady drumbeat of radio support for MOVE prisoners. He finished work the night of December 9, 1981, stepped outside the station, and discovered a policeman beating his younger brother. Mumia was shot and seriously wounded, the policeman was killed. Mumia now sits on death row in greatest need of mass support from every sector, if he's to be saved from the state's electric chair.

Kazi Toure of the United Freedom Front (UFF) was sent behind the walls in 1982. He was released in 1991.

The New York 8 – Coltrane Chimurenga, Viola Plummer and her son Robert "R.T." Taylor, Roger Wareham, Omowale Clay, Lateefah Carter, Colette Pean, and Yvette Kelly – were arrested on October 17, 1984, and charged with conspiring to commit prison breakouts and armed robberies, and to possess weapons and explosives. However the New York 8 were actually the New York 8 + because another 8 or 9 persons were jailed as grand jury resisters in connection with the case. The New York 8 were acquitted on August 5, 1985.

That same year Ramona Africa joined other MOVE comrades already behind the walls. Her only crime was that she survived Philadelphia Mayor Goode's May 13, 1985, bombing which cremated 11 MOVE members, including their babies, families, home, and neighborhood.

The following year, November 19, 1986, a 20-year-old Bronx, New York, youth, Larry Davis, now Adam Abdul Hakeem, would make a dramatic escape during a shootout with police who had come to assassinate him for absconding with their drug-sales money. Several policemen were wounded in the shoot-out. Adam escaped unscathed but surrendered weeks later in the presence of the media, his family, and a mass of neighborhood supporters. After numerous charges, trials, and acquittals in which he exposed the existence of a New-York-police-controlled drug ring that coerced Black and Puerto Rican youths to push police-supplied drugs, he was sent behind the walls on weapon possession convictions. Since incarceration, numerous beatings by guards have paralyzed him from the waist down and confined him to a wheelchair.

On July 16, 1987, Abdul Haqq Muhammad, Arthur Majeed Barnes, and Robert "R.T." Taylor, all members of the Black Man's Movement Against Crack, were pulled over by state troopers in upstate New York, arrested, and subsequently sent to prison on a variety of weapon possession convictions.

Herman Ferguson at 68 years old voluntarily returned to the U.S. on April 6, 1989, after 20 years exile in Ghana, Afrika, and Guyanna, South America. He had fled the U.S. during the late '60s after the appeal was denied on his sentence of 3½ to 7 years following a conviction for conspiring to murder Civil Rights leaders. Upon return he was arrested at the airport and was moved constantly from prison to prison for several years as a form of harassment.

The '80s brought the Reagan era's rollback of progressive trends on a wide front and a steep rise in racist incidents, White vigilantism, and police murder of New Afrikan and Third World people. It also brought the rebirth and reestablishment of the NOI, a number of New Afrikan POW's adopting orthodox Islam in lieu of revolutionary nationalism, the New Afrikan People's Organization's (NAPO) and its chairman Chokwe Lumumba's emergence from the RNA as banner carrier for the New Afrikan Independence Movement (NAIM), the New Orleans assassination of Lumumba Shakur of the Panther 21, and an upsurge in mass political demonstrations known as the "Days of Outrage" in New York City spearheaded by the December 12th Movement, and others.

The end of the decade brought the death of Huey P. Newton, founder of the Black Panther Party, allegedly killed by a young Black Guerrilla Family adherent on August 22, 1989, during a dispute over "crack". Huey taught the Black masses socialism and popularized it through the slogan "Power to the People!" He armed the Black struggle and popularized it through the slogan "Political Power grows out of the barrel of a gun." For that, and despite his human shortcomings, his particular contribution is comparable to the of other modern-day giants, Marcus Garvey, Elijah Muhammad, Malcolm X, and Martin Luther King.

AIDS, crack, street crime, gang violence, homelessness, and arrest rates have all exploded throughout the Black colonies. The prison population on June 30, 1989, topped 673,000, an incredible 372,000 increase in less than a decade, causing the tripling and doubling of prison populations in 34 states, and sizable increases in most others. New York City prisoners became so over-crowded they began using ships as jails. William Bennett, former U.S. Secretary of Education and so-called Drug Czar, announced plans to convert closed military bases into concentration camps.

The prison building spree and escalated imprisonment rates continue unabated. The new prisoners are younger, more volatile, have long prison sentences, and are overwhelmingly of New Afrikan and Third World nationalities. It is estimated that by the year 1994 the U.S. will have over one million prisoners. Projections suggest that over 75 percent of them will be Black and other people of color. More women are now incarcerated than previously. Their percentage rose to 5 percent in 1980 from a low of 3 percent in 1970. Whites are arrested at about the same rate as in Western Europe while the New Afrikan arrest rate has surpassed that of Blacks in South Africa. In fact, the U.S. Black imprisonment rate is now the highest in the world. Ten times as many Blacks as Whites are incarcerated per 100,000 population.

The '90 *and Beyond*

As we begin to move through the '90s the New Afrikan liberation struggle behind the walls finds itself coalescing around campaigns to free political prisoners and prisoners of war, helping to build a national PP/POW organization, strengthening its links on the domestic front, and building solidarity in the international arena. Although the established media concentrates on the sensationalism of ghetto crack epidemics, street crime, drive-by shootings, and gang violence, there has been a long quiet period of consciousness raising in the New Afrikan colonies by the committed independence forces. This heightened consciousness of the colonies is just beginning to manifest itself through seemingly random sparks and the rise of innovative cultural trends, i.e., Rap/Hip Hop "message" music, culturally designed hair styles, dissemination of political/cultural video cassettes, resprouting of insurgent periodicals, and the resurrection of forgotten heroes; all of which presage an oppressed people getting ready to push forward again.

The New Afrikan liberation struggle behind the walls now follows the laws of its own development, paid for in its own blood, intrinsically linked to the struggle of its own people, and rooted deep in the ebb and flow of its own history. To know that history is already to know its future development and direction.

Sundiata Acoli
Leavenworth Penitentiary, Kansas

Severed Ties;

The Incarcerated Mother

by Emilyn Laura

The surreptitious rise in female imprisonment has come to represent years of entrenched poverty, drug sweeps and corresponding quotas, and a tangled maze of bureaucracy. Behind the common, but limited view of "female crime" that the larger society attributes to drugs, prison advocates make correlations between crime and the bitter harvest of Regan policies that created a new legion of the poor.

Of 1.1 million inmates currently serving time in America – a prison population that exceeds both apartheid South Africa and the Soviet Union – women comprise approximately 50,000. A disproportionate number are single parents, whose children, whether born within prison walls or "lost" within foster care systems are also doing time. Unlike prisoners who formerly served their time and began a new life, women starting over today must challenge and win against a system built for profits of racial and gender bias.

Politicizing Crime

A little over a decade ago female arrests were far less frequent, comprising less than 1,000 inmates in state prisons and city jails. With the proliferation of drugs within Black communities, the incarceration of women began to reflect their evolution from low level users, to couriers and finally low level dealers. By 1987 the female rate of incarceration had outstripped their male counterparts. Drug related crimes committed by women in the 25 to 29 age category range from property theft involving burglary, grand larceny or forgery, prostitution, or welfare fraud; all indicators of recurring financial distress. Advocates attribute relentless rounds of cutbacks within social service agencies, elimination of job training programs for youth, and the long-standing deficit of "quality of life" basics such as education, jobs and housing as ongoing factors in the high rates of incarceration among women. Women without skills or economic means are far more vulnerable to the lure of selling drugs or sex to survive. Dr. Debra Prothrow-Stith, author of *Deadly Consequences* argues that,

> ...the scarcity of employed men in poor Black communities set in motion a train of destructive events...When large numbers of men are out of work and large numbers of families are headed by women, the rate of crime and violence in that community rises sharply...This data regarding single-parent families should not be interpreted as derogatory to single mothers...[but] highlights...the terrible stress under which impoverished single parent families live.

Statistics furnished by the Correctional Association of New York, prison advocates since 1844, indicate that more than half (66.1%) of the 3,500 women currently serving time in New York State prisons are first time drug offenders whose sentences may average one to three years. At least 75% of all female inmates across the nation are single parents who were raising, on the average, two dependent children prior to arrest.

Attorney Ellen Barry, Director of Legal Services for Prisoners with Children has worked extensively with female prisoners on the West Coast. She observes that female substances abusers seem to elicit particularly harsh sentences, invariably "for their own good." Take the case of Doris M., for example. She was sentenced to serve six months in the county jail in Oakland, California when she was seven months pregnant. Addicted to heroin, the judge made a decision to override the option of local community-based programs where she could receive treatment. Instead, she was forced to kick drugs cold turkey, received no obstetrical care for the first six weeks and at nearly nine months her stillborn daughter was removed by Caesarean section.

The mindset of this particular judge is not an abberation but one

 the attorney attributes to "...tremendous frustration on the part of sentencing judges who are aware of no other options. It also arises from a misunderstanding of the nature and treatment of substance abuse treatment and a growing tendency on the part of the general community to seek punishment for individuals involved with drugs...as opposed to treatment."

This punitive approach to drug use is further demonstrated by the political bent of the 1973 Rockefeller Drug Sentencing Laws. In January of 1990, for example, 59 women were arrested at JFK airport and detained for their alleged role as "drug mules". Held for nearly a year while lawyers wrangled over Class A-1 felony charges versus the defendants claims of coercion, eventually all charges were dismissed. In contrast, just a few years earlier, an undisclosed number of women, detained on similar charges, failed to convince authorities of coercion and received life sentences, despite the lack of any previous criminal record. Advocates argue that the mechanics of the law which carries a minimum of 15 years to life for criminal possession of controlled substances becomes a political tool in the hands of politicians, and is a prime factor in overpopulated prisons.

Children Doing Time

The entire family is impacted by the arrest of one parent. For children it may mean the loss of youthful innocence, replaced instead with guilt and worry that may be expressed in a number of ways: an infant's inability to form emotional attachment, an older child's recurrent nightmares, in teens inappropriate or abusive behavior. For parent-inmates it unleashes a pervasive and often infectious sense of failure. For grandparents it means raising a second generation of children, straining financial resources and taxing physical strength.

According to the Correctional Association, an estimated 120,000 children have already experienced the emotional shock of having a parent imprisoned. This figure, primarily based on the incarceration of fathers who rely on the mother or female family member in the role of caretaker, fails to tell the story of children whose sole support are their mothers. For these children, various aspects of parental incarceration, particularly their removal from familiar surroundings, generates financial, emotional and social upheaval that may be long in healing, Citing standard police arrests as the beginning of a long destructive process, Barry explains, "In New York City, the police department has internal regulations instructing officers to permit women to make a phone call to a relative or friend to care for the child. In reality, however, most women are barely given time to say good-bye to their children...In numerous instances children are either taken to the police station with their mothers, or delivered to emergency shelter facilities."

Irregardless of the "process" of incarceration, children tend to remain a vital, if overlooked anchor throughout booking, arraignment and sentencing procedures, vicariously experiencing in greater or lesser degrees, the degradation of their parents.

Research conducted by the National Council on Crime and Delinquency (NCCD) show that most children of incarcerated mothers remain with their maternal grandmother (65%). Another 20% are placed with relatives and friends while 17% remain with their fathers. Children may be forced to encounter the maze of family courts, welfare agencies and foster homes at various times during parental incarceration, an even smaller percentage remain entangled for the duration of their formative years. While some foster home situations work toward positive reinforcement of the relationship between parent-inmates and their children, far too many compound the tragedy of incarceration. Writing in *Mothers In Prison*, Phyllis Jo Baunach comments,

> Some foster programs tend to generate a pervasive and implicit anti-family bias…Parents are not encouraged to visit children, to maintain ties, or to meet caretakers; funds for services that might assist reunification of families are often unavailable; grievance mechanisms for parents or children are non-existent and the massive amount of paperwork often precludes caseworkers from getting to know natural parents and their needs.

Further restraints are placed on the family unit by antiquated state laws. Although laws vary from state to state, many support the notion that parental rights may be severed if a basis for abandonment can be proven. Given the sentencing structure of most prisons where inmates are held for long periods before their case is disposed of, or the unstable atmosphere generated by prison officials who tend to treat family visits as a privilege, rather than a First Amendment right, the basis for upholding parental rights is constantly eroded.

In a recent case of a single parent father in Florida, identified only as B.W. and his children, J.W. and W., persistence may provide incentive. The Supreme Court overruled a lower court decision to award the children to state agencies stating,

> a prisoner's efforts to assume his parental duties by communicating with and supporting his children must be measured against his limited opportunity to assume these duties while imprisoned.

The net effect of B.W.'s cards and letters explaining his inability to be with his children, both to them and the appropriate agencies, added emotional leverage to his appeal and subsequent victory. In New State however, parents are hampered by procedures of Child Welfare Administration (CWA) whose directives to arrange for visitation between imprisoned parents and their children are restricted to prisoners within fifty miles of New York City. This would mean that most women housed in state prisons remain outside of CWA's jurisdiction and also, outside of the lives of their children.

Finally, there is the seldom publicized, but volatile issue of women giving birth within prison. Lawsuits brought in California, Connecticut and Massachusetts read like a litany of horror stories: routine use of wrist shackles, leg restraints, abdominal shackles; lack of systematic OBYN treatment and inappropriate prison protocol and procedures have all been documented and form the basis for prison reform. There were typical cases like Linda H., for example, who was transported to the outside hospital in shackles, seated upright in a van. The baby was born in severe distress, was in neonatal intensive care for thirty-one days, and continues to have permanent disability as a result. Esperanza C. was not seen once by an obstetrician during the entire course of her pregnancy at the prison; the fetus died in utero at eight and a half months.

In New York State, establishment of Bedford Hills prison nursery came about as the result of a lawsuit. Established by penal laws more than two decades ago, prison officials failed to comply until a lawsuit, filed in 1973 by a county jail prisoner who accused prison officials with taking her child away after its birth. The lower court which heard her case ruled

> Incarceration in a jail or correctional institution *per se* does not constitute such unfitness or exceptional circumstances that require a newborn infant be taken from its mother...

Following the suit, the nursery, located in a special wing separate from the general population, created policy that allowed a minimum of ten female inmates to remain with their infants for the first year of life, with medical care, food and clothing provided by the State. The facility's 1984 follow-up report on the 28 women who gave birth while incarcerated, list robbery as the most common offense committed by women in the 20-34 age category. Again, most of the women were single mothers and in instances where the infant was released while the mother finished her sentence, the inmates family played an instrumental role as caretaker. Only two instances of infants being placed in the custody of the Department of Social Services for future foster care were reported. Overall, prison authorities concluded that when inmates were allowed to bond with their child, recidivism was markedly lower. Only three women violated parole after release.

Forging New Ties

Increasingly, imprisonment has taken on dimensions of an undeclared war on the Black family; a battle in which our children are the heaviest casualties. Bureaucracy dictates the survival of women who seek reunification with their family. Overcoming charges in Family Court, for example, requires many women who may be homeless when released, to obtain public assistance which many landlords refuse to accept. If seeking employment many women face seemingly insurmountable odds that require them to obtain a GED or job training. Without an apartment, or other demonstrated means of stability, retrieving their children from "the system" involves an uphill battle.

Growing efforts by advocates who push for alternative sentencing, halfway houses and drug treatment have begun to make some inroads. Clearly, however, the most significant fight is within. Barry maintains that real change begins "by putting a name and face on prisoners that society wishes to remain anonymous. No mater how many lawsuits we bring," she emphasizes, "we have no illusions that it will make prison a place to want to be. Prisons destroy...It's about empowering people so they don't have to be there."

Listed are a few of the many organizations in New York working to provide information, or direct services to the families of incarcerated mothers:

Ace
Bedford Hills Correctional Facility
247 Harris Road
Bedford Hills, NY 10507
(914) 241-3100, ext. 384
Prepares incarcerated women for release through mentorship and support programs

AIDS in Prison Project
Correctional Association of N.Y.
135 East 15th Street
New York, NY 10003
(212) 477-9633
Information, referrals, support and advocacy for incarcerated persons living with HIV/AIDS

Fortune Society
19 West 19th Street
New York, NY 10018
(212) 206-7070
Advocacy for prisoners on behalf of their families, HIV counseling, and support groups

The Incarcerated Mothers Program
Edwin Gould Services for Children
104 East 107th Street
New York, NY 10029
(212) 410-4200
Provides advocacy, foster care prevention counseling and vocational training

Justice Works Community
1012 8th Avenue
Brooklyn, NY 11215
(718) 499-6704
Offers comprehensive services to children of incarcerated parents

The Odyssey House
309-11 East 6th St.
New York, NY 10003
Provides educational, vocational and advocacy for former inmates. Family center provides housing for women with one or two children under age five.

Single Parent Resource Center
141 West 28th St.
New York, NY 10001
(212) 947-0221
Services for children aged 5-13 impacted by the incarceration of their parents.

Womencare Inc.
236 East 27th St., 2nd fl.
New York, NY 10001
(212) 463-9500/9506
Referrals, advocacy and mentorship programs for mothers in prison.

Legal Aid Society Prisoners' Rights Project
15 Park Row, 23rd floor
New York, NY 10038
(212) 577-3938, 3907

Women's Prison Association and Hopper Home
110 Second Avenue
New York, NY 10003
(212) 674-1163/677-1981
Provides foster care prevention, counseling and housing placement assistance.

Apocalypse 4 Ever by Ras Baraka

The sky
has been - GONE
some time now,
while the sun just sits there
and Burns!
u could see the stench
rise above the clouds and
the birds are stoned from the odor
smashing themselves into the
horizons
while naked children's feets
walk over their heads on blistered streets
    and
The stench of slow death seeps out the creases
in the earth.
THE WORLD SPEAKS HER POETRY OUT LOUD!
THE WORLD SPEAKS HER POETRY OUT LOUD!
maggots, halfeaten rodents,
and what is left of the well-to-do
fight destitutely over piles and piles
of arms legs torsos
dropped into the street
by giant welfare trucks.
while the poorer people nibble
for months at a time
peeling the flesh from the bones
of their own fingers and toes
in an effort to stay alive or die
which ever comes first.
even the peoples gods have took to
fighting in public places
cutting stabbing and gouging
each others eyes out in competition
for sacrifice and prayer.
LIFE IS A DIALECTIC!
LIFE IS A DIALECTIC...!
either you love or you hate
either you fat or you starve
either you have a house or you homeless

either you rich or you poor
either you unemployed or there is war
either you laugh or you cry
either you kill or you die!
opposites attract! opposite attract!
THA Boogey Man - He's for real
THA Boogey Man's real.
He lives in the closets of people's minds, and under the beds of people's hearts
haven't you heard the story of yacub - man.
he created monsters
ZOMBIEDRAKULAS
that drained the blood from the corner of the planet
and sucked the sky dry
until the sun just burned
every living thing in sight
and now,
NOW
niggers have fallen to their knees
praying to purple creatures
martians from way out lands
on super duper space ships
come to save dem
black asses
loud voices can be heard
(in what's left of our journeys)
    drop the bomb.
    drop the bomb.
Exterminate them all
in a nervously calm tone.
There are no more prisons
no more books
only time rotting away
THE WORLD SCREAMS HER POETRY OUT LOUD!
THE WORLD IS SCREAMING HER POETRY OUT LOUD!
The lies have sailed to the end of the seas
only to find out
after these centuries
the earth had been flattened
to preserve the status quo
and that
good does not always prevail
 sometimes evil has the upperhand...

and i wonder what will they do to my corpse
for seeing this
will they dismember me into souvenirs
drag my bloody body thru the streets
make hats coats hood ornaments
out of my memories
will they say he was a nice guy
a great man
loved children
was playfully serious
will they lie.
THE WORLD IS YELLING HER POETRY ONCE AGAIN!
THE WORLD SHE'S YELLING HER POETRY AGAIN!
gasping for air
breathing for help
on our faces
she has finally made her full turn
from nothing to nothing
from caveman to caveman
from bush to BUSH!
she has finally been conquered slaughtered
by futuristic cavemen
and is dying a slow death
gasping for air
breathing her last request on our faces
until there are no more flowers
no more trees, no more fires, no more air
no more animals, no more
living things
while little white men
in flying machines are yelling
to one another overhead
in a nervously calm tone
    DROP THE BOMB.
    DROP THE BOMB.
    DROP THE BOMB.
exterminate them all!

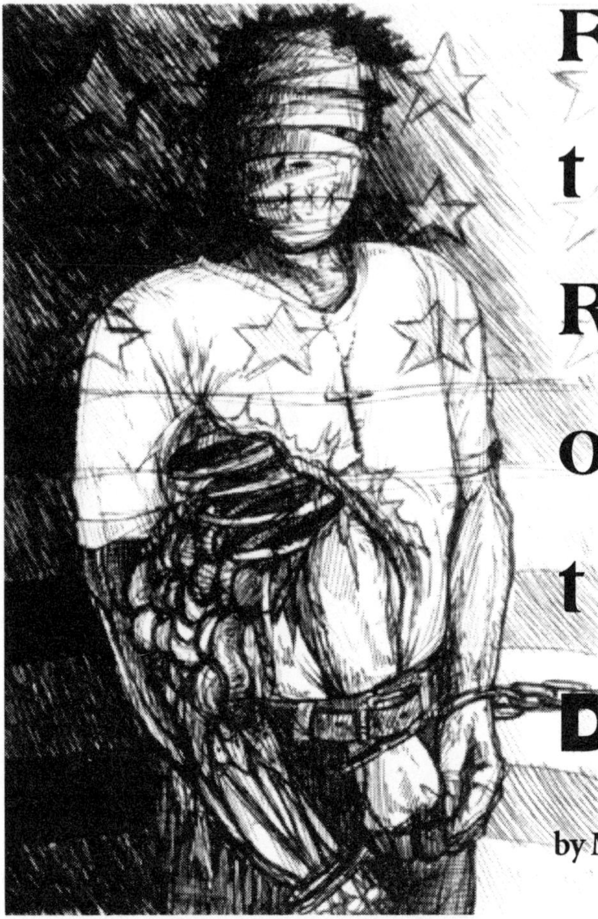

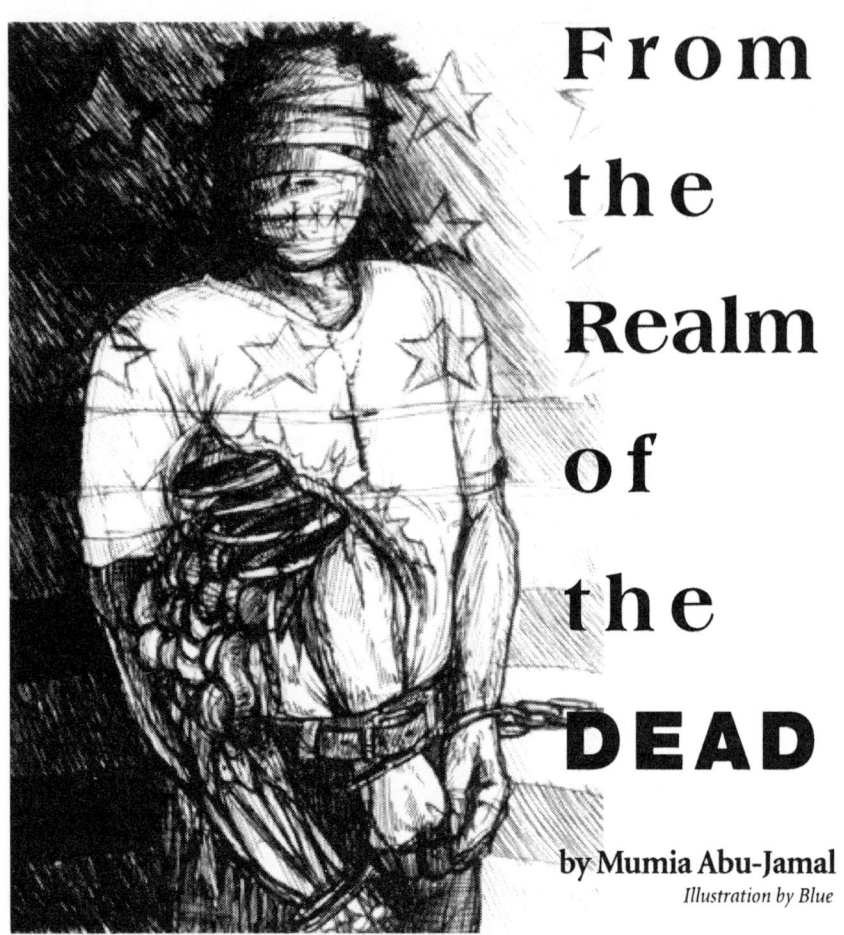

From the Realm of the DEAD

by Mumia Abu-Jamal

Illustration by Blue

"I believe that all African American prisoners are political prisoners, whether or not they label themselves as such. Because of the circumstances that got them into jail as well as the harshness of sentencing applied only to them."
-Evelyn Williams, Esq. *Inadmissible Evidence* (Lawrence Hill – 1993)

Attorney Williams' opinion doesn't merely arise from the ether; it emerges from the cruel crucible of her extraordinary life experience, as both aunt and lead trial counsel of the Black Liberation Army's Assata Shakur. It springs from her days spent in the furnaces called white courts, fighting not just for her fabled niece, but for countless blacks who tried to battle a system designed to grind them up. It comes from a brief, humiliating and enlightening stint as a prisoner, following a contempt of court citation. It coalesces from the merger of her professional and personal selves.

Lest the reader be unaware, the writer here sets forth the astonishing rates of incarceration of U.S. black males, especially as compared with the rates recently drawn from South Africa under apartheid.

Both the U.S.A. and the R.S.A. (Republic of South Africa) are white settler states which have historically enslaved and exploited Africans for material, social and psychological advantage. Moreover, both counties have historically oppressed African people to develop and maintain their settler states, thus our comparison is strengthened. Consider the following table;[1]

Table I

State	*Black Male Population*	*Black Male Inmates*	*Incarceration Rates per 100,000*
United States	14,625,000	454,724	3,109
South Africa	15,050,642	109,739	729

Put quite another way, the United States, with much less the black male population of South Africa, incarcerates four times as many of them. Rarely does a state overtly present its policy objectives, but we can infer the following from the numbers:

•the significant costs of incarceration, estimated at over $20,000 annually per prisoner, reflects an expenditure the state is quite willing to pay;

•the state, by spending an estimated $7 billion a year to incarcerate black prisoners, has chosen the most expensive of all nonincarcerative yet retributive choices, with the highest tolls in human suffering as well as lost dollars;

•the ages of those entering the system, roughly 20–29 years, reflect times of peak male sexual procreativity, thus causing disproportionate impact on reproductive strategies of a specific racial group;

•the intentional and probable effect of such disproportionate reduction of males from the reproductive realm effects a concomitant reduction in the rates of childbirth of the affected people.

So pervasive is the spectre of the state over black life that the prison has become a macabre rite of passage, a grim expectation that obstructs the road to life.

If the reader can say freely that the South African Republic (at least prior to the establishment of the Multiracial Transitional Executive Council in late 1993) is a racist state, then why is it so difficult to freely say the same of the North American Republic?

A nation, like an individual, is the sum total of its psychological, genetic (i.e., historic), social, spiritual, economic and political influences, and few can arrive that any other people have been exposed to as many, or as destructive, negative life influences as have African Americans.

It is virtually impossible to accurately track the multitudinous influences on a nation of millions, but Thomas Jefferson, widely regarded as a "founding father", drafter of the Declaration of Independence, and author of the *Religious Freedom Clause of the Constitution of Virginia,* undoubtedly had, and continues to have, enormous influence on the American mind and character.

America's third president was both a slaveowner and a prodigious writer who recorded his thoughts and firm opinions on African-"Americans" (especially men) with remarkable honestly and ambiguity.

A "revolutionary" sworn to (white) liberty, as well as owner of over 100 slaves (black), Thomas Jefferson was of the firm opinion that blacks would never become an accepted part of white American political life on equal terms:

Deep rooted prejudices entertained by the whites; ten thousand recollections, by the blacks, of the injuries they have sustained; new provocations, the real distinction which nature has made; and many other circumstances, will divide us into parties, and produce convulsions which will probably never end but in the extermination of the one or the other race. – To these objections, which are political, may be added others, which are physical and moral.[2]

Jefferson believed that among those "real distinctions" made by nature between blacks and whites, were inherent mental, intellectual, imaginative and creative inferiorities by blacks. Blacks, Jefferson wrote, were "in reason much inferior", "in imagination they are dull", and had not "even an elementary trait of painting or sculpture". Nor could blacks write poetry in Jefferson's view, even though misery is thought to be the mother of verse. "Among the Blacks is misery enough, God knows, but no poetry", he wrote.

The aim of this essay is not to further besmirch the name of Jefferson, for he is beyond such concerns now, but merely to point out how one of America's "enlightened" thought on the most pressing issue of his time.

We are in an age when a plethora of both black and white voices insist on "The Declining Significance of Race", furthering the nation that class, gender and transpersonal psychology are more central to the American Agenda. Yet, the Power of Truth is such that insistence is unequipped to halt her flow, and underlying each social, economic, political transaction lies the miasma of race. How true were the slavemaster, President Jefferson's words! They resonate over 200 years through time with a relevance that leaps centuries.

It is those "distinctions" that now color America's correctional industry, and have become so pronounced since the 1970s.

A government study of prison admissions in the United States on the basis of race[3] from 1926 to 1986 reveals a marked and dramatic rise in the number and percentage of African-Americans sent to state and federal prisons, a rate that began disproportionately high and began to boom in the 70s. A compilation from Bureau figures follow;[4]

TABLE II

	Number of Admissions to State & Federal		Percent of State and federal prisoners			Percent of State Prison Admissions only	
Year	*Prisons*	*Total*	*White*	*Black*	*Total*	*White*	*Black*
1926	43,328	100%	78%	21%	100%	75%	23%
1940	62,692	100	71	28	100	70	29
1970	48,497	100	61	39	100	57	43
1986	183,769	100	55	44	100	53	46

1990 [5] of 390,087 State Prison Admissions in 1990, from 35 states, these percentages 100% 46.0% 53.2%

While the writer acknowledges the difficulty inherent in interpreting statistical data for socio-political purposes, he argues that as relative percentile of population has changed little in the 60-year period (i.e., 10% in 1926 vs. 12% in 1986) then population growth cannot account for the phenomenal leap in African-American incarceration rates.

The 1970s marked a pivotal phase in U.S. history, as a time of the emergence of the Black Liberation Movement via militant groups like the Revolutionary Action Movement (RAM), the Republic of New Africa (RNA), and The Black Panther Party (BPP). This striking emergence, the author argues, gave rise to the often startling disparity reflected in statistics which show, in 1990[6] rates, how whites, roughly 90% of the U.S. population, can become a minority percentage (46%) of those admitted to state prisons, and how blacks (to be precise, black men), roughly 12% of the U.S. population, can balloon upwards to a majority percentage (53.2%) of state prison admissions.

Nor is it dispositive of the issue for one to infer that as the accused were criminals, duly convicted of committing felonies, claims of disparity should be dismissed.

A 1990 profile of felons[7] convicted in state courts revealed that "among persons convicted, *white felons were less likely than blacks to be sent to prison*; 42% of convicted white defendants received a prison sentence, *54% of black defendants*, and 47% of defendants of other races."

When government figures admit to such gross disparity, then who are we to deny their import?

Who are we to second guess their significance?

This entire system is but the embodiment of white will, a will still to devalue, encage and ultimately destroy Black Life.

This system reflects but the "law of the outlaw", and the adage of Evelyn Williams, which opened this essay, resounds with the ring of truth.

ENDNOTES

[1] See Marc Mauer, Americans Behind Bars – *A Comparison of International Rates of Incarceration; Cages of Steel*, p. 24 (Maisonneuve Press – 1992); Accord; Same, publ. by The Sentencing Project, 918 F St., N.W., Ste. 501, Washington, D.C. 20004; (202) 628-0871.

[2] Thos. Jefferson, *Notes on the State of Virginia* (1782).

[3] Look for footnote

[4] Id., at 5, 6.

[5] B.J.S., U.S. Dept. of Just., *Sourcebook of Criminal Justice Stat's* 1992, 1993.

[6] See Table II, last line, supra.

[7] Bureau of Justice Statistics, *National Judicial Reporting Program*, 1990; Dec. 1993, p. 14.

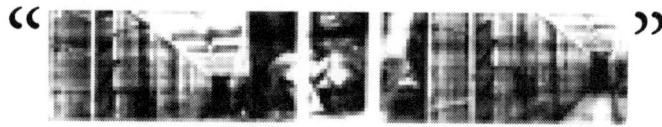

“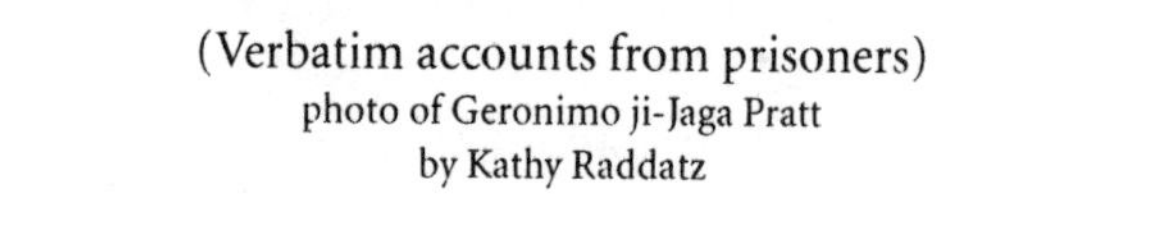”

Means

“Our Voice From Within”

(Verbatim accounts from prisoners)

photo of Geronimo ji-Jaga Pratt
by Kathy Raddatz

our voice from within

STRAIGHT FROM THE HEART

Adam Abdul Hakeem, who at 15 years of age was "forcefully recruited" by the NYPD as his partner in drug dealing and whose attempt to "extricate himself from their clutches with their drug money"–ending in a shootout November 19, 1986 with a squad of 30 "converging to assassinate him" ("I was not apprehended; I turned myself in to the FBI on December 6, 1986")–wrote NOBO several times September, 1993, after general queries about his well-being and what he would like to share with his brothers and sisters on the outside.

Hakeem's case made history. He is the only black man in the annals of the U.S. Republic to ever be acquitted after shooting ("9 – not 6 as reported – were shot") policemen in self defense. Long before the Mollen Commission came into existence, you'd think more heavy political eyebrows, both right and left, would have been lifted based on this significant fact alone.

Now in Comstock Correctional Facility (for, ostensibly, illegal gun possession charges), confined to a wheelchair after a particularly vicious "restraining" by 15 correction guards, and now 27 years old, Bro. Hakeem sent the following long handwritten note and poem, his first correspondence to us. It is indicative of his spiralling upward development:

You requested my views, as to the most significant things our community needs to know about the Penal System. You went further and said come "straight from the heart". You make it seem from that statement that things I do or say are not from my heart, when in fact they are.

In any event, some of my views are as follows:

As of this present day, most black people don't know that jails and prisons did not come into effect until blacks were released from the plantations during the Lincoln period when he issued, as you know, the "Emancipation Proclamation", on the 1st of January, 1863.

Prior to the year of 1863 you and I both know Europeans did nothing more than hang our people and just outright killed them and raped our women, killing many of them. Certainly, slavery is still in effect, clearly in a modernized manner.

The 13th Amendment to the United States Constitution provides:

"Neither *slavery nor involuntary servitude, except as a punishment for crime* whereof the party shall have been duly convicted, shall exist within United States, or any place subject to their jurisdiction". [Emphasis author's.]

This was adopted to the Constitution in the year of 1865, after the assassination of Lincoln (in that same year). The European racist Congress foresaw the need to issue the 13th Amendment to maintain some control over those they recognized as slaves, which, as you know, were and are blacks. Congress at that time realized that weapons were in the hands of blacks, who were fighting in the war with the Union (to save the Union). It was right after that war the 13th Amendment was adopted.

Congress feared in every possible way that blacks who had the firepower as well as the manpower would rebel once blacks had finish fighting the Union war and that was the last thing Congress needed to see was blacks taking over the United States.

So Congress made it clear that slavery will exist in the United States as a form of punishment for those convicted of crimes against the United States. And as you know, the only people considered slaves were blacks. And to go a step further, Congress adds further insult to injury by allowing the existence of the death penalty.

Should a brother commit a capital crime and be sentenced to death because he is found to have committed the crime? The real question is does the person who puts the brother to death get the same death sentence for committing the capital crime against the brother who he puts to death? After all, a capital crime is a capital crime according to the U.S. Constitution and certainly two wrongs plus the wrongfulness of the Constitution does not make any right.

Since my incarceration it has come to mind that all prisoners in the State of New York prison system have been sentenced to prison time and not death or savage beatings by sadistic guards. However, I've personally witnessed beatings of prisoners as well as the death of one, and when I personally intervened on their behalfs I was was attacked myself. Even had COs spit in my face and put feces in my food on numerous occasions. Solely because I intervened on brothers behalfs and will continue to intervene when need be.

One of the most significant things I've come to learn about these ruthless, deceitful, careless, deceiving, immoral, revengeful, inconsiderate, irresponsible, racist, sadistic correction guards is that they have conspired to provoke unprovoked fights with prisoner(s) to get the prisoner(s) to fight back, after he has been savagely beaten by sadistic guards. This is done by guards for several reasons:

(a) So the guard(s) can claim an assault upon his person, so he can use the assault as an excuse to go out on "sick leave" and get free pay;

(b) to keep any rebellious prisoner behind these prison walls by bringing outside court charges against the prisoner; and (c) to be able to write various fraudulent misbehavior reports to get that mandatory $5.00 surcharge from prisoners accounts (because of the misbehavior reports). After all this is a business.

One must understand that this country of America has been built off the Europeans lies and destruction. However, how can we go believing that this System will work? They say that the Department of Corrections is to correct prisoners' behavior. How in the hell can they correct anybody's behavior if they are not correct themselves.

The Penal System is built off lies and destruction. The Judges, DAs and Police lie to get us political prisoners of war (PPOW) behind these walls, then the destruction comes in when they try and even succeed in killing us behind these prison walls.

Brothers and sisters when we learn to trust ourselves that's when we will stop trusting in this system and until then, we will go on giving this system chances after chances which is leading us more and more to our total destruction.

We can't trust anybody to do what we ask of them because we can't trust our own ability to trust each other. We must destroy this system or it will destroy us.

Respectfully,
Adam Abdul Hakeem

Men In Blue

As I sit within this Prison of Pain
Searching endlessly, in mindless gain,
Reflecting life's comic outrage.

Society's laws they say I broke,
Not wanting to be the police's joke
Dealing drugs for the men in blue – as well as DAs too,
Yea, those sent to "protect" me and you …

They run the hoods citywide
Stealing young souls, and the young can't hide
Spreading terror far and wide,
The men in blue: They take our pride.

To those of us who refuse to abide,
The word hit the streets that one must fly

Patrolmen, DAs, Judges, Detectives, Inspectors: High,
Living on drug money, hands in the pie –
All saying, "Larry Davis must die."

So now I sit within this Prison of Pain
With the men in blue trying their best to torment my brain.
I took my stand – I stood with pride!
Hopefully teaching young brother and sisters
That there's no need to hide!

Through pain and suffering, one grows strong.
My strength is yours, let's move on
Fighting the drug dealing
  DAs, Judges and men in blue
Never give up, I AM WITH YOU.

Adam Abdul Hakeem
88T2550-D-1-27
Great Meadow Correction Facility
P. O. Box 51
Comstock, New York 12820-0051

NO TURN BACKS by Asha Bandele

See my people dressed in black
you know we come a long way
and we ain't turnin back
wade in the water
wade in the water children
wade in the water
you know my God is gonna trouble these waters for me
until every one of my people are free

What distinguishes this nite
is the silence
falling e z around my shoulders
a short-lived pretense 2 peace
and it's not that I'm unappreciative
it's that I'm aware...

  fast moon setting and the morning comes bringing with it statistics
that do not lend themselves to metaphor

oooh-
and if i cld
i wld write luvpoems all day
burn incense
watch my candle glow
and tell u stories of only beauty
but such choices r not mine 2 make
when the times demand of me this ritual:
the laying out of funeral clothes
the return of another blkchild
gone 2 soon
and now
now we walk
heads bowed in this world
of neutralized people
blkfaces of stone who no longer allow themselves 2 feel
and so they lie
they lie about everything to everybody
and dismiss the eruptions of afrikan volcanoes spitting maroon lava
like some freaky side show
  can't u write anything else

asha
?
doesn't anything make u happy
asha
?
baby
they
don't
know
i have this range of emotion
and i wanna be your lifetime smile
and i wanna make luv 2 you past the midnite ride your passion beyond a
frenzied dawn tease your sweat into necessary water 4 u 2 swallow whole -n- complete
-n- then make u ease -n- arch -n- stretch
baby
i
mean
i
need
2
make
u
feel...

but touch is not a simple thing
nor does it come with out a past
a present and we
we poets
blk and in desperate luv with people & possibility

we poets
blk and splitting moods
(and winning awards even)
(and publishing books even)
we poets blk
will remain in undisrupted pain
since we are apparently without even one word
within all these fancy/hip words
that can birth justice as quickly as america buries it

 we poets

blk
are reaching
and clawing
and trying
we poets
we are crying our words
we are searching our worlds
for a place 2 build a new house
a house 2 replace
this house
this house
cos this is the house that greed & historical revisionism built
this is the house that blk grandmothers shot dead in their own kitchens
and whiteboys walked free built

this is the house that blanketed diseases, the tallahatchie river, bloody
new jersy turnpikes, napalm, nuclear wipeouts of entire races and white boys walked free built
this is the house that roy innis built
this is the house that hatred built
and silence & individualism & the appointment of clarence thomas sanctioned
this is the house where blkgirls cld be so exhausted
by 16
that they'd whisper to me
listen
i don't care about nuthin
i just want 2 live
ok
/
behind the steady succession of assaults
used to be warriors
trade in the truth
4
loot
(gotta gotta get some loot yo!)
and we don't even reach 30
before giving up or else
giving out
our energy
2 any palefaced freak

who wld replace our sun
with neon
and who wld replace us!
us builders
us dreamers
us dragonslayers
us peacemakers
with deadeyed/ rythmless/ stupified/ zombie yes men
who stumble thru the univers
dribbling shit on themselves and their children
babbling new age sound-bite theories
without light
without luv
without life.

Message of POW's and Political

by Dhoruba bin Wahad

Historically, the governments of the United States and South Africa have dealt with political dissent and radical resistance to institutionalized racism in much the same manner. Under the pretense of maintaining "law and order," the U.S. and South Africa criminalize radical and progressive movements for social and political change. Here in the U.S., our movement was brutally and viciously destroyed. Our leaders were murdered, forced into exile or imprisoned.

In both the U.S. and South Africa there are hundreds of political prisoners within the bowels of their prisons. And yet the U.S. and South Africa boldly deny the existence of these freedom fighters to the world. Instead they claim these peoples' heroes are criminals.

In both the U.S. and South Africa, white skin privilege is the rule. The needs and humanity of poor people of color are for the most part ignored or denied. In South Africa racism is codified, reduced to a system of law. In the U.S. racism is more subtle and hypocritical: the odor of phony democratic idealism masks the foul stench of a racist, eurocentric system that dehumanizes us, imprisons our youth, marginalizes our women and tramples our most basic humanity.

As a former political prisoner, Comrade Mandela, you surely know what it means to be defined as a "terrorist" by a state that refuses to deal with the right of oppressed people of color to defend themselves against the racist violence, injustice and terrorism of the State. The very individuals and governments who hail you today as a "freedom fighter" in the past supported efforts to kill and imprison you. These same hypocrites defined the A.N.C. as a terrorist organization. The same white media that now hangs on your every word just a moment ago in history supported "constructive engagement" with the racist apartheid regime. This same white media has consistently distorted and stifled the righteous cause of the South African people.

Brother Nelson, I was incarcerated for twenty years for my political views and activities on behalf of the African-American community. Today there are over 100 political prisoners in the U.S. suffering under some of the most repressive conditions imaginable. Many of my comrades in the African-American liberation movement have been murdered by agents of the U.S. government, our families have been destroyed and our organizations decimated. But one day the African-American community will again have its own Intifada, its own peoples' uprising.

Today, U.S. political prisoners have no voice, they remain invisible. The A.N.C. and the anti-apartheid forces in South Africa have always kept the names and faces of your political prisoners in public view. We should learn from your example. We must not forget those who have sacrificed on our behalf. Brother Mandela I stand before you on their behalf, so that they may be heard. There's an African proverb which says if you speak the name of an ancestor they live again. Let us speak the name of our freedom fighters that they may be free again. Free Geronimo! Free Nuh! Free Herman! Free Abdul! Free Mumia! Free Leonard Peltier! Free Marilyn Buck! Free Jalil! Free Robert Seth Hayes! Free Ahmed Rahman! Free Sundiata! Free Sekou Odinga! Free David Rice! Free Kaza Toure! Free Hanif Shabazz Bey! Free Alejandrina Torres!

Our hearts and souls are with you and the freedom loving people of South Africa. It's been said that there are no strangers in the struggle for freedom, only comrades that never met. African-American political prisoners of the United States share a human experience with you that few who have not undergone long periods of imprisonment, isolation and torture for their political principles can understand. We are one in struggle! Power to the People! Amandla!

ARE HIGH TECH OPERATIVES AMONG US?

the nobo interview

A CONVERSATION with brian wronge

"I'm sitting on this park bench and this cop comes up to me, asking me where do I belong, so I tell him I'm minding my own business. The next thing I know, he's got his hand in my face so I knock his hand down; when I look up, five more of them suckers lined up. Before I know it, there it is, the usual routine: Prosecutor in court asking that I be "held over for observation" to determine my mental stability to stand trial. What did I do? Why am I here? I won't take that crap, thorazine and such. And when you try to refuse, they strap you down then shoot you with a needle. If you ever make a mistake in judgment and you allow something like that the first time, they'll send you through it again and again hoping you'll eventually break. You're a guinea pig for life."

Mind control and behavior modification through psychotropic drugs is certainly a chilling scenario. The above quote was part of a lengthy monologue expressed by a long time freedom fighter at a protest in Harrisburg in support of Mumia Abu Jamal. The injustice he has continually faced now appears tame compared to recent revelations of stealthy U.S. control and behavior modification experimentation.

Illustration by Shawn Alexander

Scientifically fixated, in the most base manner, the U.S. controlling culture has been gassed since the two greatest scientific advances in this century: the splitting of the atom and the splitting of the nucleus of the cell. With such important gains, the misdirected aim of the worldwide dominating moneyed elite has now inundated the planet with uncontrollable nuclear waste, genetic warfare and designer germs.

The amazing people discarding experiments of the 1950s was a response of the scientific community to the "cold war", which gave the U.S. government carte blanche to experiment on unknowing citizens under the guise of "national security".

The recent radiation experiment revelations uncovered by the Department of Energy (many say forceably) and the notorious CIA experiments of the 50s through the early 70s, code-named MKULTRA, clearly illustrates how thousands of Americans have been experimented on without their consent. The CIA experiments (drugs to electroshock to sensory deprivation) were known to be carried out in universities, mental hospitals, drug rehabilitation centers and prisons.

Most of the psycho/physiological experimentation in this country has been disproportionately performed on people of African descent. This began during the (overt) slavery era. Now shift from the despicable Tuskegee experiments to the case of Brian Wronge as confirmation that such furtive experimentation on African people has moved to a new level. The latest effort of the scientific community, for control elements in U.S. society, is implantation of computer devices in the body to augment, detect and direct functioning, eradicating or grossly distorting personal identity.

The well publicized 1940s experiments of physiologist Jose Delgado, reputedly done "altruistically" for humankind, involved implanting electrodes and transmitting radio signals through them to induce desired mobility and other behaviors in animals.

Microsurgery is a highly intricate, yet frequently performed speciality. Practitioners are quite capable of removing pituitary tumors through the nose and sewing tiny, injured brain nerves back together efficiently. Or leaving small metal clips on the arteries of the brain, to cut off aneurysms. This invasion is imperceptible and causes no harm to the patient.

First reported in Maitefa Angaza's "Sci-Fact-Not Fiction: High-Tech Slavery is Here" (The City Sun, December 15-21, 1993), Brian Wronge was 19 years old when he was arrested in 1979 in connection with an armed robbery in Brooklyn. He was subsequently identified in a line-up, sentenced 7½ to 15 years, and sent to Elmira Correctional Facility where he ultimately obtained an associate's degree at Corning Community College's Behind The Walls Program. Wronge says he began having problems and was transferred repeatedly after prison authorities noted his particular high aptitude in scientific subjects. It was his contention that a psychological profile was being devised for him. While being treated at Staten Island's Billy Seaton Hospital, where he was sent while at Fishkill prison in 1989, for a supposed bronchial condition, Wronge was surreptitiously implanted with paramagnetic computer chips (receptors and transmitters). He valiantly withstood efforts to kill him and many trials calculated to break his spirit – he detected mercury in his food when was returned to custody for parole violation, an infraction he says was justified. He sought CAT scan and other examinations, confirming his suspicions, immediately upon his last release.

NOBO staffer, Aton Archer, can vouch for the manipulation and unwarranted imposition of such collusion between the U.S. medical establishment and law enforcement authorities, having had a series of bizarre incidents in the late 80s, which culminated in a false mental evaluation and history being devised for him which he uncovered. He spoke with Brian Wronge recently for NOBO.

NOBO: So … Brian, how are you presently feeling?

BW: I'm feeling decently, with a few exceptions, because of my situation. I'm strong but still am having to combat this … system … that's inside of me.

NOBO: Are you feeling anxious? What's your emotional state?

BW: No, I'm feeling stable emotionally. There is just a constant stress based on my internal battle. The devices seems structured to attempt to gain control over my nervous system.

NOBO: You say you damaged the object ... how?

BW: I stuck a bobby pin in there and actually bent a servo antenna that goes up and down in the object.

NOBO: Was there anyway for you to determine you had truly made this mechanism inoperable? I understand that prior a physician ran a microphone over your body during examinations –

BW: Correct, and there was feedback.

NOBO: There was feedback. So were you able to certify that you had successfully damaged –

BW: Not completely, there are faint receptions. I believe the government and the medical establishment have devised this invasive structure, this paradigm, if you will, to effectuate the situation. If you ever were to go and report that you were hearing voices, or bizarre messages, immediately you would be written off as schizophrenic, or suffering from delusions of grandeur or paranoia ...

NOBO: Or borderline.

BW: Yeah, sealing whatever psychological diagnosis they have devised for you. The procedure for detecting such diagnoses is fully outlined in the DSM 3, which is the Diagnostic and Statistical Manual 3 for Psychologists and Psychiatrists. The medical establishment understands that if an individual reports symptoms, relaying what a person detects, and he or she is not able to verify these sounds through physical evidence, that person is to be written off as a case ... a nut.

NOBO: Do you think all the publicity you have received has successfully shielded you from being terminated by these "authorities" who devised all this?

BW: Well, it's not just publicity. In my estimation, it all seemed to occur back in 1981, when I was in college. I had written a paper in my Psychology 101 class [The Computer and the Mind; A Study in Comparison] where I described how a person can take computer analog chips and imitate the human senses and I received the highest grade on that paper. I think I stumbled upon one of the establishment's well kept secrets. I suppose they were afraid that if I were to get back on the streets with that knowledge that I could probably wreck the havoc that I am wrecking at this time. Unleashing –

NOBO: Well, you know, that's Providence. My case was not as dramatic but it was life-threatening nonetheless. The only reason I brought it up is that I think there are a lot of people that are getting experimented on and it's not only in the prisons. In this whole construct that they've created called "the homeless", there are bodies ready that have been psychologically depleted that can be manipulated.

BW: It's basically neo-slavery. It's stripping individuals of their self-esteem and character, totally debasing them basically. Using subliminal, well not even subliminal, but direct verbal motivation and other psychological ploys, to strip the individual down. After the person becomes debased, they become more malleable for mental control. Then controller becomes like parent over the individual.

NOBO: Absolutely.

BW: Yeah. Basically what I'm am facing is a just a microscopic part of the ongoing conspiracy to control the masses by the monied, privileged few. Racism is nothing but a political tool to control the masses. That's what it's all about. There is no premise for white supremacy whatsoever.

NOBO: There is no premise, it's a mental disorder. You had filed a suit in New York's Eastern District Court charging the government with conspiracy to commit murder and invasion of privacy. I know the judge has agreed to hear your case. He has put it on hold and suggests that you find a surgeon to remove a chip and a scientific researcher to identify its function. What is your progress? Do you feel there was any stonewalling on the part of the Court.

BW: Yes, I believe there is stonewalling on the Court's behalf. The medical society's behalf as well, because I've spoken to an African doctor, off the record. He stated the only reason he couldn't remove the device after observing it in my x-rays is because he is afraid of repercussions from the system. He said he would do it anyhow if the procedure was monitored by "60 Minutes" or some well known media vehicle. He said he wouldn't have to worry then if anything happens to him or his family, people would be concerned about finding out who was responsible.

NOBO: So, such individuals are afraid of repercussions from a force that is possibly the U.S. government? That's amazing.

BW: Right. They are connected or ancillary to the government, or individuals in the government. I don't want to believe that the U.S. government can sanction this kind of activity, broadcast microwave transmissions for such purposes. But, no average individual can transmit frequencies at such a high wattage and this technology is even used in satellite communication. You have to have an excessive amount of money to own such a microwave system to transmit anything, and satellite access is not available to the average Joe Blow. You have to go through FCC and that's the U.S. government. So at this point I have to say the government has some dealings in this matter. Who else has interest in mass control, with much cash at its disposal?

NOBO: Are you presently representing yourself until you can find a suitable and willing attorney? What is the status on securing an attorney or will you begin your search after your compliance with the Judge's instruction [to have a device removed and appropriate technological consultant evaluate it]?

BW: I have made steps to secure representation, but I am not at liberty to discuss it at this time. The doctor who I mentioned earlier, who wishes to remain anonymous, stated that based on his report alone I have the basis for a malpractice suit for the implantation of foreign objects placed in my body, to my unknowing. That in itself is a malpractice suit. There is the conspiracy theory and the intent to kill. We have many issues in this situation. We have invasion of privacy, because there are listening devices implanted, bugging devices implanted in my body. The devices can receive rapid or erratic transmissions so they also have the ability to incapacitate or terminate life. We are talking about the conspiracy to commit murder. Three different issues. Not to mention my criminal case where I was wrongfully incarcerated with inadmissable evidence. The Brooklyn Supreme Court had ruled that the evidence instrumentally convicting me – a lineup – was inadmissible. District Attorney Fairbanks, the Kings County District Attorney at that time, convicted me on evidence that was really inadmissable. They tried to terminate my life while I was in the prison system.

NOBO: When you returned to prison in September 1989 for parole violation – and this was due to a short term memory loss after the physical invasion –

BW: No, that was not the scenario. It was after I was released, my memory was sometimes jumbled. Having to return home after so long a time, and after being incarcerated ... there was so much input ... then, I would have to remember an appointment to go see a psychologist who would deem that I was stable enough to work, you know, whatever. I happened to have forgotten the appointment. Several occasions I had previously arrived, and the psychologist wasn't present. I was simply unable to make it by the time I recalled it. I tried to make a phone call to inform my parole officer of the fact and I couldn't get in contact. So the next day I was immediately arrested and sent back for parole violation based on something as insignificant as a justified missed appointment. Taxpayers don't seem to care about those injustices. All the misused money it took to put me back there and hold me for an additional nine months. I mean, after I got out and I did go back to see the psychologist, he says everything was alright, and that was it. All these trials seemed calculated to break my spirit.

NOBO: When you were at Elmira you were an inmate liaison –

BW: No, at Elmira I became president of the NAACP/Elmira prison branch. I was the president for one year at that facility. I was active in several types of grievances that was filed in Elmira to rebuild the infirmary. That has been rebuilt now. There was a lot of flax behind it. Petitions and everything were filed. I think if you were to go back and look at the documents you would find that many of those people on staff at the infirmary were probably terminated.

The power structure in the prison system – I don't even want to use the word "white" anymore, that's just a scapegoat mechanism to use that term when you're disgusted at the controlling elite. What we have is a collaboration of people that are working towards the same interest – controlling. Though a great many are Caucasians … and their minions.

Look at the situation with Mike Tyson, not Mike Tyson, this other guy … Larry Davis –

NOBO: Adam Abdul Hakeem.

BW: Yes, Adam Abdul Hakeem. All of a sudden he's crippled in prison, supposedly from a vicious beating, and people merely accept that without question. Cancer, strokes, heart failure, blindness, you name it, basic cell mutation can have it's genesis from microwave voltage transmissions. These devices are connected to your nervous system. The transmission – sound waves of varying frequency and speed – can be likened to a huge voltage being drawn into a small wire: you eventually burn it up. And that's what's being done – decimating and scrambling people's nervous systems. No one talks about the effect of excessive electricity on cellular tissue. It appears to be a certain scientific subject that people are not to be made aware of.

NOBO: So … this "technique" can manipulate cellular structure and cause free radicals in the body?

BW: That's what it does. It causes free radicals. Electron disorganization. Excessive, invasive electricity can disturb the molecular configuration of the cells. Strangely enough, it is my belief that there are those who are walking hand in hand with the "new technology" that are allowing themselves to be used and have consented to having reception and transmission devices implanted in them for enforcement purposes.

NOBO: Wait a minute! What are you saying? We have undercover Robocops walking around us?

BW: Those who are willing and ignorant enough to accept this process, law officials and others, might eagerly do so because then they can consider themselves unique, with capabilities far beyond mere mortal men. Many have been desensitized, programmed and mesmerized by the media, the movies, the Terminators and the like. This is most conceivable. The technology is here. This might sound like a science fiction movie, but if you are implanted with a microwave system with a frequency to augment your sleep patterns in your sleep center you can stay awake indefinitely and be subject to commands and carry them out accordingly. That is only one focus. There can be other "advantages" to being implanted with such devices. You can be a walking talking snitch implanted with a nondectectable internal bug. There are more possibilities, but I don't want to gross you out.

NOBO: Many thanks. You know, when you were in Elmira in 1989, it's ironic that in the same year, March 19, 1989, to be exact, the United Nations General Assembly passed into effect Resolution 43/173, entitled: "Body of Principles" for the protection of all persons under any form of detention or imprisonment. Principle 22, specifically states, and I quote, "No detained or imprisoned person shall, even with his consent, be subjected to any medical or scientific experimentation which may be detrimental to his health." That is the supposed, world body view on that issue. The United States sits on that body. What do you think of this?

BW: I think it's the height of hypocrisy.

NOBO: Your family and friends have been a remarkable support during this period.

BW: My family is well informed of my situation and in the event something happens they know the necessary steps to take. My friends and associates are informed as well.

I'm thankful to everyone who is appreciative of what I have to say. In order to effectuate any kind of control you must keep people ignorant of what's really going on. In society, knowledge is disseminated on different levels. Everybody doesn't have the same knowledge. We give this person a little more than the other and that's how strife is effectuated, conflict. To override that conflict is our battle to know, to become knowledgeable of ourselves.

NOBO: We thank you, Brian Wronge.

The following page has details of Brian Wronge's diagnosis ▶

MRI-CT SCANNING, INC.
FUTURE IMAGING ASSOCIATES
NUCLEAR DIAGNOSTIC RADIOLOGY ASSOCIATES

[illegible]

[illegible]
Brooklyn, New York [illegible]

Re: [illegible] – Computed Tomography Head, [illegible]

Dear Dr. [illegible]:

[illegible]

The [illegible] external auditory canals [illegible] metallic objects. The etiology of this finding is uncertain. Clinical correlation is suggested.

[illegible]

IMPRESSION:

1. BILATERAL CHRONIC OTTIS MASTOIDEA
2. BILATERAL METAL OBJECTS ARE IDENTIFIED IN THE EXTERNAL AUDITORY CANALS. [illegible] CLINICAL CORRELATION IS SUGGESTED.

Sincerely yours,

[illegible], M.D.
Board Certified Radiologist, Medical Director

IMPRESSION:
1. Bilateral chronic Ottis Mastoidea.
2. Bilateral metal objects are identified in the external auditory canals. The Etiology of this finding is uncertain, clinical correlation is suggested.

BROOKLYN, NEW YORK 11229
718-769-6800

May 30, 1991

Albert O. Duncan, M.D.
50 East 40th Street
Brooklyn, New York 11203

Re: Wronge, Brian

Dear Dr. Duncan,

MRI of the chest was performed. Multiple T1 weighted axial and coronal sequences were performed through the chest. These images reveal the presence of a paramagnetic foreign body artifact noted in the region of the left anterior chest wall at the level of the axilla. The artifact obsures most of the detail in the region, and therefore, its exact location and type cannot be discerned from these studies. Comparison with plain films, and if indicated, further evaluation with CT scaning would be helpful here.

There is no other significant osseous or soft tissue abnormalities identified.

IMPRESSION: Findings suggestive of a metallic or paramagnetic foreign body in the region of the anterior left axilla.

Thank you for referring this patient.

Very truly yours,

Norman Dinhofer, M.D.

David Dinhofer, M.D.

ND/DD:jb
Enc: All films

IMPRESSION:
Findings suggestive of a metallic or paramagnetic foreign body in the region of the anterior left axilla.

Primer to Counterinsurgency and Low Intensity Warfare

Genocide Through Behavior Modification In the U.S. Penal System

by: **Dr. Mutulu Shakur**
Anthony X Bradshaw
Malik Dinguswa
Terry D. Long
Mark Cook
Adolfo Matos
James Haskins

This is a presentation about genocide waged against the Black Nation using behavior modification in the United States penal system. It was initially drafted December, 1988, and distributed to several political prisoners in state and federal prisons to encourage support and participation for an in depth development of this work for the Research Committee on International Law and Black Freedom Fighters in the United States for input to the human rights campaign. This paper was developed by a team of Black prisoners who experienced behavior modification inside prisons and who desire to expose the immediate, prolonged, and historical effects of this government's efforts to control the Black Nation. We do not suggest the techniques used are exclusively implemented on the Black Nation solely, but there is no denying that the Black Nation is the government's paramount target.

Illustration by Shawn Alexander

Before going on we want to extend our thanks to our supporters and to those who contributed to this work. This paper was developed to bring about broader unity on this topic to collectively expose human rights violations to the world through the human rights conference of non-governmental organizations in Zurich, Switzerland.

We specifically charge that the government of the United States is practicing genocide through behavior modification and counterinsurgency and low intensity warfare techniques in its penal system, specifically, the state and federal prisons.

We submit that behavior modification practiced in United States prisons incorporates techniques from both counterinsurgency – low intensity warfare, and the science of psychology with political and military objectives. The implementation of this strategy in the United States penal system is the result of research conducted by government scientists and counterinsurgency agents who studied the theories and works of past experts in the distinct fields of behavior therapy (synonymous with behavior modification), insurgency, and low intensity warfare.

Every aspect of this behavior modification program violates the human rights of those persons subjected to it. This treatment is vehemently complained about by political prisoners and POWs. This program takes a scientific approach to target special prisoners who achieve political objectives. Each targeted prisoner is observed to determine his/her leadership potential, religious beliefs, aspirations, and most importantly, to record his/her reaction to the experiments implemented. The sole purpose of this program is for government agents to learn lessons from experimenting with political prisoners, how they suffered, reacted, then use those findings to formulate a broad plan to be implemented against the people in society at large who are the ultimate targets.

The oppressive conditions and experiments conducted in the United States penal system, implemented by this government through prison officials, are the evidence of a psychological war being waged against political prisoners[1] who come from a people involved in resistance struggles against oppression in all forms. When the behavior modification program conducted by government is viewed, in the light of the mandates contained in the "Geneva Accord", one can only conclude that the United States Government's actions are criminal and violate international laws concerning the rights of human beings. Accordingly, the United States Government's acts should be regarded as war crimes.

The U.S. Government is in violation of *Article I* of the Geneva Convention on the prevention and punishment of the crime of genocide which was approved by the United Nation General Assembly on December 9, 1948; and, the U.S. Government is in violation of resolution 260, *III*, which entered into force on January 12, 1951. In this resolution "the contracting parties confirmed that genocide, whether committed in time of peace or in time of war, is a crime under international law which they undertake to prevent and punish." According to *Article II*, genocide is defined as any of the following acts committed with the intent to destroy, in whole or in part, a national, ethical, racial or religious group; such actions as:

- Killing members of the group;*
- Causing serious bodily or mental harm to members of the group;
- Deliberately inflicting on the group calculated adverse "condi tions of life" to bring about its destruction in whole or in part;
- Imposing measures intended to prevent births within the group;
- Forcibly transferring children of the group to another group.

*(cited from *The Law of Nations* by Herbert W. Briggs.)

Subsequent to reviewed the above list of acts that constitute the crime of genocide, as set forth by the Geneva Convention, we submit that the behavior modification program being carried out in the United States penal system is a scientific form of genocide waged against black people in the U.S. It is a continuance of the nefarious tactics employed by the government over the years to keep the Black Nation subjugated.

On learning of the use of behavior modification techniques in futherance of counterinsurgency and low intensity warfare objectives, especially in light of the government's intended broad application, all caring people in any society should be shocked.

The Theory and Practice of Behavior Modification

Behavior modification is highly complex science composed of information from various sciences including psychology, sociology, philosophy, anthropology, and biology. By definition "Behavior Modification" broadly refers to the systematic manipulation of one's environment for the purpose of creating a change in the individual's behavior.

It involves a systematic effort to influence the frequency, intensity, and duration of specified target behavior." (From notes of Michael S. Rubin that appeared in the *Arizona Law Review*, Vol. 18).

During our research we discovered that behavior scientists and counterinsurgency agents of the government learned many of their tactics from studying the works of John B. Watson and B.F. Skinner. These two United States psychologists are leading authorities in the field of behavior modification.[2] We learned there are three basic types of behavior modification techniques recognized today – operant conditioning, classical conditioning, and aversion therapy.

Operant Conditioning

Operant conditioning is based largely on B.F. Skinner's work. It involves presenting a reinforcer/reward when a desirable behavior is produced to increase that particular behavior being repeated. A classic example is that of a rat being trained to depress a lever in his cage which releases food pellets. A reinforcer, food pellet, is something that increased the rate of the behavior. (See Durland's *Illustrated Medical Dictionary*, 25th Edition, 1938).

Classical Conditioning

Classical conditioning utilizes a stimulus to elicit an involuntary response/reflex. At the beginning of the program an "unconditioned" stimulus, food, is employed to elicit the reflex, salivation. A second stimulus, by itself would not produce the involuntary or unconditioned response, is paired with the unconditioned stimulus. After continued pairing of unconditioned and conditioned stimuli, the same response is obtained from the presentation of the neutral stimulus – as was produced by the unconditioned stimulus. Thus, Pavlov, was able to elicit a dog's salivation upon hearing a bell by repeated pairing of the bell sound (conditioned stimulus) along with the presentation of food (unconditioned stimulus). (See G. Kimble and N. Garmezy, *Principles of General Psychology*, 1968).

Aversion Therapy

Aversion therapy has been defined as an attempt to associate an undesirable behavior pattern with unpleasant stimulation. The unpleasant stimulation is made a consequence of the undesirable behavior. It is anticipated that an acquired connection between the behavior and the unpleasantness will develop. The development of such a connection will hopefully be followed by a cessation of the target behavior. (See S. Rachman and Teasdale, *Aversion Therapy and Behavior Disorders*).

Although all three techniques are used by prison officials in the United States penal system, aversion therapy seems to be the preferred technique. It is used with counterinsurgency and low intensity warfare. Numerous behavior therapists have confirmed there are many adverse effects associated with aversion therapy, *e.g.*, pain, frustration, increased aggressiveness, erratic and unwarranted arousal, general and specific anxieties, other various somatic malfunctions, and development of unexpected and often pathological operant behaviors. (See F. Kanfer and J. Phillips, *Learning Foundation Of Behavior Therapy*).

All behavior modification techniques are intrusive to individuals whether the effects are felt physically or psychologically. Individuals in the experiment are subjected to tampering with their minds, bodies, or both.

History shows us behavior modification is no new phenomenon in the United States penal system. However, in earlier years prison officials used more "hands-on" approach in manipulating prisoners behavior. During our investigation of many prisoners and ex-prisoners, we learned that in earlier years persons who resisted prison officials; or persons who complained of oppressive conditions, or persons labeled incorrigibles, were arbitrarily confined to mental wards inside the prison, or transferred to mental institutions for the criminally insane. They experienced severe effects of mind altering drugs, electric shock treatment, psychosurgery, the ultimate weapons used by prison officials to carry out their behavior modification strategy.

These measures proved to be ineffective in the United States penal system by the end of the 60s or early 70s. Prison demonstrations and uprisings occurred rapidly throughout the United States and coincided with the liberation movement outside prison walls. The government, concerned about group control inside the prisons, addressed this concern by using psychological warfare. Prisoners of strong religious and cultural beliefs who had organized prisoners to resist and prisoners who put up independent resistance were singled out and met with extreme oppression as targets of experimental behavior modification.[3]

We submit that Black people were the first experimental targets of group behavior modification. Current data and statistics on the prison situation support our contention that Black people inside the state and federal prisons today remain the prime targets of government programs.

During our research we discovered that psychological warfare waged in the U.S. penal system was planned as far back as the early 60s. The government foresaw Black people revolting against being oppressed, even in prison. Black people's conduct, like many people throughout history, validates the axiom "oppression breeds resistance."

Significantly, in 1961 a social scientist named Dr. Edward Schein presented his ideas on brainwashing at a meeting held in Washington, D.C., that was convened by James V. Bennett, then director of the Federal Bureau of Prisons Systems, and attended by numerous social scientists and prison wardens.[4] Dr. Schein suggested that brainwashing techniques were natural for use in their institutions. In his address "Man Against Man" he explained that to produce marked changes of behavior and attitude it is necessary to weaken, undermine, or remove the supports of old patterns of behavior and old attitudes. "Because most of these supports are the face-to-face confirmation of present behavior and old attitudes. "Because most of these supports are the face-to-face confirmation of present behavior and attitudes, which are provided by those with whom close emotional ties exists. This can be done by either "removing the individual physically and preventing any communication with those whom he cares about, or by proving to him that those whom he respects are not worthy of it, and indeed should be actively mistrusted." Dr. Schein then provided the group with a list of specific examples such as:

1. *Physical removal of prisoners to isolated areas to effectively break and seriously weaken close emotional ties.*
2. *Segregation of all natural leaders.*
3. *Use cooperative prisoners as leaders.*
4. *Prohibit group activities not in line with brainwashing objectives.*
5. *Spy on prisoners and report back private material.*
6. *Trick men to write statements which are then shown to others.*
7. *Exploitation of opportunists and informers.*

8. Convince the prisoners they can trust no one.

9. Treat those willing to collaborate in far more lenient ways than those not willing.

10. Punish those who show uncooperative attitudes.

11. Systematically withhold mail.

12. Prevent contact with anyone nonsympathetic to the treatment and regimentation of the captive populace.

13. Hold a group to ridicule consisting of prisoners abandoned by and totally isolated from the social order.

14. Disorganize all group standards among prisoners.

15. Undermine all emotional supports.

16. Prevent prisoners from writing home to family and friends in the community describing conditions of their confinement.

17. Make available and accessible only those publications and books that contain materials neutral to or supportive of desired new attitudes.

18. Place individuals in new, ambiguous situations where standards are deliberately kept unclear; then, apply pressure to conform to desired orders to win favors and reprieves from the pressure.

19. Place individuals whose will power has been severely weakened or eroded in a living situation with several others more advanced in desired thought reformation and whose job it is to further the undermining of the individuals' emotional supports.

20. Use techniques of character invalidation, e.g., humiliations, revilement, inducing feelings of guilt, fear, suggestibility, sleeplessness, exacting prison regime with periodic, spontaneous interrogations.

21. Meet all insincere attempts to comply with developed pressures with renewed hostility.

22. Arrange cellmates to repeatedly pointing out the incognity of where he/she was in the past, now in the present, and thereby not even living up to his/her own standards or values.

23. Reward submission and subservient attitudes, encompassing brainwashing objectives while lifting pressure and acceptance.

24. Provide social and emotional supports to reinforce new attitudes.

Following Dr. Schein's address, James Bennett commented, "We can perhaps undertake some of the techniques Dr. Schein discussed and do things on our own. Undertake a little experiment with the Muslims. There is a lot of research to do. Do it as groups and let us know the results."

Approximately eleven years after that historical meeting, it was confirmed that Dr. Schein's ideas and objectives were in fact being implemented inside the prisons. In July 1972, the Federal Prisoner's Coalition, in a petition to the United Nations Economic and Social Council, asserted that the Asklepieion program conducted at Marion, Illinois, federal penitentiary was directly modeled on Chinese methods of thought reform. The petition contains a point-by-point comparison between Dr. Schein's address, and the written description of goals and structure of the Asklepieion program. (See the *Mind Manipulators* by Alan W. Scheflin).

Although tactics introduced by Dr. Schein when viewed individually may not necessarily shock the conscience of society, the tactics, when executed singularly, or in total are very deleterious to persons subjected to them. We charge that the execution of the tactics are a violation of the prisoner-victim's human rights. These violations are prohibited under international law.

Many writers today who have done articles on prison behavior modification usually leave their readers with inaccurate impressions that experiments are only implemented in isolated units of prison. These writers usually mention the infamous control unit at the U.S. Penitentiary located in Marion, Illnois, as prime example. However, we want to make it clear that the experiments are conducted nationwide and there is close collaboration between the state and federal prison systems. The results obtained from having conducted these experiments are used by government agents to formulate a broader plan to be implemented against people in society at large. One of the objectives of the broader plan is altering the behavior of young people, creating conditions and situations that incline youth toward deviant and self-destructive behavior . Thus successfully derailing them from the course of resisting oppression.[5]

Subsequent to having examined B.F. Skinner's analysis of behavior one would readily conclude that United States penologists heavily borrowed information from Skinner's works in formulating their behavior modification program and in devising its specific techniques. In his book, *Beyond Freedom and Dignity*, Skinner explains that "a culture is very much like the experimental space used in the analysis of behavior. Both are sets of contingencies reinforcement. A child is born into a culture as an organism is placed in an experimental space. Designing a culture is like designing an experiment; contingencies are arranged and effects noted. In an experiment we are interested in what happens, in designing a culture with whether it will work. This is the difference between science and technology."

In unequivocal terms, Skinner's theory relates to a prison environment and society at large. Imagine a prisoner replacing the child in the situations noted above and imagine a prison as the experimental space, then one can clearly see the experiments carried out inside prisons are done with experimenters having in mind the ultimate objective of altering the culture of an entire people. The placing of a person in a designed situation for the purpose of tearing him or her down then rebuilding him or her according to the specification of an alien group is a clear act of genocide.

As Black psychologist Bobby E. Wright perfectly stated in his view of Skinner's theory, "and Black with a cursory knowledge of B.F. Skinner's experimental analysis of behavior should recognize its potential danger to our community, where every institution is under the control of the White race." (See, *Black Suicide, 1980,* Bobby E. Wright, Ph. D.).

We want to emphasize that it would be very difficult for a Black psychologist or any other psychologist not to draw a parallel between Skinner's theory and Dr. Schein's objectives as it pertains to the agenda implemented against the Black Nation.

In discussion of various tactics implemented under this behavior modification program, we know that prison officials use drugs as a method of control. We discovered most drugs used by prison officials today are far more detrimental in potency than those used in earlier years.[6] It is not unusual inside prisons today to see prisoners exhibiting "Zombie-like-behavior" as a result of the type of drugs administered to them against or with their consent. In many prisons a prerequisite for some prisoners is to take certain prescribed drugs to be released from solitary confinement. Several courts support forcible use of drugs by prison officials thus leaving the use of drugs as a hands-on tactic.

In a recent tour of the Soviet mental institutions by American Psychiatric Association (APA), included numerous interviews with detainees. It was found that most of those detained were for political reasons and they were being administered psychotropic drugs as part of a program to neutralize political dissent. Many Soviet doctors still use a broad-brush diagnosis, *schizophrenic*, to lock people up. This "diagnosis", is still commonly used in America, is a smokescreen appellation used in the government's political-military strategy to contain and isolate individuals perceived to be a potential threat to the status quo.

The APA specifically alleges that Soviet patients are treated with massive amounts of pain inducing and mind altering psychotropic drugs. They consider such dosages to have no medical value. This position gives rise to the very serious question of intent of the APA especially when light is cast on empirical investigation of the value and efficiency of drugs. (See *New York Times* article, March 3, 1989).

We submit that the APA tour and reported findings about Soviet institutions clearly represents the height of hypocrisy on the part of the United States government. We make the same contentions about practices in the United States penal system that the APA alleges with respect to the Soviet Union. If past and present tactics implemented in the United States penal system are not acknowledged, and objectives clearly recognized and understood, then we simply make way for these abuses to continue in the future, thereby, furthering the program of genocide.

It is our position that one should not consider the measure of one's feelings as the acid test[7] in deciding that experimenters have exceeded legal criterion of what constitutes violative practices. One should bear in mind that behavior modification experiments are conducted to achieve nefarious counterinsurgency and low intensity warfare objectives. The judicial branch of government continues to support daily abuses of behavior modification programs carried out in the United States penal system by not intervening to require the executive branch to cease their deleterious program and practices.

Many of the programs carried out by the Reagan administration and continued by the Bush administration that focus on suppression of the Black Nation would immediately be condemned were they exposed to public scrutiny. Of course, one such program would meet public condemnation if given wide public exposure is the behavior modification program under discussion.

The Use of Behavior Modification to Achieve Counterinsurgency and Low Intensity Warfare Objectives

Counterinsurgency tactics are the political military actions undertaken to forestall all resistance before it is strikingly manifested. The use of such tactics demonstrate clear recognition by those governing the state that unjust conditions exist and will continue to exist into the foreseeable future. Once resistance surfaces, counterinsurgency tactics are then used to effectively destroy it.

Low Intensity Warfare involves use of political/military strategy to achieve political, social, economic, and psychological objectives. Such wars are often of a protracted nature and many major battles are fought in diplomatic, economic, and social arenas in an effort to apply psycho-biological pressure on resistors. Equally important is the low intensity wars feature constraint on weaponry used and intermittent eruptions of violence. Accordingly, low intensity warfare techniques in the United States is derived from strategies formulated by Frank Kitson and Robin Evelegh.[8] The government has effectively managed to pursue this two-track strategy through military, law enforcement agencies, and prison officials.

Judging by all standards of what constitutes a low intensity war, we, the rising Black Nation, are targeted insurgents in the United States, because our people have not been standing still in response to the permanent oppression perpetrated against us by the government. Let us not forget the infamous J. E. Hoover's Cointelpro of the 60s era when he directed counterinsurgency measures against the "Black Nationalist Movement" to prevent the rise of a "Mau Mau" like group and to prevent the ascent of a "Black Messiah". These were taken from documents detailing Hoover's plan and serve as unequivocal testimony that the government formed its strategy against the Black Nation after reading about Kitson's experience, particularly in Kenya, fighting the "Mau Mau" and after having read about Kitson's use of gangs and counter gangs. Hoover's counter intelligence program (COINTELPRO) listed the following five objectives:

1. *To prevent the coalition of militant Black nationalist groups, which might be the first step toward a real "Mau Mau" in America.*
2. *To prevent the rise of a "Messiah" who could unify and electrify the movement.*
3. *To prevent violence on the part of Black nationalist groups by pinpointing potential troublemakers and neutralizing them before they exercise their potential violence.*
4. *To prevent groups and leaders from gaining respectability by discrediting them to the responsible Negro community, to the white community (both the responsible community and the liberals [the distinction is the Bureau's]), and to Negro radicals.*
5. *To prevent long-range growth of these organizations, especially among youth, by developing specific tactics to prevent these groups from recruiting young people.* (See *Political Legacy of Malcolm X*, p. 225-226, by Oba T. Shaka).

Even the Church Committee Report on Urban Unrest in the 60s era labeled participants, the disenfranchised who took part in riots, rebellions and skirmishes, as insurgents. Remember the urban unrest and Church's labeling those who participated as insurgents occurred during developments of the Black Liberation Movement. Many people of that period who participated in the struggle on various levels became social prisoners, political prisoners, and prisoner of war.[9] In many cases those imprisoned were jailed as a result of tactical maneuvers carried out by the government to suppress resistance of the people in society at large. As one prisoner of war stated, "Prisons are a fundamental pillar of state power. Their main function is suppression of all internal threats to the State." (See *Sun Views* by Sundiata Acoli). The implementing of counterinsurgency and low intensity warfare through behavior modification is geared to destroy the captive Black Nation.

We submit that the captured Black Nation was, and remains a prime target of the government's strategy of behavior modification counterinsurgency and low intensity warfare. The evidence of implementing the government's strategy is evinced by exceptionally harsh treatment inflicted on Black prisoners in the United States penal system–especially those prisoners committed to the Black Liberation Movement–the struggle for self-determination.

It is important to understand that prisons in the United States have always been operated primarily by White administrators and armed with mostly White prison guards. This combination of factors renders Black prisoners excessively vulnerable to and a prime target of unbridled racism and brutality. Additionally, the government itself is deeply rooted in racism.

Let us not overlook the fact that there are prisoners from other oppressed Nations inside the United States and from the Caribbean Islands who, as they fight for their national liberation, are also targeted by this government's strategy of counterinsurgency and low intensity warfare. One indication of commitment and determination possessed by these brothers and sisters is reflected by many political prisoners and POWs from their struggles locked inside the bowels of the United States penal system.

The Puerto Rican National Liberation Movement in Puerto Rico and in the United States of America has been a prime target of the United States Government. The government has used the most severe tactics of counterinsurgency and low intensity warfare against them for over a half century. Since United States troops invaded the island in 1898, the people have used every method within their reach to terminate the colonial type structure designed and imposed on them by colonizers, specifically the United States Congress.

The United States has violated the most basic principles of a people. The United States is cognizant of its wrongfulness and it is aware that people of the world, airing their views through their representatives in the United Nation General Assembly, side with the struggling Puerto Rican people. In fact, this statement was issued during that struggle, "The General Assembly … reaffirms the legitimacy of the people's struggle for liberation from colonial and foreign domination and alien subjugation by all available means, including armed struggle." (See U. N. General Assembly Resolution 3030 (XXVIII).

The American Government assassinated certain members of the Puerto Rican Movement; it tortured and maimed political prisoners; it used frame-ups resulting in imprisonment; it transferred Puerto Rican leadership from the Island of Puerto Rico to prisons deep inside the United States. Thus, denying leadership the opportunity to community *with persons in the ongoing movement.*[10]

An example of United States' imperialism and United States' efforts to control and alter behavior of people resisting oppression becomes startlingly clear when we observe the handling of Black and Latin freedom fighters from the Caribbean Islands who are incarcerated inside the U.S. penal system. Many of these prisoners are politically opposed to the "puppet regimes in their Caribbean Islands that America controls." Consequently, these dissident prisoners also become targets of the government's counterinsurgency and low intensity warfare.

Let it be understood that in light of the geo-political and economic objectives the United States is carrying out in developing nations, many social crimes committed on these islands are a direct result of America's intervention.[11] After arriving on United States soil many prisoners from

Caribbean Islands become socially, politically and culturally active in United States prison systems and their experiences incline them to create unbreakable bonds with Black freedom fighters inside the United States.

When White Anti-Imperialists Participate in the Resistance

Mentioning Blacks from the United States and the Caribbean Islands, mentioning Puerto Ricans from the United States and from the Island of Puerto Rico – all of whom are freedom fighters of color, gives rise to the question: are White anti-imperialists prisoners also targeted by the government's programs?

When White anti-imperialists are charged and brought before judicial tribunals, many American judicial members suggest that because the White anti-imperialists are not victims of oppression, they have no justification for participating in the resistance. This position is clearly a nullification of the "Nuremberg principle." This principles specifically states ...

It is natural for a caring human being to sympathize with, support, or align with those who resist being oppressed. When White anti-imperialists get involved in resistance soon thereafter they are placed in prison because this government is so deeply rooted in racism and feels compelled to discourage Whites from aligning themselves with Blacks. Treatment inflicted on anti-imperialists are sometimes just as severe as that meted out to Blacks and that treatment is often exceptionally cruel. These tactics are aimed at sending the message to North American Whites to stay clear of the struggle.

The government is concerned with determining why this phenomenon exists, and in altering the behavior patterns of captured White anti-imperialists. The government seeks thereby to prevent the growth of the ranks of White people who fight against oppression.

Persons Arrested as Grand Jury Resistors Are Counterinsurgency Victims

Another not to be overlooked tactic used by this government against most liberation movements is imprisonment and inflicting harsh treatment on grand jury resistors. These comrades are clearly not guilty of or even charged with any crime. They are incarcerated because they refuse to violate their principles that prohibit them from collaborating with the government.[12]

Many times grand jury resistors are not members of a particular movement. They are usually the friends or relatives of the revolutionary who is being inquired about or they are sympathizers of the cause. So their imprisonment is clearly a tactic designed to intimidate. What we see here is another aspect of the counterinsurgency strategy that encompasses the objectives of determining the resistors' leadership capabilities and level of political development and dedication.

Grand jury resistors are given a subpoena; thrown into jails and prisons, and subjected to psychological and emotional distress ... all this is done in order to facilitate the breaking of the targeted revolutionary's will thus suppressing the movement. For the government to execute all these measures actually consummates the marriage between behavior modification and counterinsurgency low intensity warfare.

Isolation and Sensory Deprivation in Prison: An Attack on the Larger Black Community

What really needs to be considered is truly of paramount importance. The United States government officials so effectively utilize their penal system as the primary tool for repressing and subsequently crushing all dissent. Mercilessly destroying the minds of countless people, and, their souls, after a slow death offered on the altar of "real politic."

We submit that, first of all, the science of politics is not truly grounded in morality. Political scientists and politicians in general simply utilize a lot of false laudatory moralizing to build a convenient facade to cleverly conceal their real designs.

In the politician/oppressor's dealings with the oppressed, when the question is raised regarding what guiding precept to embrace, morality looses out to expediency, doing that which conforms to the cynical spirit of Machiavelli. History speaks all too clearly in confirmation of this.

So, it is against the backdrop of these brutal realities that we examine the question of imprisonment in general and isolation and sensory deprivation in particular. What is isolation and sensory deprivation, and how does it impact upon its victimized subjects? This is a deep question that encompasses very subtle and deep emotional, psychological, and physiological realities.

We charge that at present, and for some time now, there is and has been a very clear and systematic program of low intensity warfare perpetually in motion in the prisons across America. This program, brutally alive and well, is no mere accident, no loosely controlled haphazard affair. It is part of a precise, coordinated, careful and well-thought out program that embraces the most scientific and subtle techniques of brainwashing, of psychological infiltration, of menticide. It is a program for the ruthless manipulation of people's minds, for forcing them to conform with scientific and archetypal patterns of broken subjects.[13] Their scientists have meticulously worked out intricate details of this practice through experimentation, deduction and inference.

They have refined details on how to create a controlled environment, on how to impregnate the environment with certain subtle messages to trigger thoughts and behavior patterns in their controlled subjects.

Isolation and sensory deprivation, as it was practiced in the "Auschwitz and Dachaus concentration camps" scattered across America, is a definite aspect of the oppressor's controlled environment. They know that through isolation, through systematic removal, inclusion, or manipulation of key sensory stimuli, they can attack a prisoner's mind and reduce him/her to a warped, subservient state characterized by feelings of lethargy, listlessness and hopelessness ... in short, a prisoner develops feelings of being more dead than alive.[14]

They combine the practice of tampering with sensory stimuli with a deficient diet, a diet lacking key nutrients indispensable to proper functioning of a well-integrated personality. The diet consists of meals that have acceptable appearances, but are nutritiously deficient. After eating a few meals one finds oneself getting hungrier and feeling lethargic. Being on such a diet promotes depression and ultimately gives rise to thoughts of self-destruction. All of this is intentional. All of this is based on a very clear, scientific program, one of the best programs their "think tanks" could devise. They know exactly what they are doing; they know precisely what their experiments, their scientific applications, will entail. In this, as in other areas, they are again in violation of international standards.[15]

It is clear, unequivocally clear, that this is a cruel brand of psychological and emotional torture that violates human rights and the U.S. Constitution's prohibition against cruel and unusual punishment. These measures rival methods used by Nazi Germany. Right now there are literally thousands of people being subjected to this program. It is an essential feature of the American penal system. A penal system which is designed to break minds, to create warped and aberrated personalities. Isolation and sensory deprivation play a distinct role in this.[16]

All prisoners are targeted. Even staff become victimized by the same system they blindly uphold. *You cannot dehumanize people without becoming dehumanized in the process.* Yes, all prisoners are targeted and the harshness of their treatment varies only in degree.

They concentrate intensely on political prisoners because political prisoners have the clearest understanding about the true nature of things, about the exploitative relationships that prevail. They concentrate extra hard on political prisoners because she/he has the greatest potential for awakening and organizing other prisoners.

Isolation and sensory deprivation have always played a unique role in the government's perennial war on political prisoner. Through isolation and sensory deprivation, through being confined within a limited space, through the denial of privacy, through lack of natural light and fresh air, through the lack of intellectual stimulation, lack of comradeship, through the lack of undisturbed sleep, lack of proper health care, lack of education and recreational outlets – the lack of these things that contribute to fueling life – reduces one to an existence of lifelessness.

This is war. This is a war of attrition and it is designed to reduce prisoners to a state of submission essential for ideological conversion. The next option, in deadly sequence, is to reduce prisoners to a state of psychological incompetence to neutralize them as efficient, self-directing antagonists. That failing, the only option left is to destroy prisoners, preferably by making them desperate enough to destroy themselves.

The purpose of this isolation and sensory deprivation is to disrupt one's balance, one's inner equilibrium, to dehumanize the prisoner, to depersonalize, to strip away the captor's unique individuality.

We note that amongst the many effects of the process is the disruption of the biological time clock, neuropathic disorders, biochemical degeneration, depression, apathy, chronic rage reaction, defensive psychological withdrawal, loss of appetite (or the opposite extreme), weight loss and the exacerbation of pre-existing medical problems.

These things are real, frighteningly real, as many, many, documented cases prove. All are part of a very clear, scientific program operated by the government and is designed to crush, dehumanize, and decimate those held captive.

This implacable, relentless attack by the United States government is a very clear violation of fundamental human rights. These violations constitute an issue we must all immediately confront. This terrible malady is already in its most advanced state and everyone is affected by it. In addition, it is to the peril of the whole nation the longer people procrastinate on taking a just stand on this issue.

There are relevant international bodies that exist to uncover and redress human rights violations.[17] What we ask, those of us who have been victimized, is where are the stringent voices of those international bodies as day in and day out, our rights, our dignity, are offended and trampled on over and over again? Is everyone so inexorably chained to partisan politics that they reframe from applying their conscience until given the nod by party bigwigs? The world can see what goes on in the tomb of America as Black people are being slowly strangled and suffocated to death and are reeling drunkenly under the tyrannical whip of oppression.

Yes, the world can see what goes on. Yet there remains a deadly chorus of silence, a conspiracy of silence.

We charge the American government with genocide. In clear, unequivocal terms, we charge the American government with genocide against captive Black people in America who are perpetually under siege. We charge genocide, infanticide and menticide, which is perpetrated via institutionalized racism.

The voracious jaws of oppression and exploitation constantly feast upon our people. Additionally, every aspect of our existence is determined and controlled by another people, by a brutal enemy intent upon our total annihilation. We see the emissaries of death wreaking havoc in our ravaged communities by further eroding the quality of life (already at a subhuman level) and by further contributing to the horrendous deficiency of life-supporting stimuli.

The funeral pyre burns on and on. Our youth stumble through the wilderness of confusion, hopelessness and feelings of insignificance. Their young and vulnerable bellies are bloated with the plague of self-destruction, miseducation, rejection, feelings of worthlessness. Our youth are receptors of a defective social system that was not designed with the best interest of our people at heart.

The government of America knows exactly what it is doing; it has mastered the techniques of mass control. It knows how to build into an environment certain stimuli that will set in motion a desired process that takes on a life of its own, with the hand that originated the process becoming less and less visible. *The withdrawing of the hand results in the people mistaking the effect for the cause.*

Before this process can be properly cultivated to fruition, it first of all becomes necessary for the oppressor to develop ways to determine what the oppressed will think and when they will act. The first step in determining these things is to systematically destroy anything and anybody who might provide an alternate frame of reference. First of all attacking and destroying that people's history and culture. Second, given the oppressed something warped and twisted in place of what has been destroyed. Keep in mind the oppressor knows what negative experiences the oppressed are subjected to and the oppressor knows what trashy ideas are stuffed into the heads of the oppressed.

In connection with his brother, Amilcar Cabral, noted "that oppression or domination of a people is only secured when the cultural life of a people is destroyed, paralyzed, or at least neutralized." Parenthetically, it may, in fact, be the case that the different forms of oppression experienced by African peoples are determined by the emphasis placed on destroying, paralyzing, or neutralizing the culture of the people under domination.

We hold this government responsible for the conditions of our people. In places like Chile, Argentina, Paraguay and South Africa, they have done it blatantly (and we must not forget that it was, and is , the United States government which finances and trains practically all of these oppressive regimes); they do it crudely, and blatantly with gun and truncheon.

In America, they do it through psychology, theology, philosophy, biology, through the refinement of sophisticated behavioral sciences, and we see the evidence of its effectiveness. All of the institutions of America serve to further uphold and perpetuate this oppressive order; all of their sciences are drawn into this nefarious enterprise and subordinated to it.

Brother Wade Nobles has expounded on this saying: "The ideas of science do not develop in empty space, or even abstract space where there is supposedly nothing but ideas. The ideas, interests, application and definition of science goes on in a human world, and human life is social. There is, therefore, no science which is not part of a social science. Similarly, when the social reality is defined by racism and oppression, there can be no science which is not, in part, oppressive and racist. Just as science and technology have gone hand-in-hand in the last three hundred years to assist in the development of the Western World, so, too, does it seem apparent that social science, as a political institution, now serves to maintain the advantages obtained by technological superiority of the Western World.

Where the connection between science and society once was in science's devotion to the creation and use of technical and industrial power, science now serves Western society in the creation and use of theories and ideas designed to control the use of power in general by oppressed people. In fact, where power before was defined by creation of ideas and ability to have people respond to ideas as if they represented the respondent's reality."[18]

The allegations we make are very clear; even many of their own establishment figures admit as much. Statistics always fall short of fully conveying the entire picture but even the ones that are out present a most bleak and shocking picture of what is happening to our people. Cited here are just a few of these statistics.

It is estimated that one-third to one-half of Black men up to age 24 are unemployed; many are caught in a cycle of drugs, homicide and suicide. They say that employment among Black men was 84% in 1940, but only 67% in 1980. Today one-third of all Black men are either unemployed, or completely out of the labor market. This is more intense than during the great depression. In the past 25 years, the employment rate of young White men has remained constant while Blacks dropped from 52 to 26 percent in the 16 to 19 age group and from 77 to 55 percent in the 20 to 24 age group.

It is estimated that a young Black man has one chance in 21 of dying from homicide while the typical American has a 1 in 133 chance. More Black men died from homicide in one year, 1977, for instance, than died in the entire Vietnam War, and we believe there have been many such years.

In 1987, the Bureau of Justice estimated that the number of prisoners in this country reached 546,659. It has been estimated that from 1975 to the year 2000 the total prison population will quadruple and the number of Black prisoners is expected to increase tenfold.

Moreover, on closer inspection of the statistics shows that the rates of imprisonment accelerated after the social upheavals of the late 1960s era. In 1969, 120 cities burned during the Black rebellion. In 1983, the imprisonment rate per one hundred thousand people was 713 for Black people (even greater now); compared to 114 for White people, and it goes on and on.

The Further Erosion of Constitutional Protection

We submit that it would be a meaningless exercise to litigate the charge of human rights violations in the United States Courts, especially in view of the fact that the executive branch has virtually usurped the discretionary powers of the judicial branch thus making it impossible for us to receive relief.

Even the Supreme Court of the United States has closed its eyes and ears to these human rights violations. As Alvin J. Bronstein states in his introduction to *Prisoner's Litigation Manual*: "The courts have returned to the hands off doctrine."

Over the years, prisoners have put forth the effort to engage in legal battles regarding constitutional violations, prison conditions, and treatment. (Moreover, it was hoped that the occasion of being in court could be used to expose the United States penal system to the international community).

The courts, for a brief period listened to prisoners' complaints and at times sustained their allegations of constitutional rights violations. However, as a result of pressure applied on courts by the executive branch, the independence of the judicial branch was erased and consequently, prisoners were left deprived of institutional guarantor of the protection of their constitutional rights which really means prisoners exist in a constitutional void.

Conclusion

In every stage of these oppressions, we have petitioned for redress in the humble terms. Our repeated petitions have been answered mainly by repeated injury. A nation, whose character is marked by every act may define a racially oppressive regime, as unfit to receive the respect of a free people.

America's national mentality demonstrates poor judgment and irresponsibility in dealing with people at both a domestic and foreign level. America appears self-centered in her search for immediate gratification and failure to make long-range goals that benefit humanity.

As we note the 1962 meeting with Dr. Schein and his objectives, recall the infamous J. E. Hoover' memo, directing counterinsurgency against the Black Liberation Movement. It is evident that Kitson's experience in Kenya, fighting against the "Mau Mau", emerged as a strategy of the U.S. government's counterinsurgency objectives.

We encourage and promote a thorough investigation by the International Human Rights Commission.

[1] When the term "political prisoner" is used in this paper it is not limited to those who are incarcerated as a result of their political beliefs, actions, or affiliations. The term includes persons in prison for social crimes who became politicized inside prison walls and who oriented their lives around the struggle for social justice and national liberation. Such persons as Malcolm X, George Jackson, The Attica Warriors, and the many other men and women of yesterday and today's struggle would be encompassed in the term.

[2] John B. Watson was the founder of behaviorism in the United States in the 1900s. He rejected mentalism, and introspection and advocated a purely objective psychology ... B.F. Skinner was a pivotal figure in psychological behaviorism. Much of his work has centered on the process of operant conditioning.

[3] We want to emphasize that prisoners who resist outside of an organization framework are expressing dissatisfaction with the social situation although their expressed reason for having done so does not include the use of terms commonly articulated by a conscious resistor. As one writer stated while addressing this issue, "criminality itself is a form of unconscious protest, reflecting the distortions of an imperfect society, and in a revolutionary situation, the criminal, the psychopath, may become as good a revolutionary as the idealist. (See *War of the Flea*, p. 113, by R. Tabor).

[4] Information concerning that historical meeting was found in the "Mind Manipulators" by Alan W. Schefin. (See *Library of Congress* cataloging in publication data); additional information was found in a pamphlet on "Breaking Men Minds" behavior control in Marion, Illinois.

[5] Many behavior scientists will attest to the fact that situations can be contrived in such a manner that they will influence people to engage in self-destructive behavior. Therefore, the United States government must be held accountable for contributing to the behavior of the oppressed.

[6] The drug thorazine (chlorpromazine) was the first anti-schizophrenia drug used in the United States and was generally given to prisoners in earlier years. This drug clearly produces a "Zombie-like-behavior" in the individual. Furthermore, it is used as the standard against which the newer drugs are compared. (See Multimodal Behavior Therapy, by Arnold A. Lazarus). Although, thorazine is still being used by prison officials today, new drugs called prolixin (fluphenazine) and haldol (haloperiodol) are more preferably prescribed. Prolixin has a relative milligram potency of 70:1 to thorazine, and haldol as a potency of 100:1 to thorazine. Both drugs produce drastic mental and physical side effects.

[7] According to the *Webster Third New International Dictionary*, the definition of "acid test" is a severe or crucial test, as of value authenticity or effectiveness.

[8] Frank Kitson was the commander of the British counterinsurgency force in Northern Ireland for many years, and before that he was an officer in many of Britain's lost colonial wars, *e. g.*, Kenya, Aden and Cyprus. Most of his examples of low intensity operations are drawn from Britain's war in Ireland the United States war in Indochina. One of his strategic techniques was the use of the gangs. The rise of gangs in the oppressed communities in America partially reflects the successful use of his strategy by past administrations. The corollary to the use of gangs is the emergence of an increasing clamor for law and order. Kitson's book, which is entitled *"Low Intensity Operations"* (1971), is the basic manual of counterinsurgency methods used in Western Europe and North America.

Robin Evelegh has written a book that forms the basis of the revised British strategy used in Ireland. His approach to suppressing insurrections is also widely favored by the secret police in the United States. However, Evelegh's suggested methods for smothering an insurrection are presently being hotly debated in ruling class circles. (See *Peace Keeping in a Democratic Society: Lessons of Northern Ireland* (1978) by Robin Evelegh).

[9] A committee chaired by Senator Frank Church made an overall evaluation of

the riots and rebellion that swept the United States during the development of the Liberation Movement in the 60s era.

[10] Again the U. S. Government is clearly violating international standards by transferring Puerto Rican and Caribbean political prisoners into prisons deep inside the United States. The United Nations has established clear provisions against this sort of practice. On March 3, 1989, the U. N. General Assembly passed into effect Resolution 43/173 which is called, "Body of Principles For the Protection of All Persons Under Any Form of Detention or Imprisonment." Under its listing of principles, specifically U. N. Resolution 43/173, Principle 20, the following is stated: "If a detained or imprisoned person so requests, he shall, if possible, be kept in a place of detention or imprisonment reasonably near his usual place of residence."

[11] The exploitative and brutal control the United States wields over the Caribbean Islands is evinced by the cowardly attack on Grenada, the intervention of the election during Manley's administration in Jamaica, and the continual colonization of the Virgin Islands. One salient consequence of U.S. exploitative and brutal control over the Caribbean is the major influx of Rastafarian and progressive prisoners from the Islands into the United States penal system.

[12] By the American government taking punitive measures against grand jury resistors it violates accepted standards that were enacted prohibiting the use of such measures. On March 19, 1989, the United Nations General Assembly passed into effect Resolution 43/173, entitled: "Body of Principles" for the protection of all persons under any form of detention or imprisonment. Under its listing of principles, U.N. Resolution (A/Res/43/173), Principle 21, Number 1, the following is stated: "It shall be prohibited to take undue advantage of the situation of a detained or imprisoned person for the purpose of compelling him to confess, to incriminate himself otherwise or to testify against any other person."

[13] Through experimentation, deduction, and inference all of which is empirically verifiable through repeated experimentation and arriving at the same results in conformance with the projected model or worked out archetype, their scientists are able to work out and develop the precise formula that will enable them to direct and control people's behavior with mathematical precision.

[14] See *Covert Action Information Bulletin*, Issue Number 31, wherein Susan Rosenberg speaks about the horrendous conditions she, Silvia Baraldini and Alejandrina Torres were confined under the Lexington High Security Unit.

[15] U. S. Resolution 43/173, Principle 22, passed into effect on March 19, 1989, states the following: "No detained or imprisoned person shall, even with his consent, be subjected to any medical or scientific experimentation which may be detrimental to his health.

[16] See *The Mind Manipulators* by Alan Scheflin. It contains information on some of the techniques used on prisoners. Here is a telling list of the chapters: "Assaulting the Mind", "Tampering with the Mind (II)", "Ruling the Mind", "Amputating the Mind", "Pruning the Mind", "Rewiring the Mind", Blowing the Mind", "Castrating the Mind", "Robotizing the Mind".

[17] We do not mean to imply that these international bodies have not done some outstanding work. We acknowledge that these bodies have monitored certain regions and countries and they have called attention to human rights abuses occurring in those areas. What we do charge, however, and feel most strongly about, is that these same international bodies have been virtually silent with regard to the brutal treatment of Blacks in America, a people who have never had any real rights in America. We are calling attention to this neglect.

[18] See *African Consciousness and Liberation Struggles: Implications for the Development and Construction of Scientific Paradigms*, Wade Nobles

LONG TERM PAROLE

A "lifers' group", in any prison, is primarily developed to protect and advance the interests of lifers and other long term prisoners, specifically around the issues of goodtime legislation, parole reform and temporary release problems.

In 1988 the Woodbourne Prison Long Termers Committee Newsletter was created by founding members of the Woodbourne Long Termers Committee: Darryl King, John Benizio, Ralph Richman and Ratton Hall. After Darryl King was "shipped" to another institution in 1990, the Newsletter was discontinued. However, shortly thereafter, John "Snake" Massey was transferred to Woodbourne and he subsequently resuscitated the Newsletter. Below are a few excerpts from the Newsletter regarding parole and "life behind bars".

Elmo Reborn

Elmo has served over twenty years in prison for murder. At one time he was an extremely dangerous and angry person. The years have mellowed him. He is now a peaceful and loving man.

I've known Elmo for a long time. I've known the brute and I now know the saint. I hadn't encountered him for many years. Our paths crossed again a couple of years ago and I was amazed at the complete transformation of this man.

The Elmo of old thrived in the microcosm where violence was the order of the day. He was a functional illiterate and his range of reason was limited. He was not stupid, and he had a certain skill and cunning which he used to propel him through the quagmire of his existence.

Raised in an inner-city ghetto, Elmo was a product of his environment. He was a strict adherent of the "Urban Survival Tip" which says, "The violent are cool; the non-violent are suckers". It's an adage that was instilled into him at a very young age. As a child, he was beaten by a group of kids after school. He went home and tearfully told his grandmother what had happened to him. He was admonished for his weakness, given a bat and instructed to find those boys and "beat the shit out of them". He did...

-Charles Frazier, 71-B-0122
John White, 82-A-4444,

Simple Equation

Why do people commit crime? This is a complex question but one could safely conclude that poverty is a significant variable. In 1983 it was reported that 50% of all jail inmates had annual incomes of less than $5,600 prior to their arrest [see Bureau of Justice Statistics, Report to the Nation on Crime and Justice: Second Edition, March 1988]. Another contributing factor was the epidemic of substance abuse, which permeated the nation as a whole and inner city ghettos in particular. Finally, lack of adequate education limits one's range of opportunities as well as limiting one's range of reason. There is a simple equation that I use to illustrate this point: Ignorance + Frustration = Anger + Violence.

This formula is as valid for the root causes of violence in our inner city urban areas as it is for society's response to that violence. Ignorance and frustration has driven our society to embrace the revenge concept of capital punishment. It also demanded that certain prisoners never be released even though they pose no threat to the community and even though they may provide solutions that would stem the increase of violence in our society.

There is a perception that society bears no responsibility for violence that exists in impoverished communities. The Long Termers Committee has endorsed the notion of Community Corrections. Our approach advocates the idea that qualified long term prisoners be encouraged to do community service in the areas of aggression control, substance abuse and education. Long term prisoners presently run effective programs in prisons, in the areas mentioned. We understand the problem and we have viable solutions…

-Elmo McCargo, 73-A-1112

Prison Is

PRISON IS A PLACE where the flame in ever man burns low. For some it goes out, but for most it flickers weakly, sometimes flashes brightly, but never seems to burn as brightly as it once did.

PRISON IS A PLACE where you can go for years without feeling the touch of a human hand, where you can go for months without hearing a kind word. It is a place where your friendships are shallow and you know it. …

PRISON IS A PLACE where you forget the sound of a baby's cry. You forget the sound of a cat's meow or the sound of the dial tone on the telephone.

PRISON IS A PLACE where you see people you do not admire and you wonder if you are like them. It is a place where you strive to remain civilized, but where you lose ground and know it. …

PRISON IS A PLACE where you go to bed before you're tired, where you pull the blanket over your head when you're not cold. It is place where you escape … by reading, by playing cards, by dreaming or by going mad.

PRISON IS A PLACE where you fool yourself, where you promise yourself you'll live a better life when you leave. Sometimes you do, but more often you don't.

PRISON IS A PLACE where you get out some day. When you do you wonder how everyone else can be so calm when you're so excited. When the bus driver goes over twenty-five miles an hour you want to tell him to slow down, but you don't because you know it's foolish …

– Alexander M. Marathon, 79-D-0127

Rehabilitation

Today there are many individuals coming into the prison system who are uneducated, unskilled and very impressionable. All that they've heard, when they first walk through the prison's gates. Shortly after their arrival they learn that there is very little expected of them by the Department of Correctional Services. Should they desire, they can spend their time doing nothing that would prepare them for a positive transition back into the community. Many find themselves rewarded with temporary release, by DOCS, or release at their earliest date, by the Division of Parole.

The DOCS, in conjunction with the State Division of Parole, are constantly releasing "defective products" back into the community. These individuals are liabilities to the community and possess no viable skills to compete in the work force, which leaves them dependent upon social services, or leads them back to the negative factors that brought them to prison in the first place. They cannot teach the youth of the community because they do not know themselves what is actually wrong. One would think that the best candidates for release on parole or temporary release would be those whom have taken advantage of their time while incarcerated to rehabilitate themselves. Those are the ones who know the problems that exist within the communities. Those are the ones who know the problems that exist within the communities. Those are the ones that are capable of competing strongly within the work force. In total, these are the men and women who are capable of helping to rebuild our deteriorating neighborhoods. But they are also the ones whom the DOCS utilize as stabilizers within prisons around the State. They are the teachers/instructors' aides and the stabilizing forces between facility staff and the younger prisoners…

– Ronald West, Vice Chairman, 79-A-2138

Growing Old in Prison

As a Latino and continuous victim of the arbitrary and capricious nature of the Parole Board's discretionary power I must say that I'm tired of a parole system that is out of touch with the reality of prison and crime in our society.

While it is true that crime in our society has been growing at an

alarming rate, violent crimes has become almost common place; the problems and causes are drug abuse, poverty, lack of education, broken homes, etc. We could point fingers all we want but the reality of the situation is we have young men and women in prison that will be returning to society one day. What do we do with them? Do we educate them with skills that will enable them to become assets to our society or do we just give up on them.

Before I go any further let me ask you, the reader, a question. Have you ever done anything when you were young that had gotten you into trouble with the law or something which you were ashamed? I have asked this question of many professional people and most answered yes. Look at our President, he smoked marijuana when he was young. Does this make him a POT HEAD or UNQUALIFIED to be President of the United States, or does this make him human in the eyes of the people, to admit to a mistake when he was young? What would have happened if President Clinton was arrested for smoking marijuana? Do you think he would have become President? Many people make mistakes in their lives, or do things under stress or peer pressure that they would not normally do. Sometimes these mistakes can be corrected, other times we have to live with the consequences of our unthoughtful actions.

What the Parole Board fails to realize is that the nature of crimes will never change. All we could hope for is that the prisoner realizes his mistakes and tries to change his ways. When a prisoner is hit with two (2) years because of the nature of the offense it dampens their spirit, yet these prisoners continue. Two (2) years later they are hit again with two (2) more years, due to the "nature of the offense", and this goes on and on, sometimes up to ten (10) years or more.

We complain about the recession in our country, but yet the Parole Board is spending millions of your tax dollars housing long term prisoners that could better serve society if they were released. At present, the average cost to keep a prisoner in prison is about $30,000. This writer has been hit twice for a total of four (4) additional years. In essence, for that period, I am costing you, the taxpayer, $120,000. For ... ? ...

– *Tyrone Garcia*

Parole vs. Long Term Prisoners

There are approximately 72 prisons in New York State and parole hearings are held monthly at 95% of those prisons. There are 19 Parole Commissioners who move around the state on a regular basis. So, how much time can a person spend in the community, which they are pledged to serve, determining the ills of that community or the concerns that the community has would say very little.

Long term prisoners are not trying to diminish the seriousness of their offenses (although there's evidence that quite a few are really innocent), but they want a fair chance when they met with parole officials concerning their release. Statistics will show that long term prisoners are the best risk when given parole, they have a very low recidivism rate. Many of them, on making that transition are working in the communities trying to instill values, principles and morals in the younger generations so that they will not have to take this route to be educated. Long term prisoners are not interested in perpetuating a system, but they are interested in saving tax dollars for the taxpayer by returning to their communities as assets and participating in the process of rebuilding. Rebuilding through the development of our youth through renovation and viable interaction; all becoming valuable resources for a more effective community...

– John Massey, Chairman, 71-A-0264

PRISON IS A PLACE
Woodbourne Long Termers Committee
Woodbourne Correctional Facility
Pouch 1
Woodbourne, New York 12788

HOT ICED A.M. NITE *by Leticia Benson*

Flirtin is a e-z step\ aspecially\if u know ta holler
when that feelin\ thumpin out grip n grind grooves.
Watchin all them bone shakers\ do the belly roll...
Wall holders: heads cocked back in 40 degreezin mack style.
Mojo workers: hips motionin in a way can't nobody who
aint in it testify to.
Freestylers: arms floatin up and down\ aimin to be heard
and played on\ like brass buttons\ under a master musicians fingertips.
Yeahhh... its all goin down here tonite
but the big umph got SWEETEST FINGER in they bowl o' gravy...

Her eyes favoritizin his and him doin a right back atcha nod.
Them. Mixin mergin\ candle in the corner\
3 a.m. winterness scoochin through a cracked window.
Feel good music goin on n on n on n on...
Maybe somebody else seein um\ maybe not
but that aint part of they matterin
(whether a crowd gone givum the snap up or suck teeth sayin
"they needta take that shit home this aint no coochie house")
Ya see\ approvin commin from the inside\ workin itself to the
outside\ goin upaside and downaside\ throughout the whole\
entire room.
Them. And that pure light in the corner shimmien its bud
servin up all the flavor of a cracklin fireplace with 10, 000
switches and twitches.
UmHuh... that's all the RARA they need.
The heats pilein on now like drum beats in a Gelede' celebration.
They move\ wantin to disappear\ fill up every bit of space\
creation knows. Hookin up to Ancient World\
under a Love Jones lip lock spell. Smilin\ cuz unspoken words\
leavin um SaNCTiFiED! MEsMeRiZEd! HYPnoTIZeD!!!
Them.
Touchin\ comin down now\ holdin on nice\ knowin quivers and quakes
under skin\ gone do um real good\ for a next 100 years.

On Refusing Parole

by Safiya Bandele and ibn Kenyatta

Getting banged on the head with a billy club after being falsely accused of not paying his fare in 1974, ibn Kenyatta grabbed the transit cop's gun to save his life. Convicted of [attempt(ed)] murder (before blacking out from the beating the two exchanged gunfire, the cop was shot three times, Kenyatta twice), he ultimately received 15 to life.

Since 1988 Kenyatta, a New Afrikan, has repeatedly refused to appear before the parole board. He wants an unconditional release. His woman/ fiancee of 17 years, Safiya Bandele, supports this struggle and heads up The Coalition to Liberate Kenyatta (P.O. Box 470-912, Brooklyn, New York 11247 (718)493-3698 ext. 243).

Images of his remarkable artwork, which have been reviewed and exhibited in major publications, are shown on page 123 and on the following pages. Kenyatta's refusal to appear, to many, just seems plain wrongheaded. But Kenyatta says, no, there is a well thought out strategy to his actions (like his stylized disregard for the English language). Kenyatta and Bandele decided to collaborate and devised this second/third person "dialogue" to give the African community insight into his/their position(s):

Kenyatta should take parole because he could be much more effective on the outside.

Effective how? Effective doing what?

Raising issues about prisons.

Why can't You raise the issues?

We could but it would mean more coming from him, since he spent all those years behind bars.

Is that like: our people like to be "entertained"; would like to say – "Look at him, spent all those years locked up, etc.?"

Actually, Kenyatta would be more effective inside if there was a movement out here of folks saying: "Kenyatta is still behind bars, still upholding his principles and we want him out! Do You want him out? What are You going to do, to help?

Prison issues are related to every other issue in our community. What issue are You working on? Do You see how prisons relate to Your issue? What's happening with the issue You are working on? Any movement?

Why not? Prisons relate directly to homelessness, AIDS, police brutality, the miseducation system. The work to Liberate Kenyatta is about his kastruggle [case struggle] to demonstrate the connections of our struggles in our own community here in the U.S. and around the world.

Well, you know, my organization is about…

Cool. Y'all ever talk about prison issues Why not? Do you see the connections? The political, social, and economic connections? The connections it has on us as a people? Your own daughter, son, mother, brother, father?

And isn't it also true that when Kenyatta leaves prison another Black (African) person takes his kage [cell]? So what changes? Nothing!

Kenyatta is a strong brother and our communities need strong brothers, particularly ex-prisoners.

Strong brothers are out here. Strong brothers (and sisters) are getting out of prison every day. How are they using their lives to help the community? How are you using yours?

Many folks are working hard, struggling to help brothers and sisters to get parole. Most of our political prisoners want parole. Many have been unjustly denied parole. And here Kenyatta is refusing to consider parole. It's really hard to support his position.

Yes. Definitely. Many, if not most prisoners want parole. And our movement supports them. Kenyatta's position is not recommended for everybody. For example, Kenyatta doesn't necessarily see Lifers refusing parole. It's the prisoner's choice. It's how s/he wants to use her or his life. We strongly support Political Prisoners/Prisoners of War. And we're saying: this is our position. If you can support us, fine – we need your support. If you can't, or won't, then we still wish you well in your work.

I don't mean to appear mean or insensitive by saying this, and I hope you won't take it that way, but Kenyatta's position sounds like maybe he's really afraid to come out on parole.

Don't mind my feelings. You wouldn't believe how many instant replays i've had with this issue. i've had to listen to worse. One sister, who used to be my friend, even said to me that Mandela had already done what Kenyatta is doing – taking a principled stand by staying in prison. And even Kenyatta has heard it from other prisoners.

His response is to tell them that only a fool wouldn't be afraid to come out here where we're at. Black men's life expectancy is greater for survival in prison than out here in the streets of Harlem or Brownsville.

But that isn't why Kenyatta is refusing parole. He asks "parole to what?" There was nothing here for the majority of men and women who went to prison in the first place. There is even less today for them when they leave prison – with $40.00 – on parole – to return to the community as ex-offenders.

Yes, but ...

The state's game is that of a surrogate Godfather. When they offer prisoners parole, they can't refuse. But when prisoners say "No!" to parole, to the state's game, they (prisoners) take control of how the game is to be played. The prisoners' "No!" forces the state into having to look at community leaders/representatives in order to negotiate another relationship for power-sharing in prisons, criminal justice, poverty, unemployment, etc., – the funding of our own badly needed inner city infrastructure.

We in the community can then make it plain to them that we're now wise to the fact that by them building prisons in upstate New York and sending our men and women (and our children!) up there that we're no longer fooled by this. African and Latino prisoners may be "paying their debt to (white) society" but they damn sure ain't paying their debt to the African and Latino communities.

We ought not to ever forget that u. s. prisons serve as another extension of the repressive arms of government used by the dominant minority classes who run this country. So, we would not be organizing ourselves in this struggle in order to "make a living" from prisons, but to work towards eradicating them.

Yeah, all that sounds good. But what's wrong with parole? It is a "legitimate" way out of prison.

The federal penal system has no parole. Why does the state penal system have parole. It's a $1.4 billion annual failure system. It needs changing (or abolishing). And have you ever asked yourself or questioned why they are given parole in the first place? Parole is granted not out of concern for prisoners but because the prison system needs the bed space. The kage.

Think of the prison system as a human body. The garden that feeds this system is the Black and Brown communities. This body (prisons) "eats" Black and Brown people by ingesting (incarcerating) them in prisons and eliminates them through parole conditional release, or maxing out (serving the maximum sentence). Since the majority of prisoners come out on parole, refusing parole would mean stopping the shit. It would constipate the system. Create a cesspool. A sewer. Change would come. Or the body would bust.

Think about it – the court system, the city/county/jails, etc. – everything stopped. Stagnant. Once this is grasped by our people it becomes a form of community empowerment.

We must begin to understand that for us, the oppressed, refusing parole is a political act. It is a legitimate form of strategy in our struggle to be free, to educate, politicize and raise the revolutionary consciousness of African people.

The African community does not benefit economically from the billions spent on the parole system. It's a challenge for our community to use these dollars for the community. We must demand this. The community should be responsible for programs dealing with incarcerated prisoners as well as programs for those ex-prisoners who are daily returning to us. Just as prisoners should be responsible for their attitudes and behaviors towards the African community. Will we choose empowerment or continued disenfranchisement?

O.K., I see your position. But you're such a beautiful African woman. Kenyatta should get out so you two could be together, have a family...

True. i'm beautiful. He's beautiful. And through an arduous journey we are together now. We would love for our two beautiful bodies to come together to (pro)create freedom. We have family. We are family. "We two are a multitude," Kenyatta always says. But, will You help us?

There is power in decisions
Kenyatta and i have made ours
What is YOUR decision?

"The First Modeling Class"
Graphic Art

"de Black Angel"
charcoal

Voice: Paul Robeson
pencil

"Who's Gonna Take the Weight?"
ink and brush wash

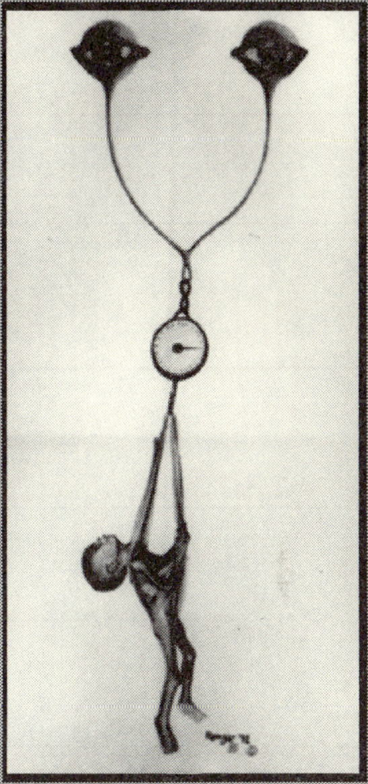

Political Prisoner ibn Kenyatta's work is frequently "challengin the kultural malaise in U.S. society."

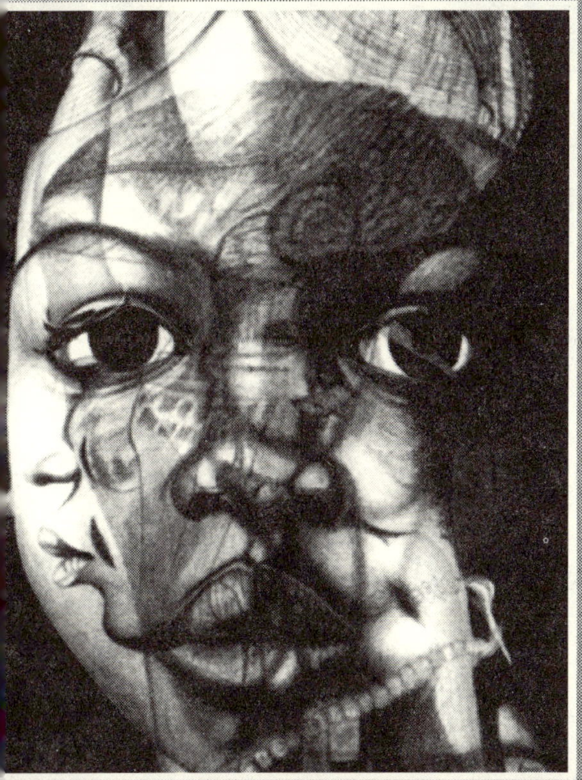

"She Nigma"
pencil

Illustration by Shawn Alexander

Non-Traditional Approach to Criminal and Social Justice

by Eddie Ellis

Beginning in the middle 60s to early 70s, there was a fervent burst of consciousness throughout New York state (and, indeed, this nation's) prisons.

A number of men who had been influenced by, or actively contributed to, the sweet street cries of Black pride and justice of the time, found themselves behind bars examining the capitalistic philosophy of the penal and criminal justice systems.

Study groups inside the prisons emerged, particularly at Greenhaven, Auburn, Sing-Sing and Attica. After the Attica uprising of September, 1971, prison officials, "getting wise" to this activity, determined to contain this dynamism among certain inmates by shipping a sizable number to one facility, Greenhaven. (Many conscious prisoners consider the word "inmate" or "resident" docile and obfuscating, like "superintendent" for "warden" or "facility" for "prison".)

At Greenhaven, most of these men, many were lifers, developed what they called the Think Tank. After exploring certain questions related to self-determination, they successfully promoted their requirement that prisoners were entitled to more than high school equivalency certification as a road to successful rehabilitation.

Greenhaven became the first penal institution in the nation to develop college study for its prisoners in 1973. The Think Tank also created and advanced call-home programs and conjugal/trailer visits for prisoners and their loved ones, aiding in the stabilization of the family unit for prisoners everywhere in the U.S.

Soon there was a great deal of flux around the Think Tank membership as individuals were moved back and forth between various institutions. In 1975-76 the Think Tank was phased out, primarily due to these erratic transfers.

Those active brothers remaining at Greenhaven at the time, the remnants of the Think Tank, were Charles "Hasaan" Gale, Cardell "Blood" Shaird, Larry "Luqman" White, Lawrence "Bubba" Hayes and Eddie "Kabaka" Ellis. As a core group, they commenced to correspond and develop data with other leaders and conscious prisoners in various institutions. They began to understand that there was no ideological basis for people to do prison work (study, research and analysis) around an Africentric or Pan-Africentric perspective. This was significant. It became increasingly clear that those who were keenly aware of the varying crime producing elements in their communities, had no voice in addressing and thwarting those elements.

Putting aside the (self-serving) social and political analysis of European sociologists, psychiatrists and penologists giving reasons for crime in the urban centers of the nation, particularly Black and Latino neighborhoods, this group began to clarify the full symbiotic relationship of politics and economics behind the imprisonment of people of color. Out of their examination came the "Non-Traditional Approach to Criminal and Social Justice". This study was heavily assisted by Carl D. Berry, Dept. Superintendent of Programs at Greenhaven – considered the most progressive prison official in the nation at the time – who "ran interference" with various levels of prison administration and provided outside resources for the brothers to fully develop their work. Chief among those resources was Dr. Gary Mendez, Director of Criminal Justice for the National Urban League. To date, Dr. Mendez is still supportive of the prison reform aims of the Non-Traditional Approach; he has developed his own think tank in Washington, D.C. around issues related to the survival of black males: the National Trust for the Development of African American Men.

Eddie Ellis, after serving 23 years, and Lawrence Hayes, after serving 20 years, are now both out on work release and parole, respectively (however, the other three "major architects" remain, active, in various prisons). Ellis, a former member of The Black Panther Party and survivor of the Attica insurrection of 1971, who is presently developing a prisoner education, research and advocacy organization called the Community Justice Center in the village of Harlem, New York, details below the present philosophies and goals of the Non-Traditional Approach to Criminal and Social Justice.

Extensive research has been done at Greenhaven Prison over the past ten years, in conjunction with data from numerous studies and reports, supporting the following:

•Racism is alive and well in New York City and state, along with a horrendous crime and drug problem in African American and Latino communities that appears to have defied all solutions to date.

•There has been a massive failure of basic institutions serving Black and Latino communities. The dysfunction of criminal justice and prison system is one outstanding example of institutional failure.

•People who control these institutions either don't know what to do or refuse to do what they know to be right.

•Black and Brown communities have little or no control over institutions which determine their quality of life, a major reason why these institutions are dysfunctional.

•Problems of poverty, crime and drugs are the direct result of, among other things, institutional failures which create crime generative factors that lead to prison or death.

•Fundamental assumptions which guide and govern these failing institutions and on which social and criminal justice theories, analysis, decisions and policies are based, are no longer valid. Demographics of both inner cities and prisons have changed dramatically over the last 25 – 50 years, while the assumptions have remained sacrosanct.

•There is a direct identifiable socio-economic, political, cultural and community specific link between prisons and the communities from which the majority of prisoners come. This link demonstrates a direct relationship between the two.

•Interpretation of statistics, raw data and other research relating to social and criminal justice problems has been fatally flawed. It is evaluated based on incorrect assumptions and further misshaped by a perception and world view that is essentially, if not exclusively, a white, middle-class, Euro-centric norm, grossly distorted by race and class.

These factors illustrate our belief that solutions to problems we face as Black and Latino people are not attainable using conventional or traditional methods. There are no prison problems, *per se*, which do not have their origins in the communities from which the majority of prisoners come. If we attend to the solving of community problems, prison problems will become solvable also.

Our recommendation is the creation of a "non traditional model" that establishes an ideological framework for a major departure from traditional theories and assumptions about crime and prisons. By developing an Afro-Latino perspective which defines and gives meaning to our own reality, as we experience it. Such a model is designed to move away from general, establishment approaches and definitions to one which is community specific, which evolves from unique cultural norms and socio-economic conditions of our communities. It reinterprets social and criminal justice issues, theories, concepts, terminology, problems and solutions in an Afro-Latino context.

Background

The problem of crime and drugs has become so pervasive and so insidious it now threatens to destroy the inner city Black and Latino community. Over the past 15 years, despite all efforts to the contrary, the problem has become progressively worse. Black people are the major victims of crime, primarily victimized by other Black people. The only solution to this problem, law enforcement officials, politicians and the media tell us is harsher and longer sentences, building more prisons and declaring "war" on the criminal, whatever that means. None of these solutions remotely resemble the answer and none have proven successful.

Few people really know what to do; no one wants to admit, however, that they don't know. Those who should know, perhaps do know, seem afraid to offer new insights or suggestions that break with traditional thinking. The communities most affected are least consulted. The criminal justice apparatus and the state prison system are controlled and operated mostly by white authority figures and the inner city communities have become American bantustans.

There are more African American and Hispanic people in New York state prisons today. The prison population has grown at a rate which staggers the imagination in its implications for communities of color and would offend the knowledgeable observer. Prisons have become the ultimate weapon in a system of social control called the "legal system", whose function is to deal with people who are actually or potentially disruptive to the social order. Otherwise, how do you account for the fact that although Blacks and Latinos combined comprise less than 25% of the general state population, they represent *85%* of *all* state prisoners *and 75%* of the state prison population comes from New York City? Further, that the 75% from New York City come from 18 specific State Assembly districts: 29, 32, 33, 40, 42, 43, 55, 56, 57, 68, 69, 70, 71, 73, 74, 76, 78, 82. All these districts are primarily composed of people of color.

Empirical evidence seems to confirm that prisons are being constructed in New York State as "warehouses" for society's considered Black and Brown undesirables. The working poor, "underclass", and particularly young males from ghettoes and barrios of New York City have been classified and written off as not having any significant labor role in the new technological service oriented economy. Thus, prisons have come to be used as devices of social control. The war on crime and drugs is little more than a war on the Black and Latino poor, whom white sociologists and penologists (some Blacks too) blame for their own condition.

Simultaneously, the rapid expansion and construction of prisons in rural, white, conservative, Republican, upstate communities in New York state, has spawned an entire new and booming "clean" industry. White workers displaced because of the decline in "heavy" industry or as a result of technological changes in the workplace now find employment and economic opportunities in prison growth which provides primary jobs, second incomes in many cases, contracts and other financial benefits to them. Underlying this complex matrix, consciously or unconsciously, is the ugly presence of racism. While the keepers are all white, the kept are all Black and Brown.

The Historical Perspective

The theoretical and analytical basis of our model for non-traditional solutions, arises from an Afro-Latino historical perspective. This perspective offers us another way of viewing our history both as people of color and as prisoners. It opposes the view that dominant society has given us. This new perspective or "new view", is the beginning of a process that allows us to speak for ourselves and in so doing commence a practice that leads to our own empowerment. It affords us an opportunity to create a "new consciousness", which is the first step in an act of empowerment that offers us identity, purpose and direction. This new consciousness is the key force, the life-giving energy, which allows us to begin transforming ourselves from whoever or whatever we were that caused us to be in prison in the first place, into self-conscious, progressive, social activists, even while behind cold, steel bars.

Our historical perspective covers a 50-year period, from 1940 to 1990, and traces the growth of Blacks and Browns in prisons today. It provides a historical account, from our perspective, of how we got to this point in time. More importantly, it identifies social conditions which account for (so-called) "minorities" in prison, develops the connection between the broader society and prisons, explains the policies and priorities of prisons as government institutions, traces the changing needs of institutions generally as the people served change in complexion, and instructs us why the character of an institution must change as the people it serves change. Finally, it proposes that a transformation in the prisoners' self-image and conscious behavior creates empowerment, and shows that prisoner empowerment can only be linked to the empowerment of our home communities, so both must cooperate together. It then establishes the framework for the direct relationship between prisons and the Afro-Latino community.

The Direct Relationship

The numbers alone (85% Blacks/Browns in state prisons; 75% from New York City) in the first instance establishes the direct connection between our communities and the prisons. Each feeds off the other and is affected culturally, socially, economically and in many other ways by one another. The flow of people from the community into the prisons, and from the prisons back into the community further establishes the direct relationship. This flow is now above 25,000 per year, going and coming. Finally, the root of the direct relationship is in the fact that because of institutional failures in our communities, certain factors arise which we call "crime generative factors". These begin with racism, the primary cause of institutional dysfunction and leads to family breakdown, undereducation, un/underemployment, poverty, welfare, hustling, crime, drugs, prison or death. These conditions are present in over 90% of people in prison today and constitute the cement which binds us to our communities.

The *direct relationship* constitutes the basis by which we propose that there are no prison problems, only community problems. Once we begin to address community problems, prison problems will also be addressed. Prison policies can no longer simply address individual failures or infirmities, instead they must include crime generative factors and institutional failures; so-called rehabilitation cannot and does not work, not because of the frequently offered traditional reasons (prisoners have no work history, no work ethic, etc.), but because the concept of rehabilitation in prison, as it relates to Blacks and Browns, does not consider crime generative factors or institutional failures. Hence, even if rehabilitation were possible, the "cured" or rehabed prisoner would only be released to an "infected" environment and become infirm again. This explains the true nature and reasons for recidivism. The direct relationship establishes the need for a non traditional approach to criminal and social justice issues.

Empowerment Theory vs. Rehabilitation Theory

Empowerment Theory is a concept that prisoners maintain must be incorporated into all prison programs, classes and activities. The primary goals of the Non Traditional Approach, from an Afro-Latino centrist perspective are expressed in Empowerment Theory. This theory is a direct contradiction of the theory of rehabilitation. Empowerment Theory says we must instill in our youth of color not just a skill, trade or education, but also we must instill in that prisoner the responsibility to go back into the African and Latino community, upon release, with the idea in mind and heart, to combat socio-economic conditions (the crime generative factors) that contributed to their imprisonment in the first place. Empowerment Theory replaces Rehabilitation Theory because it adds "surplus explanatory value".

Whenever a new theory or model (paradigm) is developed, in order for it to be accepted and for it to demonstrate its validity, it must explain everything or nearly everything in the discarded model and more; it must also be able to explain things that the discarded model cannot. This is its "surplus explanatory value". The utility of any new model is that it presents another interpretation (and sometimes new data also) which alters the old model such that it no longer remains useful. Empowerment Theory is just such a model when compared to Rehabilitation Theory.

Empowerment Theory is based on a societal approach to addressing an offender's so called criminality. It is a theory based on the socio-economic conditions that engender illegal behavior; it is designed to produce structural and systematic transformation in community as well as in the prisoner. Transformation, Empowerment Theory says, must occur not just inside the individual, as maintained by Rehabilitation Theory, but equally if not more importantly, it must address how the individual transforms the society, which in this case are communities of color to which each offender returns. Empowerment equips the individual to undertake the role. Thus general rehabilitation must be supplemented with empowerment to be effective, hence general rehab theory plus empowerment theory equals the non traditional approach.

Rehabilitation Theory operates on the basic assumption that the individual alone is responsible for his or her attitudes and responses to racism and oppression; that societal factors do not play any role in determining behavior or attitudes. This theory says that the individual's behavior was wrong and seeks to change or correct that behavior, usually in a situation that does not consider the impact of crime generative factors. Inherent in the theory of rehabilitation is the concept that it seeks to "correct" the individual such that it returns him or her to a state or condition that he/she was in previously, or should have been in, prior to the objectionable behavior, hence re (return) /habilitation (to dwell).

With African Americans and Latinos, their condition prior to objectionable behavior was one of a disadvantaged, second-class citizen or resident alien, in relationship to full and unobstructed access to the benefits, rewards and power in society. This lack of access, clearly was a factor which contributed to the objectionable behavior. Therefore to "treat" or attempt to "correct" the objectionable behavior without also dealing with the lack of access or the crime generative factors, is a sure prescription for failure. Rehabilitation Theory was viable 40 years ago, when the prisons were predominantly populated by whites. They had access to benefits, rewards and power in general society, yet choose not to avail themselves of it. Their behavior can therefore be described as deviant. The same is not true for today's prisoner who is Caribbean, African American or Latino. Thus the focus of prison efforts must change to accommodate the new demographic realities with which they face. Failure to recognize and act upon these new demographics essentially, has rendered the Rehabilitation Theory obsolete. Therefore, the goal should not be to rehabilitate but to "empower" the prisoner to change the conditions within the community.

Empowerment Theory maintains that in addition to employment and family care, once the prisoner re-enters the community (indeed while he or she is still in prison) they must be responsive and responsible for civic duties. This involves being taught about socio-economic conditions and how the crime generative factors impact on their lives, as well as devoting a specific number of hours per week, while in prison and once on the street, towards some community, civic or organizational activities which are directed towards combating crime generative factors. This concept must be built into all prison program initiatives and educational activities both inside the prisons and outside in the community. It needs to be a condition of parole and be incorporated into earned incentives which permit the reduction of a prisoner's sentence for participation in such programs.

The Non Traditional Approach

Our Non Traditional Approach begins, as it must, with *truth telling.* This is the starting point. The truth as we see it will differ from the general or traditional assumptions about truth. It will also differ from "truth" as seen from some other non Afro-Latino perspective which is why developing our own perspective was so important.

The Non Traditional Approach says that racism and classism has locked most of us out of the economic mainstream, hence education must have a unique, dual role. It must offer the tools needed to address these specific problems and it must also empower the student to cope with two worlds: one in the general society and another in his/her community. This approach says that we must reassess the entire system to determine what the new needs of our people are and how curriculum can be structured to meet those needs. General education is not enough, which is why the schools and prisons are failing. Education must be community specific and Afro-Latino centric.

The difference between general and community specific is that general makes the individual fit the policy, whereas community specific makes the policy fit the individual. Taken one step further, our approach proposes that because of the direct relationship, all areas of the community's life and the institutions erected to serve it must be re-examined with the idea in mind of the community taking control. This should be the goal of the social activist prisoner as well as the community representatives with whom he/she works. The first step towards this goal should be efforts directed toward community control of the prison, since they are institutions which serve our communities almost exclusively.

Traditional vs. Non Traditional Approaches

Prisoners themselves have been developing alternative concepts and programs designed to address the implications and consequences of the grossly disproportionate numbers of Blacks and Latinos in the New York State prison system. We call the concept "The Non Traditional Approach to Criminal and Social Justice." The uniqueness of our approach is that it is community specific and non traditional, in the sense that we are challenging the conventional wisdom and assumptions upon which the entire criminal justice system is built.

The Non Traditional Approach posits that race and class distinctions have created a special place in society for African people and Latinos such that any educational efforts, whether in prison or in the community, must address this reality. The direct relationship connects the prisons to the community; the non traditional approach establishes the theoretical basis for specific community action. Essentially, the non traditional approach says that success in America is measured by how closely one can fit into a prescribed "traditional" American model. All of the policies and procedures that governs America and which determine success are based on this traditional model. This is true whether we are talking about religious or educational policy, social or economic policy, culture or criminal justice. Sadly enough, the traditional model is exclusionary in that people of color can never fit comfortably within the model, without fundamentally altering the basic essence of who they are in terms of ethnicity, history, culture and language. This is because the traditional approach is general, it is white and middle class. It maintains that one size fits all, that institutions must shape the people they serve and its foundation is grounded in a Eurocentric world view.

These have been the guiding assumptions for prison policy making for the past 40 years. When prisoners were predominantly all whites, up until the 1960s, these policies were valid and produced the desired results. Now that the prisons are 85% Black and Latino, these policies are no longer viable and have created unresolvable contradictions between policy makers, administrative enforcers, prisoners and the communities from which the majority come. The prisons are operated by white, rural, upstate, conservatives and populated by Black/Latino, urban, downstate, liberal youth.

Our Non Traditional Approach is custom tailored to the majority of people it is intended to serve. Instead of being general, the nontraditional approach is community specific. It focuses on Latinos, Caribbean and African Americans rather than on whites. It is aimed at working and "underclass" sensibilities rather than at middle-class values. It maintains that policies must be made to fit the people served and that one size does not fit everyone. It says that people shape institutions, not the other way around, at it is grounded in an Afrocentric world view.

By Afrocentric we mean that our approach is rooted in African and African American history, culture, language and experience. It draws its reflection, analysis and proposed solutions from the experience's strengths and weaknesses. By community specific we mean since prisons are 12% Caribbean, 37% African American and 36% Latino, and because 75% of the prison population comes from specific state Assembly Districts in New York City, any analysis or proposed solutions must be "specifically" designed to address this reality and these specific communities. Non Traditional simply means that we are questioning, critiquing and rejecting the "traditional" methods of criminal justice and prison policy making, since by every possible measure, and by New York State's own admission of 47% recidivism, these traditional policies have been a failure for the past 20 years.

Essential Program Components

Our research and analysis has led us to identify three essential characteristics common to most prisoners, which we believe play significant roles in why we are in prison in such disproportionate numbers. This research is the product of our own life experiences, individually and collectively, and reflects the prisoners perspective of his own situation. Our commonality is expressed in:

1. Crime generative attitudes from which self destructive value systems are developed that culminate in negative behavioral responses to racism and other urban socio-economic and environmental conditions.

2. The ethnic status of Caribbean, Latino and African American people in this country, defined as second class citizens, based on race and class, as expressed by custom, tradition, culture and law (both *de facto* and *de jure*), creates low self esteem, lack of group worth, and collective and individual self hatred as expressed in Black on Black crime.

3. The total lack of understanding about a collective Pan African identity, which accounts in great measure for the absence of any sense of community and the development of an "anything goes" mentality in acquiring material consumer goods.

Men enter prisons and spend years there, yet root causes of their behavior are never confronted because neither the state or the local administration offers any programs, or even a viable theory, which deals with our specific problems. As a result, we ourselves have had to design, develop and implement programs and classes, from our Afrocentric, Non Traditional Approach, which we believe begins to address many of the attitudes, values and behavior patterns that led to our illegal activity and eventually prison.

Socially conscious prisoners at Greenhaven and other prisons are struggling with these problems redirect our lives into productive activity. We have gone about as far as we can on our own. We now need the assistance of professional educations, curriculum specialists, historians, researchers, legislators and community organizations, to complete the creation of a new comprehensive and holistic approach to the problems we face as African people. We need the prison equivalent of the Curriculum of Inclusion.

Such an approach must seek to reverse the entire theoretical basis upon which the traditional system rests and in its place construct new theories that are community specific. This implies community input and control – though its elected representatives and others – of prison, parole and probation policy making and of the $3 billion criminal justice and prison budget. Because of our disproportionate numbers in the system, we have a moral, legal, logical and ethical right to this control. We may be able to do a far better job than is presently being done – we certainly can't do any worse. The sheer numbers alone justify our seeking control, since we are the people and the communities most affected.

In applying the concept of community specific to development of non traditional approaches, we have identified three essential program themes that address the specific character of Caribbean, African American and Latino communities to which the overwhelming majority of the prison population will return. These three essential program themes must (1) address the crime generative attitudes of prisoners, (2) address the ethnic status of prisoners, and (3) develop a sense of community in prisoners. Our efforts to develop non traditional approaches focus on specific needs of our communities as well as on the individual. Massive input from community representatives is required. We believe our efforts are in direct response to findings of the recent The Sentencing Project and the Correctional Association of New York reports, both clearly show the devastating impact of the criminal justice system, the implications for Caribbean and African American community and strategies for more effective policies and programs.

Community Specific

The concept of "community specific" has as its underlying premise the relationship between the state prison system and Caribbean, Latino and African American communities. That system directly affects the social, economic, political and even cultural life of these communities of color. This is demonstrated by the "direct relationship". Community specific postulates that in order to assure the system operates to benefit our communities, the rule of measure applied to all system initiatives is whether or not the focus is specifically geared to that particular community. In other words, does the system's initiatives impact in a beneficial way on the communities most affected; do the people most affected have a major voice in decision making; are key administrators and officials of the system held accountable to those most affected. Are the system's basic operating policies designed to accommodate the "specific" and unique needs of the particular community the system serves.

When we discuss the concept of "community specific" we begin from the basic premise that the state prison system owes the community which it claims to serve the following:

1. To address the crime generative attitudes of prisoners;
2. To provide relevant and realistic education and training programs for prisoners;
3. To address the release potential of prisoners; and
4. To address conditions and specific character of jurisdiction from which the majority of prisoners come and to which they will return.

Remedial approaches to these problems must not focus primarily on individual level responses or personal efforts to the exclusion of social level responses and institutional efforts. The responses to crime and the impact of the criminal justice system must be "personalized" by communities most affected. By "personalized" we mean to move beyond the "traditional" passive role assigned the community by the state in its posture as the major player in the criminal justice system. The communities most affected must become empowered to assume a more active and direct role. This is the underlying premise of the concept of community specific.

The operational philosophy of DOCS as spelled out in its major directive on prisoner activities and organizations states:

The Department of Correctional Services encourages constructive interaction between inmates and community. The involvement of the outside community exposes inmates to a great variety of activities and, at the same time, provides the community with a greater awareness and understanding of the correctional system. Participation in group activities can help the individual inmate develop increased self-respect, consideration of others, and a better perspective of his/her own role in society.

However, this directive, in the traditional manner, then goes on to establish a set of rules, regulations, policies and procedures designed to accomplish the exact opposite. It is directives and policies such as these, we need to review, directive by directive and policy by policy, to determine if they are "community specific" and what their significance will be upon

African and Latino community. It is our position that few of the programs currently existing anywhere in the state, remotely meet the unique needs of the African and Latino prisoners, except those limited few that prisoners themselves have created. To deprive, black and brown prisoners of their right to constructive and meaningful program activity while in state custody is to also deprive the community by way of the direct relationship and the 47% recidivism rate. To this end, we seek community assistance in effecting the kinds of policy changes, developing programs and implementing non traditional ideas sorely missing.

Historically, some of our greatest leaders have spent time within prisons and emerged stronger and wiser for the experience. We recognize the enormous debts that we owe to communities from which we came and to which we must return. We are not only seeking to turn our lives around, but in the process, we seek to become role models for our youth, both inside and outside. Further, we seek to link community empowerment elements to offer our services and experiences towards developing solutions to the problems we all have in common as a people.

We firmly believe that since 25% of Black youth between the ages of 20–29 are already in prisons, we must convert these places from warehouses for the "living dead", into universities of learning, self identity, sense of community, commitment to social change and empowerment. While this vision is expansive, those of us who have been imprisoned for many long years realize that it is our only hope to salvage our youth and it is our last chance. All else has failed and will continue to fail using traditional approaches which do not understand the true nature of community specific problems. There are no prison problems, only community problems that impact on prisons.

Conclusion

The destiny of Black and Latino community is intimately tied to that of the prisons by virtue of back and forth movement of tens of thousands of prisoners per year. Our analysis through the historical perspective, direct relationship and non traditional approaches establishes another direction for both prisoners and their home communities which is Afro-Latino centric and community specific. Our analysis demonstrates that prisons traditionally and currently are operated on the basic assumption that the individual's behavior was wrong and thus seeks to change or correct that behavior.

With Blacks and Hispanics, their condition previous to the objectionable (criminal, anti-social, deviant) behavior was one of a disadvantaged, second-class citizen, in relationship to access to full benefits, rewards and power in society, which directly contributed to the objectionable behavior. Our non traditional approach says the goal should not be to rehabilitate a prisoner but instead to empower him or her. Empowerment, in non traditional terms, means to transform; to equip the prisoner with the ability to transform themselves from what they have become, into what they can be. Empowerment means taking control of one's life and the circumstances of their environment that he or she has a voice in decisions that impact on and/or relate to him or her. Our non traditional approach seeks to create that empowerment in the prisoner, in the prisons and outside in the community so that African American and Latino people can acquire the capacity to realize their will even with opposition from others. Working collectively, prisoner with community, such a goal is not only realistic but attainable. It is our sincere expectation that we can begin the dialogue and the preparation needed to commence this process.

When basketball isn't enough

by Holly Bass

When basketball isn't enough
young men take to the streets
with bullets and guns.
When asphalt
is the only thing you see
for miles around
like frontier plains
and even the walls
begin to look like
asphalt
creeping up around
you, rising up
closing in–
the surge builds
you begin to feel
stir crazy
you realize you have
nothing to pioneer. nothing
to conquer
but your own streets.

and when sex and drugs
and music and basketball
cease to fulfill you
you begin to look for
new ways
to release the
pit of anger rising
in your stomach
like cancer
sinking
down
like a heavy stone

(and they say that young black men wouldn't understand
a philosophical dialectic)

When the more you reach out, the less
there is to hold onto
distance becomes measured in time
and time by the steady
rhythm of a siren.

yes, you are along way from home.
On these days
when basketball isn't enough
homicide and suicide
become the same thing
you pick up a bullet
and a gun
locate yourself in the
mirror of other
and pull.

Race, Class and Incarceration:

The Political Economy of Prisons by Keith Jennings

Introduction

The discussion of crime and violence in the United States is often presented as a "Black thing". The statement that we "have to deal with violent criminals," could implicitly be read, "we have to deal with the Blacks or the Latinos." The racist words, once decoded, lead to a perspective among white Americans that we have to build more jails and prisons. A similar opinion exists among many people of color whether victim or perpetrator of crime and violence.

The contemporary debate about violent crime has been projected in a simplistic manner, as the number one issue facing the country. There is no mentioning of "white on white" or "white collar" crime which cost the country $500 billion. It is quite interesting that such a view is expressed at the very time that the most recent data show a decrease nationally in violent crime.

This essay seeks to bring some clarity to the debate, and focuses on the interconnections between race, class and incarceration. It is entitled "the political economy of prisons" because as institutions, jails and prisons clearly express the reality of those interconnections and show the working of the state's repressive and coercive apparatuses.

The analysis of available data suggests that the intersection between racism and class repression, undergirded by a right–wing philosophical interpretation of crime and policy prescription, collectively have made the United States the modern day "prison house" of nations. Racism and class oppression also provided for the expansion of internal national security laws that mirror the civilizational crisis U.S. society is currently experiencing.

The analysis shows that several hidden factors leading to this state repression are related to the structural changes occurring in the U.S. economy, in particular the impact these changes are having on the Black working class. Finally, evidence of workable alternatives to incarceration is presented.

The problem of violence, crime and punishment in the United States over the past decade has led to overload of the criminal justice system. In state after state prison construction has become the number one industry and budget item. The federal system has nearly tripled the number of persons incarcerated. This has increasingly meant that many of those who may have been "turned around" are today being written off. Even liberals are now saying that some people cannot be rehabilitated. While many people may still believe that prison "teaches a lesson," and therefore inherently prevents future crime, that is a false assumption and mistaken conclusion. One of the clearest reasons to begin to make a critical analysis of the current crisis is because prisons do not rehabilitate or correct the offenders sent to them. In fact, prisons can't rehabilitate, especially when that is not their focus. Today the national recidivism rate averages more than 35 percent.[1]

The need for changes has been recognized by most people involved in the criminal justice system not only because of the systems failures but also because of cost, both human and financial. Seventy percent (70) of all the prison space in use today has been built since 1985, at a cost of $32.9 billion. The average annual cost to house a prisoner is close to $25,000 and in a maximum–security facility it is close to $100,000.[2] At the same time, many communities have witnessed the devastating effects of higher incarceration rates on young people. The destruction of a number of communities is clearly correlated to the severity of sentencing, but this is often a dismissed fact because of the "get tough on crime" mandatory sentencing approach lauded by many policy makers (only concerned with being re–elected). In some instances, this has given rise to anger, frustration, fear, and distrust of the criminal justice system. It is especially true for communities of color who are also the main victims of crime and criminal behavior.

The search for a way out of the crisis is difficult because of the fundamentally punitive nature of the criminal justice system in the United States. Therefore, when communities begin to deal with issues of crime and justice, the focus is often narrowly posed and understood. A properly educated and informed community would be empowered to respond to concerns about safety as well as the failures of the criminal justice system.

The gravity of the criminal justice crisis is best highlighted by the following statistics:

1) Since 1980 the number of sentenced inmates per 100,000 residents has risen nearly 130 percent. During this period, per capita incarceration rates have grown most rapidly in the Northeast (increasing by 167 percent) and the West (increasing by nearly 163 percent). The per capita number of sentenced prisoners in the Midwest climbed to 119 percent and the rate rose 68 percent in the South (this region already had the highest rate of incarceration therefore the increase was not as great).
2) In 1990 more than 4.1 million people were under the care or custody of correctional agencies, giving the United States the highest incarceration rate, per capita, of any country in the world
3) The 56,686 additional inmates added during 1990 was equal to a need for about 1,100 new prison beds every week
4) African Americans, Latinos, Native Americans and Asian Americans constitute 61 percent of the persons under the supervision of the criminal justice system in 1990
5) In 1990, 36 correctional agencies reported construction

costs exceeding $5.7 billion for an additional 112,729 beds

6) In 1990 it cost $13,911,187,659 to operate the 52 federal Correctional agencies in the United States. Another $4.7 billion was reported by 44 agencies for capital expenditures for a total of $18.6 billion in one year
7) Between 1980 and 1989 the growth rate for female inmates out distanced that for males and grew by more than 200 percent.
8) Since 1985 the number of adults arrested for drug violations has increased by 74 percent and the number of arrests for sales or manufacturing of illegal drugs has grown by 137 percent
9) In 1990 almost 40 states were under court order to relieve overcrowding by releasing prisoners
10) Over thirty states are experimenting with military style boot camps or shock incarceration for juvenile offenders
11) Teen age curfews have been introduced in a number of major urban areas with parents being penalized for violations of $1,000 fine and six months in jail[3]

When coupled with the deteriorating economic situation in the country, plant closures and relocations, the loss of manufacturing jobs, state fiscal crisis, and the growth in temporary low–wage high tech jobs, many county governments have had to make choices between budgetary commitments to incarceration and prison construction and commitments to subsidized housing, job training, medical care, drug abuse treatment and education. At the local level some officials have begun to look to prisons as the growth industry to help their community. One chamber of commerce official, in commenting on prison construction in his state said, "the state is giving us two prisons. That's 2000 jobs! That's like apple pie."

Most new prison construction across the country is occurring in rural white communities. State prison populations by race reflect the disproportionate incarceration of people of color and the institutionalized racism in the administration of justice. For instance, the State prison population at Mississippi's Parchman prison is close to 95 percent Black. Louisiana's Angola prison is almost 90 percent Black. 70 percent of the prison population in the state of Georgia is African American. The recently passed "two strikes you're in" provision and mandatory 10 year sentence for first time violent offenders, will likely increase significantly the rate of incarceration of blacks will in that state.[4]

The overwhelming majority of the people imprisoned are usually young and poor. More than 35 million crimes are committed each year, yet only about 450,000 people are sent to jail or prison. Two–thirds of all those who are sent to prison did not graduate from high school and half were unemployed at the time of their arrest. Some may have even been falsely imprisoned or received a sentence disproportionate to the crime they were convicted of. For example, according to the ACLU, the mandatory minimum sentences for crack cocaine is a prime cause of race–based disparities. The sentences are 100 times more severe than penalties for power cocaine. Ninety-one percent (91) of those sentenced for federal crack offenses were African American, while only 3 percent were white. Such drastic disparities are amazing when compared to statistics which reveal that whites constitute a much higher proportion of crack users: 2.4 million (64.4 percent) compared with 990,000 African Americans (26.6 percent), and Latinos 384,000 (9.22 percent). Moreover, simple possession of over five grams of crack, the weight of 2 pennies is a felony and guarantees an automatic sentence of five years for a first time offender. Yet, possession of the same amount of powder cocaine, is a misdemeanor and requires no jail time.[5] It is true then that "Contrary to popular belief, the seriousness of a crime is not the most crucial element in predicting who goes to prison and who does not."[6]

African Americans males are six percent of the U.S. population, however they comprise more than 50 percent of all prison inmates. In the California Youth Authority system, 75 percent of the young people held in custody are young people of color. In addition to determining who goes to jail and prison, racism in the administration of justice also is felt in terms of prison sentences. African Americans, Latinos, and Native Americans receive on the average much longer sentences than whites. For example in the federal prison system, African American sentences are 20 percent longer than whites for similar crimes. These facts are not only limited to men of color.

Women are five percent of the total prison and jail population in the United States. However, of that total more than 60 percent are women of color. And the rate of imprisonment for women during the 1980s rose faster than that of males. To a degree it paralleled the disproportionate growth of the numbers of women living in poverty.

Institutional racism is not alone in determining who is incarcerated. Social and economic class factors also play key roles in determining who goes to jail and who does not. Many middle class whites normally receive suspended sentences, probation or may be released on their own recognizance. According to a Joint Economic Committee study in 1976, the link between chronic unemployment and criminal involvement is well established. In 1983, for instance, 47 percent of all those jailed were unemployed at the time of their arrest. Seventy one percent earned less than $10,000 a year.

Perhaps one of the more classic examples at the state level of warehousing the poor and racial disparities intersect is Texas, where there are striking racial disparities. Black citizens in Texas are arrested, imprisoned, and sentenced to death in numbers that are vastly disproportionate to their representation in the population.

The greatest disparities occur in Harris County, the largest county in the state, which includes the city of Houston. The following are illustrative of the racial disparities in Harris County's criminal justice system:

1) in 1991 the incarceration rate for Black people was nine time greater than whites;
2) in the same year 61% of all imprisoned offenders were black, although only 17% of the county's population is black;
3) in 1991, 73% of all people sent to prison for drug offenses were black;
4) 56% of offenders sent to death row are black;
5) among people on death row from Texas who were sentenced to death for crimes that occurred when they were teenagers, 73% are black.
6) African Americans make up only 12% of the population of the state of Texas yet are 48% of its prison population.
7) Whites on the other hand, make up 63% of the general population, yet are only 29% of the prison population.

The everyday experience of African Americans confirms that the criminal justice system often operates in this manner. However, these racial disparities—pervasive and stark at a statewide level, and much worse at the level of Harris County—should not be brushed aside as somehow endemic to the criminal justice system in this country and therefore tolerable as the Supreme Court has done. This form of insidious and odious influence of racism in Texas *criminal* justice system is repeated across the USA.

Two disturbing trends occurring at the national level are also worth noting. The first is the growing move toward maximum security incarceration, or what has been referred to as "marionization."

The federal prison in Marion, Illinois implemented in 1983 a series of "security " measures ostensibly to stem violence. The results were permanent measures which included 23 and one half hour "lockdown," i.e. confinement to cells daily. According to court documents, prisoners are forbidden to socialize with each other or to participate in group religious services. Inmates who throw food or otherwise misbehave in their cells are sometimes tied spread–eagle on their beds, often for hours and inmates generally but always in the control unit, are subjected to a rectal search. In Florida's "supermax," prisoners are held in windowless cells from which they are allowed out only three times a week for ten minutes to shower. The rest of the time they are alone in the cell.[7]

There are close to forty "maxi–maxi" facilities in the United States today. The major one are really political prisons touted to house the most feared and dangerous prisoners.

The second trend is privatization of jails and prisons. It is equally as disturbing and in fact harps back to the days of the "chain gang" when convict labor was leased to the highest bidder because in spite of the thirteenth Amendment to the U.S. constitution involuntary servitude was legal as punishment for crime. More than 90 percent of southern chain gains were African American men.

Privatization of many government operated systems is being pushed by the privately controlled media and corporations as a more efficient way to run things, this includes prisons.

The principal organization in the business of private prisons in Corrections Corporation of America (CCA) based in Nashville, Tennessee. The second major corporate entity is the National Corrections Corporation of Santa Fe, New Mexico.

Privatization of prisons was pushed in the mid 1980s and today several local, county and state jails and prisons are privately run. The Immigration and Naturalization Service has also contracted with private firms to run several detention centers.

Privatization has been opposed on a number of grounds. First, privatization poses the threat of profound conflicts of interest because private prison operators would profit from keeping people in prison, not from finding ways to return them to their communities; second, labor rights would be violated, i.e. public employee unions have opposed privatization because they see it as a move to undercut or even eliminate union representation for prison employees; and third, a possibility of a combination of privately operated prisons working with private prison industries would reduce public accountability and state oversight thereby making the probability for severe human rights abuses inevitable.

Who profits from the $100 billion prison industry? Corporate and governmental interests mainly. The companies involved range from firms specializing in prison architecture, to for profit medical firms, to Coca–Cola Company ("Time Goes Better With Coke!"). According to Michael Kroll, author of *The Fortress Economy*, "the corporate world is extensively involved with prisons. San Quentin offers more than 250 products for prisoners to purchase, from cupcakes and fried pies to perm–cream relaxers and pinup calendars. In 1984, Unicor, the federal prison industries, earned a net profit of $18 million on $210 million in sales. This profit rate was made possible by the low level of prisoner wages, between $0.44 and $1.10 an hour. Moreover, the inexpensively produced road signs, missile components, military blankets and supplies, mailbags, and executive furniture for government officials subsidized other divisions of the federal government."[8]

Prison labor is perfect for employers with seasonal labor needs and late night or weekend shifts. Prison labor is increasingly desired by private industry because prisoners are legally denied rights that others workers enjoy. Prisoners cannot unionize. They are not covered by workers' compensation, their health care is subsidized by the state. They are not covered by the Fair Labor Standards Act.

Several observers have even argued that prison labor is now emerging as a complement to the emerging division of labor and international movement of jobs because prisons, with their abundant supply of cheap labor (a captive labor force), are an attractive alternative to foreign based production.

The exploding prison population represents one of the most significant human rights abuses in the United States. Since 1980 the nation's prison population has tripled. At present approximately 1.4 million people are incarcerated at any given time and according to Human Rights Watch as many as ten times that figure in the course of any one year.

At the federal level there has been tremendous growth in the number of incarcerated persons. And, according to the Watch this means that every week more than 1,200 more persons are imprisoned and have to be "housed, fed and clothed in the nation's prison facilities." Further:

> The predictable consequence of this vast influx into U.S. prisons is extensive overcrowding. Double–bunking is the order of the day. Facilities built to single–cell the population have instead assigned two prisoners to the same cell; more beds have been crammed into open dormitory space; triple–bunking in these dorms is not unknown. Facilities never designed for housing people are opened overnight for prisoner occupancy. When fifty or sometimes a hundred or more people are housed in one gigantic room, it is difficult to dream of complying with the... respect to prisoners' dignity.[9]

As part of this trend the American Correctional Association adopted a standard which allows prison authorities to house medium security offenders in open dormitory settings. What this means is more "beds have been crammed into open dormitory space" and in a facility like Rikers Island jail complex in New York City, dangerous and nonviolent inmates are housed fifty to a room, and all use the same bathroom that for security reasons cannot have doors or curtains for privacy.

Overcrowding depletes resources necessary to keep prisoners occupied and to maintain adequate staff supervision and control. However, according to the ACLU, in spite of these problems, U.S. authorities are continuing to provide dormitory housing for increasing numbers of more dangerous prisoners, because of the great cost savings involved.

Prisons conditions of another type are illustrative of the problems associated with overcrowding and the system itself. The documentation of brutal beatings, torture and cruel and unusual punishment abound.

 Beatings by police in holding areas is commonplace. "The use of weapons and even deadly force on unarmed sentenced prisoners is a frequent occurrence in prisons across the country." In addition, the endemic violence and threat of violence is obviously not restricted to prison authorities. Inmate - on -inmate violence coupled with racial hostility aggravate the situation. One court case found that inmates had regularly suffered slashings, burnings and other forms of violent injuries. Another case, noted that many inmates failed to report assaults for fear of retaliation.

Much of the violence inside prison walls is connected to inadequate staffing, failure to adequately monitor shower areas, unchecked abuse, sexual assault and torture and increasing gang activity.

Finally, with respect to prison conditions, "double bunking and "triple bunking" occurs. In other words, cells built for one person houses two or three people. Many state prison systems are operating under federal court orders due to the severe overcrowding which is as high as 200 percent capacity is states such as Ohio.

A United States Sentencing Commission study concluded that the kind of disparity and discrimination that the Sentencing Reform Act was designed to reduce has actually increased. African American offenders were 21 percent and Latino 28 percent more likely to receive at least the mandatory minimum prison term. Thus, the system's focus on African American youth is a key element in the entire process. The interaction with police is normally the first point of contact.

Focus on black youth.

In 1994 close to 50 percent of the national prison population is African American. Much could be made of such a startling fact. In addition, when one considers that in 1990, handguns were used to murder 10 people in Australia, 13 in Sweden, 22 in England, 68 in Canada, 87 in Japan and 10,567 in the United States it should also be clear that 12 years of getting tough on crime, reviving the death penalty and tripling the prison population has not solved the problem of crime and violence in the country.[10]

The war on drugs launched by the Reagan Administration in the mid 1980s spelled doom for Black youth and actually amounted to a war on the Black and Latin communities. Clarence Lusane, author of Pipe Dream Blues: Racism and The War on Drugs, argues that poverty and alienation are chief causes leading to a number of children, young men and women opting to deal drugs. He says, "the crushing impact of poverty leads to alienation and low self– esteem. Consequently, when a whole community faces this condition, in an atmosphere that promotes identity through material consumption, social deterioration becomes inevitable. Alienation shatters the spirit and destroys the ability to love oneself and others. The escalation of violence and the devaluation of life is rooted in the isolation and nihilism symptomatic of our consumer society."[11]

The beating of Rodney King and the Los Angeles rebellion have forever removed the blinders from the eyes of many poor people with respect to the true nature of the US criminal justice system and the role of the police in society. Harassment, terror, torture, brutal beatings, shootings, stop and frisks, and verbal abuse are "standard operating procedures" for many police forces operating in national minority communities across the USA. The sad fact is that racial discrimination continues to be a primary factor in American life and in the US criminal justice system.

Spiraling imprisonment is but one measure of the magnitude of the problem. Young Black men are incarcerated at higher rates in the United States than in Apartheid South Africa. In fact, it is almost impossible today to separate police misconduct from race and incarceration. To most officers of the law, the typical criminal suspect or "public enemy" is a young Black or Latino male.

African–Americans are suffering from a peculiar form of human rights abuse known as collective punishment. This punishment is imposed by a repressive public policy, a reactionary law and order ideology and the nationally endorsed war on drugs, which in reality is a war on people of color. Typical of the convergence of these issues are statistics compiled in 1992 for arrests on drug related charges in the city of Baltimore, Maryland. Of the 13,000 people arrested 11,000 were Black men and women most of whom were young.[12] Similar statistics can be produced for most urban areas. However, nationally 80% of drug users are white. Black men and women also account for 46% of the individuals awaiting trial in local jails or serving short sentences there. They make up 47% of the state and federal prison population. They comprise 41% of prisoners on death row. According to the NAACP Legal Defense Fund, approximately one in four African American males between the ages of twenty and twenty–nine is incarcerated, on probation, or on parole. Overall, more than one million African Americans are either behind bars or a violation away from being behind bars.[13]

Such staggering numbers are a mirror of the institutionalized racial discrimination in America and throughout the entire criminal justice system.

The humiliation heaped upon Black youth is connected to cynical government policies of social control and political repression. The police and prison systems were started for those purposes during and after slavery. Today, in a number of urban, suburban, and rural jurisdictions with heavy Black populations, the police are perceived as, and act as an occupying force, monitoring the behavior of colonial subjects and swooping in at will, with sophisticated weaponry, to ensnare and leave as quickly as they appeared, yet hardly ever responding to the real safety needs of the community. Regular and sometimes massive sweeps through Black communities are conducted by the various police forces (including the F.B.I.) and sanctioned by public officials in the name of crime fighting. Whole communities have be cordoned off and anyone entering and exiting questioned. And more often than not the police have contributed to the problem of crime and violence through their increasingly militaristic responses and their overt or covert involvement in the drug and weapons trade. In some cities white racist gangs have even been identified as being part of the police departments.

The protection of property and white people from the designated "menace to society" is a key motivating factor in police abuse of African Americans. Thus, strip searches, excessive use of force, the use of attack dogs and constant harassment are aimed at reminding minority youth who is the real authority is on the streets. Fourth amendment protection against unreasonable search and seizure is frequently violated for people of color, especially young African American men.

Stories abound in community after community that the police regularly use detained African American males to "break–in" rookie cops in the appropriate techniques of brutality and "what is expected of them in street encounters."[14] Other youth are reminded of what may have happened to a friend who decided to resist. Perhaps his/her entire family was abused, arrested and subsequently charged with assaulting a police officer and resisting arrest. Worse still, maybe his or her friend was found hanging in jail and their death ruled a "jail house suicide" similar to the 50 people found hanging in Mississippi jails during the past five years.[15]

Recent national hearings held by the NAACP in cities with disgraceful records of police brutality, revealed an alarming pattern of complete disregard for the law and human dignity by officials sworn to uphold the constitution. Numerous accounts were detailed where arrest quotas existed and where Black youth were routinely harassed and intimidated. One recurring example cited was the policy of discouraging Black youth from "hanging out" at shopping malls or tourist attractions such as Atlanta's "Underground." In most instances the police approach the youth, ask them if they have any money on them to shop at the mall. If they respond yes often their money is taken from them by the police and they are told to leave. If they say no, they are told to leave the premises or be arrested. Either way the mall is off limits to Black youth because they are "bad for business."

The fact that one's skin color represents "probable cause," suggests that the use of deadly force against minority residents is a logical extension of systematic abuses aimed at national minorities because after all it is "people of color are making the society too violent." For example, in a six month period in Miami, there were 10 police shooting casualties, nine of whom were Black.[16] The reality is that the police have increasingly come to rely on race as the primary indicator of both suspicious conduct and potential danger.

When the forces of racism and police militarism combine to dehumanize Black youth, not only are patterns of excessive force ignored but the pervasiveness of police harassment is also officially dismissed. It is dismissed mainly because unreasonable searches and seizures and other abuses are tolerated by prosecutors, judges, the media, politicians and even some in national minority communities on the promise of safe neighborhoods. By law police are not suppose to be able to stop people on the street without cause. However, in the context of "drugs, guns and the popular perception of a crime epidemic," being a Black youth is cause enough for the police. According to the SCLC, the aim of many officers who conduct "field interrogations" and "stop and frisks" is often to accomplish one thing, that of humiliating anyone who attempts to undermine police control of the streets. Hence, tight handcuffs, being shoved into a police wagon or car, being slapped with a nightstick, kicked between the legs, or suffering humiliating public strip searches all have become part of the American way of life for Black youth.

The pattern of police brutality against African Americans is directly related to the deteriorating socio–economic conditions and abandonment of the central cities by the federal government. African Americans and their movements for social justice have borne the brunt of the right wing propaganda attack. The massive unemployment problem, according to conventional wisdom, is caused by affirmative action. The decay in "family values" can be blamed on lazy "welfare queens" and unsafe streets; violence and skyrocketing crime has been blamed on young Black people.

There is a relationship between impoverished living conditions and crime. Unfortunately, addressing the root causes or sources of criminal behavior is not the objective of the police, the "dirty workers" of the US criminal justice system. Homelessness, joblessness, drug addiction, AIDS, death and despair have meant a nightmarish existence for a significant sector of the American population. Little wonder that many minority youth have rejected the existing social contract and mythical "American Dream" that does not recognize them or their humanity.

For African Americans there is no choice. The struggle for freedom and social justice will and must continue in spite of the new complexities and the collective punishment being meted out by the repressive apparatuses of the state. While it is logical that the front line troops of the system of oppression would continue to act in an intensified politically repressive manner, that type of social revenge has to become totally unacceptable and responded to in the best tradition of social protest. Moreover, the police who consciously attempt to instill fear, and conformity to oppressive conditions, in African American youth will ultimately fail. In fact, the opposite effect will occur. The social anarchy present in many urban settings will eventually give way to the type of organized fight–back that the repressive behavior of the status quo keepers sought to hold in check. This response will ultimately take on an overt political character such as that in Northern Ireland.

As long as Black youth are scapegoated for all the system's failures and anti–social behavior blamed on an "underclass" pathology, America is on the fast track to nowhere. At the same time, the practical realization that "the cost of freedom is much less than the price of repression" could save the soul of this country.

Changes in the economy

The changing economy and the impact of globalization on the economy has provided some stimulus for the growth in incarceration. African Americans and Latino were largely concentrated in the auto, construction, steel, and manufacturing sectors of the economy. Today those sectors no longer can employ as many persons. Global competition, downsizing, plant closures and recruitment of higher skilled labor has left blacks and Latinos either underemployed or unemployed. The one sector that is growing is the service sector. For African Americans and Latino this means jobs in McDonalds or Burger King. Even in the service industries racism plays a very important role. McDonalds for instance was documented as paying inner–city workers an average of one dollar less per hour than their suburban counterparts. The inner–city employees were overwhelmingly Black and Latino.[17]

The result of these objective changes and their impact is that a large part of the American social fabric has been rendered economically useless and therefore socially expendable.

Crime Bill and Black people

The $22 billion Clinton Crime Bill calls for several draconian measures to combat "crime." The following are some of the main features of the bill which are likely to pass:

1) it would authorize the death penalty for more than 60 new offenses,
2) mandate that children as young as thirteen be prosecuted as adults which would eviscerate the country's juvenile justice system (a provision submitted by Sen. Carol Moseley Braun)
3) extend mandatory minimum sentences including mandatory life imprisonment for third time felons ("three–strikes")
4) adopt constitutionally questionable "anti–gang" provision which are overly broad and subject to racial bias in implementation
5) make inmates ineligible for Pell grants, destroying one of the few avenues for education and rehabilitation

6) build 12 regional prisons in states agreeing to implement mandatory sentencing provisions
7) adopt "alien terrorist" measure that could lead to secret trials and deportation of unsuspecting accused immigrants

A bill with the above described public policy options is really the "crime" that should be opposed. And the politicians supporting such a bill should be exposed, especially those whose constituency is likely to suffer the most from such punitive legislation. This Crime Bill offers a cynical view that "symbolizes the abandonment of any hope of rehabilitation for even the youngest offenders."[18]

African American congressional representatives John Conyers (Detroit, Michigan) and Craig Washington (Houston, Texas) who offered an alternative Crime Prevention and Criminal Justice Reform Act, argued in the *Washington Post* that the Senate crime busters got it all wrong. First they ask, "Does anyone remember that when President Clinton came to office he asked for $30 billion to meet the urgent crisis in our cities?" Obviously the point is that not one dollar could be found and the emergency stimulus packet was defeated. Next, the two Congressmen say, "yes our cities do need more police0 but our cities also need jobs and job training to target the very people who are trapped in a cycle of crime and violence."

Our prisons are filled beyond capacity. The statistics are grim: The United States currently locks up more people per capita than any other nation on Earth. There are more young black men in prison today than in college. For every Latino male with a BA, there are 24 behind bars; if we are going to spend $22 billion, let's have a serious discussion about how that money can be spent. Our failure to address urban issues guarantees that crime, violence and drug abuse in the inner city will continue and will only get worse.

The Clinton Crime Bill will accentuate the harsh impact of racial disparity. In the area of capital punishment for instance of those targeted for death under a Congressional enacted law for murders committed by drug dealers, between 1988 and 1993, 73 percent were African American and 13 percent Latino. In fact, as of September 1993, all of the death penalty prosecutions reportedly approved by the Clinton Administration have been African American.

With the unprecedented growth in imprisonment during the 1980s, the idea of alternatives to incarceration, which recognize that simply locking people up is not the correct or even an effective response to crime or rehabilitation should have received more attention. Moreover, the economic burden on state and local governments, in terms of building, maintaining and operating prisons and jails should have been a major motivating force. However, the elimination of probation at the federal level and the "lock' em up, throw away the key" mentality did not allow for this.

Nevertheless, a number of reform advocates have called for a continuum of responses, with probation at one end, and a range of community based alternatives (some more restrictive than others), and temporary incarceration, such as boot camps, at the most restrictive end. According to Temple University criminologist Kay Harris, "like incarceration itself, many of the emerging programs are based on a repressive, crime control ideology which is used to rationalize substantial intrusions on individual liberty and autonomy, ongoing intervention in the minutiae of offenders' daily lives, an atmosphere of distrust, a lack of due process protection and an emphasis on the tenuousness and revocability of any privileges or benefits grants."[19]

Part of the debate among reform advocates is whether or not punishment has to be a core component of any program. Often grassroots community level voices and values are missing when many of the programs are being developed and implemented. In fact, several researchers have argued that it is important to consider whether striving to secure individual deterrence, incapacitation and obedience through electronic monitoring, peer and official surveillance, blood and urine testing, drugs, warrantless searches, humiliation and intimidation are the kinds of community based corrections or alternatives to incarceration that are needed.

If it is true that the reconstruction of the economic and social vitality of the nation's cities is dependent upon a more effective and rational crime policy then it is equally true that community survival must be linked to alternatives to incarceration.

At the grassroots level alternatives to incarceration can provide a means for offenders to repay their victims and communities; can prompt rehabilitation and reintegrate them into the community and normally this can be done at a relatively low cost.

The cost of alternatives or combination of alternatives such as literacy training, job training and placement, curfews, drug treatment, counseling, community service, intensive supervision, home confinement, restitution and others, vary among jurisdictions. However, almost all are significantly less expensive than the average cost per day of incarceration.

Shortly before his assassination Martin Luther King Jr. suggested that the country need to undergo a radical restructuring of its social, political and economic order. The organizational expression of this was the "poor peoples campaign" aimed at challenging the inherent inequalities of capitalism with a diverse, democratic grassroots based movement of people. However, Dr. King also stressed the need for a "revolution of values."

King's revolution of values spoke to the triple evils of racism, materialism, militarism. He said,

> we must rapidly begin the shift from a thing oriented society to a person oriented society. When machines and

computers, profit motives and property rights are considered more important than people, the giant triplets of racism, materialism and militarism are incapable of being conquered. A civilization can flounder as readily in face of moral and spiritual bankruptcy as it can through financial bankruptcy. True compassion is more than flinging a coin to a beggar; it understands that an edifice which produces beggars needs restructuring.[20]

Conclusion

The United States is experiencing its deepest social crisis since the great depression. The fact that more than 1.4 million people are incarcerated at any given point of the year and ten times as many during the year suggests that the administration of justice needs overhauling. However, the process of overhauling the system should not overlook the fact that racism in the administration of justice has caused close to 70 percent of those imprisoned to be African American, Latino and Native American.

The level of violent crime in communities of color cannot be ignored and definitely not romanticized as the first step toward revolution. Large sectors of the community live in constant fear. The trauma brought on by gun violence is connected to growing mental health related problems among the youth. Moreover, the high incidence of suicide has been correlated to the "outlaw culture" whose foundation was laid and ultimately determined by consumer society. At the same time the violence of the society brought on by repressive public policy cannot be excused either. The crisis of white leadership and its blind desire to complete the restoration of white supremacy today is better characterized as "tyranny of the majority," and may led to a neo–fascist option in the United States.

The decision of the state to warehouse its surplus people of color populations in rural white communities for economic reasons creates a dynamic similar to that of the poor white overseer watching the enslaved Africans for the rich white master.

There is a dire need for a national youth policy other than prison construction and boot camps. If the federal and state governments are unable or unwilling to invest in children and youth then the community, with a new vision of responsibility and obligation, and hope in a better tomorrow must do so. Capitalism in terminal decline has never before been experienced. The continued debasing of the labor force and the creation of millions of marginalized and socially expendable people, living in misery, will continually lead to repressive public policy, lower standards of living and the existence of genocidal conditions in national minority communities.

African Americans may not have cornered the market on many things but we can lay claim to our superior ability to survive. The contemporary challenges to that ability have never been as great since the days of slavery.

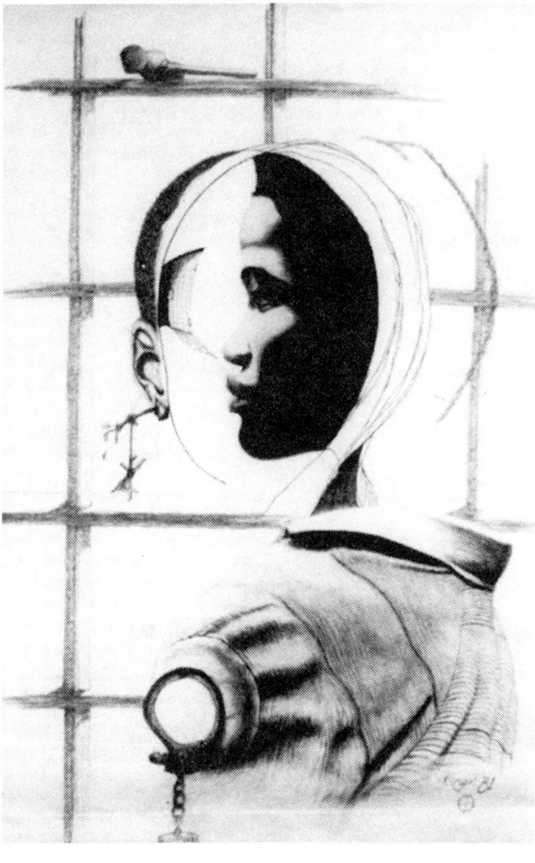

"de Judicial Lynching of Eve"

Several black youth were implicated in the murder of a white man in Florida; all accepted guilt and plea bargains, except Eve Postell, who was merely present and felt she was least culpable in the murder... she subsequently received 114 years to life.

ENDNOTES

1 "lock 'em up and throw away the key," TIME MAGAZINE, February 7, 1994, p. 55

2Ibid

3 Bureau of Justice Statistics 1990 and National Black Police Association Testimony before House Judiciary Committee, Subcommittee on Crime and Criminal Justice, February 22, 1994

4 Interview with Gilda Williams, Southern Center for Human Rights, February 25, 1994

5 ACLU Report on Racial Bias in the Criminal Justice System February 9, 1994, p. 3

6 The Fortress Economy: The Economic Role of the U.S. Prison System, American Friends Service Committee, p. 5

7 Human Rights Violations in the United States. Human Rights Watch and American Civil Liberties Union, December, 1993 pp 108–111

8 The Fortress Economy opt cit p.17

9 Human Rights Violations in United States, opt cit p.102

10 Greg Moore, "CBC Tackles Crime Bill," Black Political Agenda, January/April p. 4

11 Clarence Lusane, Pipe Dream Blues: Racism and the War on Drugs. Boston: South End Press, 1991 p. 26

12 Blacks and The Criminal Justice System, The Sentencing Project, 1991

13 NAACP Legal Defense Fund Annual Report 1992

14 Beyond Rodney King: Police Brutality in the United States, NAACP April, 1992

15 The Jackson Advocate, March 1993

16 NAACP opt cit

17 Lusane, Pipe Dream Blues opt cit p.27

18 Children's Defense Fund Testimony before The House SubCommittee on Crime and Criminal Justice, February 23, 1994

19 Kay Harris, "Strategies, Values and the Emerging generation of Alternatives to Incarceration." Review of Law and Social Justice, NYU vol XII p. 151

20 Martin Luther King Jr. Where Do We Go From Here: Chaos or Community? Boston: Beacon Books, 1967 p. 186–187

Friday Afternoons

by Susan Y. Arauz

At the little red school house–
across the street from the projects,
down the block from the Malt liquor billboard,
around the corner from the precinct,
They never noticed

How we tried to kill each other
Over stepped on feet, smudged sneakers
Being stingy with the homework
LIKE affairs gone bad
Insults scribbled on desks
Talkin' about mothers
– especially on a Friday afternoon.

Screeched curse words
Eager, growing crowds
Audience participation
Gritted teeth
Racing hearts
Fierce kicks, vicious bites,
Swinging fists committin' the
murder of a people
on a Friday Afternoon.

SPARE A LITTLE CHANGE

BY KIMBERLY HEADLY

I STUMBLE THROUGH THE CARS
OF THE JABCD TRAINS
PLEADING, "SPARE A LITTLE CHANGE"
AND YOU DON'T LOOK UP
"SPARE A LITTLE CHANGE," I SAY
AND YOU CLOSE YOUR EYES.

WHAT MOST PEOPLE DON'T UNDERSTAND
IS THAT I'VE BEEN WAITIN'
FOR CHANGE TO BE SPARED
UPON ME FOR QUITE SOME TIME–
NOT MONETARY CHANGE
BUT REVOLUTIONARY CHANGE.

I'M TIRED OF LIVING THE LIFE
OF A PANHANDLER
BEING MANHANDLED BY COPS
BY THE SYSTEM
BY RACIAL SUPERIORITY
AND THE CAPITALIST MAJORITY
"SPARE A LITTLE CHANGE," I SAY.

THE WORLD IS TOO BLIND
AND PEOPLE ARE NOT KIND
TO MY SITUATION.
SO WHEN I SAY: "SPARE A LITTLE CHANGE"
I'M TALKIN' ABOUT A REVOLUTION
OF THE SUFFERING, DEPRIVED
THE HOPELESSLY DENIED,
MASSES
BROKEN INTO CLASSES
OF STRUGGLE.

CHANGE HAS BEEN LONG OVERDUE
AND I AM UNDERPAID!

Political Prisoners

by Winston Grady-Willis

One of the most telling legacies of the governmental assault waged against the Black Panther Party and other radical Black political organizations of the late 1960s and early 1970s was the effort to imprison many of its key activists. The Federal Bureau of Investigation, in conjunction with state and local law enforcement agencies, conducted a fierce campaign to incarcerate the most tenacious and dedicated activists of the Black liberation movement. This legal repression continued after the Party's actual demise as an effective national radical African American activist organization.

Black radical activist and scholar Angela Davis knows something about being incarcerated for one's political beliefs. She had remained behind bars as a political prisoner in an outrageous attempt on the part of the federal government to implicate her in the August 7, 1970 revolt led by 16-year-old Jonathan Jackson at the Marin County Hall of Justice.[1] She offered this definition of political imprisonment in 1971:

> There is a distinct and qualitative difference between breaking a law for one's own individual self-interest and violating it in the interests of a class or a people whose oppression is expressed either directly or indirectly through that particular law. The former might be called a criminal (though in many cases he is a victim), but the latter, as a reformist or revolutionary, is interested in universal social change. Captured, he or she is a political prisoner.[2]

There are as many as 150 political prisoners and prisoners of war (POWs) *currently* being held in US. prisons. That group includes Puerto Rican activists (who consider themselves prisoners of war engaged in a colonial liberation struggle), African Americans from the Black liberation movement, Native American freedom fighters, and radical White activists. The largest number of those incarcerated for political activity are Blacks. The bulk of them were associated at one time or another with the Black Panther Party.[3]

Since political prisoners have not been acknowledged officially in this country, activists have almost always stood trial for specific "criminal" offenses. Dhoruba Bin Wahad, a former Panther 21 member and political prisoner of some 19 years, has asserted that most people in the US. operate under the false assumption that all prisoners are criminals who have been afforded due process. US. law enforcement agencies "have *consistently* criminalized the legitimate movements of oppressed people, and in so doing have...rendered the activists that come from these movements 'criminals'..."[4]

The imprisonment and 1927 deportation of Marcus Garvey for mail fraud was a classic example of the criminalization of a Black activist in this country. In February of 1951 scholar activist W.E.B. DuBois, Garvey's principal rival during the 1920s, found himself handcuffed and in court during the height of the Cold War for his activities in behalf of world peace. Authorities indicted him for an unusually overt political offense: "failure to register as an agent of a foreign principle." As radical scholar Gerald Horne has noted, that the elder DuBois (who was acquitted due to mass public support) could be arrested at all was proof positive that one cannot truly "comprehend the Cold War itself without comprehending its sharp racist edge."[5]

DuBois did not hesitate to make the necessary connection between his brief period of detention and the plight of the overall African American prison population. "We protect and defend sensational cases where Negroes are involved. But the great mass of arrested or accused Black folk have no defense."[6] For many African Americans the institutionalized racism of the court system has become even more firmly entrenched. So much so, that it has become part and parcel of the criminalization of poverty itself in this country.[7]

DuBois' concern with the general African American prison population was significant because of the often inhuman treatment Black prisoners have been accorded in this country. This may help to explain why Black prisoners as a group have tended to be more politicized than other inmates.[8] A clear case of a Black prisoner who became politicized–indeed, radicalized–while in prison was that of George Jackson. When 18, Jackson had been sentenced to an indefinite term for the 70-dollar robbery of a gas station. The imprisoned Jackson not only went on to be named field marshal of the Black Panther Party, but founded a guerrilla group called the People's Army.

George Jackson, along with comrade inmates John Cluchette and Fleeta Drumgo, composed the Soledad Brothers. Prison officials had the three inmates indicted for the retaliatory murder of a White prison guard at Soledad. Given the organizing activities of the Soledad Brothers, the rationale behind the indictment was a political one. George Jackson died on August 21 1971, a year after his brother Jonathan's death, at the hands of prison guards at San Quentin prison. He took three guards with him. Jackson died having spent the entirety of his adult life in the California prison system.[9]

The legal cases of most African American political prisoners associated with the Black Panther Party resemble that of Geronimo ji Jaga (Pratt). Geronimo was a highly decorated combat paratrooper while in the Vietnam War. He became disillusioned with US. intervention in Vietnam, however, and returned to his native Louisiana a changed man in 1968. He left the South to attend UCLA as a student in the High Potential Equal Opportunity Program. He also joined the Black Panther Party.[10]

The Panther leadership named Geronimo ji-Jaga Pratt leader of the Los Angeles office of the Party after the January 1969 US shootings at UCLA He "became instrumental " in forming the Afro-American Liberation Army (later changed to Black Liberation Army), an underground military cadre. Geronimo went to trial for the robbery and first degree murder of Caroline Olsen, a White woman who had been playing tennis with her husband Kenneth on December 18, 1968. The murder occurred in Santa Monica at the same time the FBI was aware that Geronimo ji-Jaga was in Oakland on Party business. In the confusion and distrust surrounding the Newton-Cleaver rift (Geronimo was in the Cleaver camp) no one in the Newton faction would testify at Geronimo's trial on his behalf. Geronimo ji-Jaga is the only political prisoner in the US. acknowledged by human rights group Amnesty International.[11]

One of the US. government's most extensive efforts to repress a Black activist came against former Panther and Black Liberation Army activist Assata Shakur (JoAnne Deborah Chesimard). Shakur went to trial on eight separate occasions on seven different charges between April of 1971 and March of 1977 before being convicted of killing a state trooper during a May 1973 shoot-out on the New Jersey Turnpike. This despite her being seriously wounded during the confrontation and unable to fire a single shot. The conviction resulted, of course, from perjured testimony and withheld evidence of FBI counterintelligence activity.[12]

Before Shakur's imprisonment police detectives had kept extremely close tabs on her. "I would look out my window and there, in the middle of Harlem, in front of my house, would be two white men sitting and reading the newspaper. I was scared to death to talk in my own house" When police tried to link Shakur to a 1971 bank robbery in New York City she became, in the tradition of Angela Davis, one of those listed in the FBI's Most Wanted List. Anyone who knew of her whereabouts was in line for a $10,000 bounty.[13]

Attorney Lenox Hinds has written that Assata Shakur "understates the awfulness of the condition in which she was incarcerated." The revolutionary Black activist was not allowed books or exercise. During both time she spent recovering from an injury to her median nerve from the turnpike shooting and her later pregnancy, prison authorities undertook a concerted effort to deny her adequate medical attention

As a female prisoner Shakur was also subject to vaginal as well as anal strip searches. She spent a great deal of time in solitary confinement and was always under 24-hour surveillance. At one point Assata Shakur spent four consecutive months in solitary confinement in the Middlesex County Jail for Men in New Jersey. Lengthy periods "in the hole" had a profound effect on her:

> "When someone asked my name I stammered and stuttered. My voice was so low everyone constantly asked me to repeat myself. That was one of the things that always happened to me after long periods of solitary confinement: I would forget how to talk.[14]"

Assata Shakur's nightmare as a political prisoner ended in 1979 when she escaped from prison and fled the United States to receive political asylum in Cuba. During Shakur's years in the Party one of the comrades she respected most was Dhoruba Moore, known today as Dhoruba Al-Mujahid Bin Wahad. It took Bin Wahad 19 years before he set foot outside a prison a "free" man. If authorities have their way, he will be back again.

Bin Wahad was a self-employed painter and "artist for the free press" before joining the Black Panther Party in New York City. An articulate Panther leader, he had assumed the post of field secretary for the state of New York by the time he and other defendants went to trial in the Panther 21 case in October 1970. At one point Bin Wahad jumped bail during the trial when he suspected that Huey Newton, in the midst of the leadership rift with Eldridge Cleaver, wanted him dead. "We were right in the middle of madness that we couldn't understand," Bin Wahad explained. "We felt we were going to get killed by someone and we didn't know who." In February of 1971 the FBI sealed the issue by sending to Oakland via special delivery a bogus letter that claimed the New York Panthers "were conspiring" to murder Newton.[15]

The FBI stepped up its efforts in New York after the acquittal of the Panther 21 in May 1971. President Richard Nixon, Attorney General John Mitchell, FBI director J. Edgar Hoover and assorted local law enforcement officials launched a counterintelligence campaign ostensibly aimed at securing indictments for a number of recent police killings at a 28 May meeting at the White House. As part of this newly established NEWKILL investigation, Dhoruba Bin Wahad and other New York Panthers were primary targets because of their support for the underground Black Liberation Army.[16]

When police arrested Bin Wahad and other Panthers for the armed robbery of a Bronx social club on June 4, they provided themselves with a NEWKILL opportunity. Police charged Bin Wahad with attempted murder in the machine gunning of patrolmen Nicholas Binetti and Thomas Curry on May 19, 1971. Law enforcement authorities savored the arrest because the policemen were wounded near the home of Manhattan district attorney Frank Hogan, the man who unsuccessfully prosecuted the Panther 21. The Black Liberation Army claimed responsibility for the shooting, which occurred on the birthdate of Malcolm X.[17]

Dhoruba Bin Wahad's 1973 conviction (after two mistrials) on the attempted murder charges was a clear-cut case of state legal repression. The Panther leader had received a 25 years-to-life sentence for a crime he maintained he did not commit.

Twelve years of litigation by Bin Wahad and his attorneys revealed prosecutorial misconduct and an FBI cover-up. Bin Wahad was able to obtain through the Freedom of Information Act over 300,000 pages of FBI documents which indicated that he was the victim of a sophisticated act of political repression. One, the key witness for the prosecution, a paranoid schizophrenic who had been kept in "protective custody" for 20 months, perjured herself on the stand. Two, another prosecution witness recanted his testimony. And three, the district attorney's office had withheld evidence during Bin Wahad's trial.[18]

The overwhelming evidence in Dhoruba Bin Wahad's favor led to a reversal of his conviction in March of 1990. The former Panther leader is a free man, at least for the time being. Bin Wahad's release and hard-fought right to a new trial did not erase, however, the memories of being held as a prisoner of conscience for nearly 20 years.

Bin Wahad recalled that solitary confinement and the sensory deprivation it insured placed him and other incarcerated activists in a "prison within a prison." Having spent 8 of his 19 years as a political prisoner in solitary confinement, Bin Wahad was well equipped to elaborate on its significance as a mechanism of control.

Tyranny is very strange. The tyrant, despite the access that he or she may have to the instruments of power and control, always fears the individual who will speak out against their prerogatives or their tyranny–whether this individual is armed or just has the clothes on his or her back...But when an individual does not care about the coercive instruments of the state, and calls into question the moral and ethical credibility of the tyrant, then the tyrant has a very serious problem. And the way that they deal with this problem is by isolating this individual as if he or she has a virus, as if he or she has something that's contagious.[19]

Dhoruba Bin Wahad got the chance to deliver the message that there are political prisoners in the US. facing such draconian measures to Nelson and Winnie Mandela during a June 1990 Harlem rally welcoming the South African couple. Bin Wahad was speaking for imprisoned comrades Sundiata Acoli, Bashir Hameed, Abdul Majid, Geronimo ji Jaga , Sekou Odinga, and countless others when he told the Mandelas that "African-American people and their movement for liberation have been criminalized just as the ANC [African National Congress] was criminalized by the racist, fascist regime in South Africa."[20]

Bin Wahad's statement to the newly freed Nelson Mandela as one former political prisoner to another served to fluster President George Bush and other government officials. The former Panther's remarks were almost as embarrassing to the powers that be as Andrew Young's admission in 1979 that there were "hundreds if not thousands" of US. political prisoners–this in the midst of President Jimmy Carter's international human rights campaign.[21] "Almost" because Bin Wahad's remarks should not have come as a surprise. The same cannot be said for Young, who as US. ambassador to the United Nations, overstepped the bounds of being a good house Negro.

Primarily because Dhoruba Bin Wahad has not silenced himself since winning his release from prison, local and state authorities have sought to imprison him once again. In December of 1991 the New York State Court of Appeals ruled in a 4-3 decision to narrow the ability of a defendant to obtain a new trial in cases where prosecutors withheld evidence and all appeals have been exhausted.[22]

Two 1992 US. Supreme Court decisions may also hamper the efforts of political prisoners to overturn their convictions. The high court ruled in a 5-4 decision that federal prosecutors do not have to present a grand jury with evidence indicating that a defendant might not be guilty. In another 5-4 decision the Supreme Court ruled that a state prison inmate not be granted a fact-finding hearing to reopen his or her case at the federal level unless there is "substantial proof" that such a hearing is necessary.[23]

The state appellate court's decision overturned the March 1990 lower court ruling granting Bin Wahad a new trial. Bin Wahad's attorneys were thus hit with the burden of proving in a hearing that the evidence withheld in the 1973 trial substantially effected its outcome. Prosecuting attorneys pressed to postpone two such hearings–scheduled for February and April of 1992 to determine Bin Wahad's "parole status" and petition for a new trial–because of the overwhelming presence of community activists. The former political prisoner and his lawyers considered the postponements a "peoples victory" since they were afforded more time to build his case. "If it was not for all of you," Bin Wahad told supporters after the April postponement, "I wouldn't be standing here today."[24]

The legal odyssey of Dhoruba Bin Wahad has profound implications for current political prisoners. The final outcome of his case will have a direct bearing on the legal struggles of others, most notably those activists from the Black liberation movement incarcerated in New York state. One such case involves the New York 3–Herman Bell, Anthony Bottom, and Albert Nuh Washington. These former Panthers have been fighting for a new trial since their 1975 conviction for the Harlem murders of two police officers in the spring of 1971. COINTELPRO and NEWKILL documents obtained through the Freedom of Information Act indicate that prosecutors also suppressed evidence at the trial of the New York 3.[25]

The New York 3 and other African American political prisoners will have more of an opportunity to win their court cases if a movement takes form in support of these freedom fighters. Dhoruba Bin Wahad has noted that current activists in various grass roots movements "will themselves suffer vicious repression from the status quo unless they deal with the issue of political prisoners up-front..."[26]

Political prisoners–in addition to being dedicated freedom fighters–are some of our best movement teachers. They certainly will provide more direction than the growing crop of "revolutionary" opportunists who claim to represent the aspirations of marginalized Black people. If they remain incarcerated and forgotten, however, their lessons will go unlearned. And that simply cannot happen.

Those of us who consider ourselves activists in this day and time cannot overlook the need to press for the release of political prisoners. In struggling to win the release of and make conditions better for imprisoned freedom fighters in the US., grass roots organizations such as the Campaign to Free Black Political Prisoners/P.O.W.s in the United States (New York City) and Freedom Now! (Chicago) have begun to expose the issue. What other concerned activists do to confront this continued injustice by against repressive forces remains to be seen.

Communication
Soaks Through Thirsty Soil,
A Healing Rain

Brothers In Chains:
It is our duty to fight for our freedom.
It is our duty to win.
We must love each other and support each other.
We have nothing to lose but our chains.

Loneliness in prison arouses sensations that alternate between thoughts of suicide and piercing spasms of pain. A prisoner's life slips away slowly and more freely with each moment of isolation. His life's journey has left a haphazard, rocky trail. He periodically backpedals and plunges into cracks of darkness, as he attempts to negotiate over ebbing waves of light.

Prisons are physically cold, harsh places. They are dark and smelly; where all emotions are subdued. A lid is put on one's spirit. Where sincere human contact is absent; where inhumanity is rampant.

Negative days are shoved in your face in the nights' stillness. Your innocence lies buried in a dirty, encrusted tomb. Yet the jewel (human heart) does not lose its luster, and can resurrect and project a vibrant stream of warmth past empty steel cages, dim hallways, a maze of security gates into...your living room. If so bidden. The prisoner realizes that if he does not seek positive reinforcement from the outside he will die, physically or spiritually. She has a lot of inventions swirling around her head and she needs to express them...somehow.

Prisoners are resuscitated with correspondence that serves to let them know two very important things: they are not alone and they have not been forgotten.

When the prison gates slam behind a prisoner, he does not immediately or necessarily lose his human qualities. His mind is not soon closed to ideas; his intellect does not cease to feed on some interchange of opinion; his yearning for self-respect does not end; nor is his quest for self-realization concluded. If anything she is compelled to fortify her identity and self-respect in the dehumanizing prison environment. Whether an Ezra Pound, a Faiz Ahmed Faiz, or a frightened young prisoner writing his family, the poet and the prisoner need a medium for self-expression.

A prisoner realizes that this entreaty to nudge a disinterested and media drugged public to correspond will be an incredible attempt to vault above accepted false perceptions and veils of confusion and denial. All black and all colored and all poor face *some* form of lock-up or lock-out due to the present ruling order. But *even* they still accept the stigma: "they're all bad; they have what they deserve; they don't deserve a second chance."

This is irrational and untrue. Why? Because many notable beings have been confined to prison and have made great contributions to society:

Among men, there was Joseph, a diligent servant, who was falsely accused of rape by the lascivious wife of the captain of the guard of a House of Pharoah in Ancient Egypt – still serving his (true) Master well, he was later elevated to captain of the guard to the keeper of the prison (Genesis: 39); Jesus the Christ was in prison prior to his crucifixion (St. John: 19); Eldridge Cleaver constructed his clarion call of the day, *Soul On Ice,* behind bars (amazingly, the Supermasculine Menials still complacently do what they're told for a price; the Omnipotent Administrators still enforce selfish policy with cold, heartless science); Martin Luther King wrote remarkable work from the Birmingham County jails; and, of course, everyone knows Malcolm's genesis in prison was astounding. Being behind bars does not necessarily equate with bad behind bars.

Complete autonomy (rugged individualism) is some kind of warped ideal that is promoted in this culture, which in reality can never exist. We are all interrelated. We/I/A prisoner(s) are/am/is asking for your help.

In The Struggle,

Arthur Sullivan
87T0945
Drawer B
Stormville, N. Y. 12582

Keith "Kichaka" Bush
#76B-0980
Drawer B
Stormville, NY 12582

Special International Tribunal on Human Rights Violations of Political/POW Prisoners in the United States

Illustration by Blue

Conditions of Confinement

Testimony by Jill Soffiyah Elijah, Esq.

During the past three decades there has been a steady increase in the number of people imprisoned because of their political views and actions. Many of the Black/New Afrikan political prisoners and prisoners of war came from the Black Panther Party and/or the Black Liberation Army (BLA). Numerous members of the Puerto Rican independence movement have been similarly targeted by the United States. Activists from the Native American movement and the disarmament movement, including plowshares, have likewise been targeted and incarcerated. Numerous north american anti-imperialists have also been the subject of governmental attack.

As the prison population becomes more politicized, the level of repression to which it is subjected is heightened. Prison rebellions have increased and many prisoners who were targeted as organizers or leaders within the prisons have been subjected to beatings and lengthy periods of total isolation. Such is the case of the Reidsville Brothers, who, in 1978, participated in a rebellion by Black prisoners at Reidsville Prison and demanded an end to guard brutality, degrading living conditions and racist attacks by white inmates. The prison officials retaliated with beatings and solitary confinement.

Stark in its illustration of this heightened repression is the Attica Prison Rebellion, which occurred in 1971. In response to demands from prisoners who had taken over Attica seeking more humane treatment, the then governor of New York State, Nelson Rockefeller, ordered the state troopers to retake the prison by force. This order was given despite on-going negotiations for a peaceful resolution of the Attica situation. In essence, Gov. Rockefeller ordered the mass murder of 43 people; 34 prisoners and 9 guards. Rockefeller's barbarism was rewarded later when he was selected to serve as vice-president to Gerald Ford.

It is clear that the attitude of the U.S. government towards prisoners' concerns is one of intolerance and indifference. The imposition of egregious conditions is part of a systematic effort to destroy any visible signs of resistance. The intent of the government in imposing these conditions is two-fold; destroy the will of the political prisoner and send a strong message to supporters and followers that their resistance will be met in kind.

The United States government continues to deny to the world that there are political prisoners within its borders. It maintains this position at all cost. Recall the almost immediate removal from office of the then U.S. Ambassador to the United Nations, Andrew Young, when he publicly acknowledged the existence of political prisoners within the U.S.

Back in the 1970's, brother Jalil Muntaquin, one of the New York Three, recognized the significance of raising the issue of political prisoners held within the U.S. in the international arena. Thus, in 1976, he launched the National Prisoners' Campaign to petition the United Nations. This effort was widely supported by political and progressive prisoners. It resulted in a petition being submitted and discussed in Geneva, Switzerland. This work formed the impetus for Lennox Hinds, Esq., and the National Conference of Black Lawyers to invite the U.N. Commission of Jurists to tour numerous U.S. prisons and interview political prisoners. Their findings raised serious questions about the treatment and reasons for confinement of the many political prisoners they interviewed.

In the following text, I will discuss various prison conditions and the manner in which they are applied to political prisoners and prisoners of war. I will not attempt to discuss each prisoner. Rather, as a particular condition is explored, specific examples will be cited to illustrate the point.

Type of Sentence

As a general rule, political prisoners have been given the harshest sentences possible. Journalist Mumia Abu-Jamal, a former Panther and staunch supporter of MOVE members whose home was bombed by Philadelphia police, was sentenced to death for defending himself and his brother from a vicious beating by local Philadelphia police. Johnny Imani Harris was also sentenced to death for his role in the protest prison rebellion during which a guard died at the infamous Atmore Prison. It was only after years of court battles that Gary Tyler was able to get his death sentence commuted to life imprisonment.

Haniff Shabazz Bey, one of the Fountain Valley Five, was sentenced to 8 consecutive life sentences plus 99 years for his role in the attack on the Rockefeller-owned golf course in St. Croix, Virgin Islands. Despite glaring evidence maintained in FBI files that Geronimo ji Jaga (Pratt) was framed for murder, he was sentenced to life imprisonment. Although he has an exemplary prison record, he has been denied parole on 9 separate occasions.

Larry Giddings was sentenced to multiple life sentences plus 75 years. Carmen Valentin received 90 years for seditious conspiracy. For similar charges Ricardo Jimenez received 90 years and Lucy Rodriguez was sentenced to 80 years. Marilyn Buck was recently sentenced to 10 years consecutive to her already lengthy 70 year sentence. David Gilbert and Judy Clark are serving 75 year to life sentences.

Donald Taylor, a former member of De Mau Mau, which was a clandestine self-defense organization within the U.S. Marine Corps in Vietnam formed to defend against racist attacks from white troops, was sentenced to 150 to 200 years without parole. Each of the MOVE defendants was sentenced to 100 years. Leonard Peltier is serving two consecutive life sentences.

Jihad Abdul-Mumit, a former Panther and BLA member, was sentenced to 14 years for a parole violation that did not involve a new arrest or prosecution. The New York Three (Herman Bell, Jalil Muntaquin and Albert Nuh Washington) are each serving 25 years to life sentences. Also serving similar sentences are Bashir Hameed, Seth Hayes, Teddy Jah Heath, Abdul Majid and Baba Odinga.[1]

Number of Years Served

All of these political prisoners and prisoners of war were arrested as they entered the prime of their lives. Some, like Jalil Muntaquin who was only 20 at the time of his arrest, were just entering adulthood. They have spent lengthy periods of time behind bars and those who are eligible have been denied parole.[2]

Preventive detention is also used as a tool to incarcerate political prisoners and prisoners of war. Thus Joe Doherty has been held for over 7 years without trial in a pre-trial holding facility in New York City. Numerous Puerto Rican *independentistas* were held for nearly three years as pre-trial detainees before the court finally ruled that they had to be released on bail.

Laura Whitehorn spent nearly 5 years in preventive detention.

Solitary Confinement and Administrative Detention

In the early sixties, a meeting of social scientists and prison wardens was convened by the then director of the Federal Bureau of Prisons, James V. Bennett. The main speaker for the convention was Dr. Edward Schein, a social scientist. He presented his theories on brainwashing and the application of such techniques to modify behavior within the prison population. Amongst the many techniques suggested by Dr. Schein were the following:

1. physically remove the prisoner to an area sufficiently isolated in order to break or seriously weaken close emotional ties;
2. segregate all natural leaders;
3. prohibit group activities that do not fit brainwashing objectives;
4. systematic withholding of mail;
5. create a feeling amongst the isolated group of prisoners that they have been abandoned by and totally isolated from the community;
6. undermine all emotional supports;
7. preclude access to literature which does not aid in the brainwashing process.[3]

Director Bennett urged the conveners to experiment with Dr. Schein's theories within their respective institutions.

Approximately a decade later, the "experiments" that grew out of that meeting in 1961 began to emerge all around the country. The glaring similarities between Dr. Schein's techniques and the treatment received by the vast majority of political prisoners and prisoners of war serve to enforce the belief that there is a thinly disguised attempt on the part of the U.S. government to psychologically and physically destroy them.

Marion Penitentiary in Illinois is the highest level security prison in the country. This is where the first control unit was established. Its main focus is sensory deprivation and solitary confinement. A disproportionately high number of political prisoners and prisoners of war have been sent to Marion. Many of them have had lengthy stays in the control unit there. The control unit consists of small soundproof box-type cells.

Since 1983, the entire prison has been on lock-down status. This means that all prisoners are locked in their cells 23 hours a day. They are only let out of their cells for one hour to shower and take recreation on the tier. Twice a week, for two hours at a time, outdoor recreation in a small caged-in area is permitted at the whim of the guards. The drinking water is contaminated and many of the inmates have developed unexplained tumors and illnesses.

The cells at Marion consist of a stone bed and a toilet/wash bowl. No contact visits are allowed with social visitors. All legal visits are monitored by video camera and guards. All meals are taken in the cell. No phone access to lawyers is permitted unless the prisoner can prove that the lawyer wants him to call. Only 2 ten-minute calls per month are permitted to family and friends. Marion is the epitome of the implementation of Dr. Schein's theories on behavior modification.

Sekou Odinga was immediately designated to Marion upon being sentenced to 40 years plus life. After spending 3 years at Marion in lock-down status, he was transferred to Leavenworth in general population.[4] When he arrived, Sundiata Acoli was there, having already spent 5 years in solitary After being accused of escape charges, Oscar Lopez-Rivera was transferred from Leavenworth to Marion and held in solitary confinement for a lengthy period of time.[5]

The Bureau of Prisons' (BOP) answer to Marion for women was the high security unit (HSU) built underground at Lexington Penitentiary, in Kentucky. Appendix B. As an experiment, political prisoners Silvia Baraldini, Susan Rosenberg and Alejandrina Torres, were held there until a (length of time) district court judge ruled that their continued incarceration there was violative of their first amendment rights. He also stated that the facility was close, if not violative, of constitutional protections against cruel and inhuman treatment.[6] Every movement of these women was audio and video monitored. The unit was completely isolated from the rest of the prison. The BOP admitted that this facility was not being used for punitive measures for short durations of time, but, that it was the facility where these women would spend the duration of their lengthy prison sentences. Bright lights stayed on 24 hours a day, all walls were painted off-white, and no interaction with other inmates was ever allowed. Strip and cavity searches by males guards was common place. The physical health of each of these women deteriorated significantly during their stay at Lexington. Amnesty International has condemned Marion and Lexington.

Prior to his transfer to Marion, Sundiata Acoli had spent 5 years in the Management control Unit (MCU) of Trenton State Prison in New Jersey. He was the first prisoner sent there. At MCU Sundiata was locked down 24 hours a day in a cell that was smaller than the space requirement set by the Society for the Prevention of Cruelty to Animals for a German shepherd dog. No contact visits were allowed. All meals were taken in the cell. Strip searches were required every time he left the cell for any reason. Cavity searches were frequently imposed. In 1979, just months before the liberation of his co-defendant, Assata Shakur, he was secretly transferred during the middle of the night to federal custody at Marion. Sundiata remained at Marion 8½ years before he was transferred to Leavenworth.[7]

Members of the Black Liberation Front, a group organized in Pennsylvania State Prison to fight for religious freedom, political awareness and protection of human rights, were labeled as "terrorists" in 1973. As a result, Joseph Bowens "Joe Joe" was held in the control unit for 5 years, Russel Shoats was similarly held for 3 years and Clifford Futch "Lumumba" was held in a control unit for 14 years.[8]

Frequently the prison administration will engage in games of deceit in an effort to mask their political motives. Chui Ferguson-El spent 8 years in federal custody in general population without any disciplinary infractions. Upon his transfer to Pennsylvania in 1989, he was immediately placed in segregation. In response to this author's inquiry, the state prison officials stated that he would spend the balance of his sentence in administrative segregation because, "he had previously been shown to be a threat to security while in federal custody at Lewisburg Penitentiary." In response to Chui's inquiries, prison officials stated that he would not be removed from segregation until he cut his dread locks.[9]

Near the end of 1988, Bashir Hameed, a member of the BLA and a well respected Muslim leader amongst the prisoners, was placed in solitary confinement at Shawangunk Prison, located in New York. Prison authorities admitted that he was being placed there because of his leadership and organizing abilities. As of this writing, Bashir is still being held in segregation.

In early April of 1990, Abdul Majid, a member of the BLA, was put in solitary confinement (the box) because of "his status in the Muslim hierarchy", according to prison authorities. He was condemned to a year in solitary at the Great Meadows Correctional Facility in Comstock, New York. The "box" is a 6 x 8 cell where Abdul is locked in for 23 hours a day. Recreation is twice a week, alone in a fenced cage that is 6 x 9 feet. Showers are only allowed twice a week unless a social visit is planned. Social visits are only permitted once a week.

Many of the political prisoners and prisoners of war held in New York State have been handled according to a Central Monitoring Classification (CMC). Last Spring, New York State passed legislation which implemented more lenient guidelines for the use of administrative segregation. Within the past year, Shawangunk opened a control unit for men which is very analogous to the HSU at Lexington. This unit, known as CSU for close supervision unit, is a totally self-contained prison within a prison. The guard to prisoner ratio is extremely low. Every single move of these prisoners is closely monitored. Everyone must be in a program for 8 hours a day. No one moves to another area of the unit without an escort. The entire unit takes recreation separate from the general population and that usually occurs at night. There is a small yard where the men are allowed to take recreation, and twice a week they are escorted to the larger yard. Meals are eaten in a separate cafeteria. The men who have been placed here have been told that there is no way out for them. This is where they will serve out the balance of their sentences. Included amongst the men in CSU are Maliki Shakur Latine, Herman Bell, and Al Musadug Yusef of the Williamsburg Four. It is clear that the intent of the CSU is to identify and destroy political thought and organizing amongst the prisoners.

The Bureau of Prisons is building a maximum security (maxi-maxi) prison in Florence, Colorado that threatens to rival Marion. Marion is being downgraded to a level 5 facility. Florence is designed so that one guard can control the movements of numerous prisoners in several cell-blocks by way of electronic doors, cameras and audio equipment. Total isolation is virtually guaranteed at Florence.

The BOP has already opened the replacement of Lexington's HSU in Marianna, Florida. It remains to be seen what repressive measures will be taken against the women political prisoners who will be held in that facility. The State of California has constructed its own Marion in Pelican City on the northern border of the state. Like the other close supervision units, Pelican City is reputed to maintain small group electronic monitoring.

In the federal system, the BOP monitors and controls the transfer, temporary release and community activities of most of the political prisoners and prisoners of war through its Central Inmate Monitoring System (CIMS). (The regulations for the CIMS are found at 28 C.F.R. §524.70 et. [seq., Appendix D.)]

Distance from Family and Friends

In keeping with the suggestion of Dr. Schein that behavior modification can be achieved by separating a prisoner so as to weaken his emotional ties, most of the political prisoners and prisoners of war have been confined far away from their families and supporters. For instance, many of the Puerto Rican independentistas have been incarcerated in BOP facilities which are far removed from their homeland, Puerto Rico. Geronimo ji-Jaga was incarcerated in northern California for many years. He had a well organized support committee based in the San Francisco Bay Area. In retaliation for his offer to testify on behalf of Filberto Ojeda Rios, Geronimo was transferred to Tehachapi Prison which is located in southern California.

Nuh Washington is confined in Wende Correctional Facility located in the far north western corner of New York State. His parents, lawyers and support committee are all located in New York City.[10] Mutulu Shakur, who spent his entire life in New York City, is incarcerated in Lompoc, California.

Punitive Transfers

In order to understand the punitive nature of a transfer, it is necessary to first understand the disruption that it causes in a prisoner's routine. When a prisoner is transferred, he/she is placed in administrative segregation, usually for one month. During this time, they cannot work and whatever work status they had previously achieved is lost. No educational program can be pursued during this time and prior educational credits are not transferrable. Personal items are frequently "lost" and many weeks may pass before a new visitors list is established for the prisoner. During this waiting time, visitors are usually frustrated by being refused visits even though they were previously approved on another facility's list. Additionally, friendships and contact with other inmates are destroyed.

During his 4 years in state prison, Ricardo Jiminez has been transferred 6 times. Herman Ferguson has been moved all over New York State in the past 30 months. Similarly the New York Three have been moved around New York in "musical chairs" fashion since their confinement.

Torture

Upon their arrest, many political prisoners and prisoners of war were beaten and tortured. When Guillermo Morales was captured in Mexico a few years ago, electric nodes were attached to his genitals and he was repeatedly electrified during a lengthy brutal interrogation at the hands of U.S. agents. When Kazi Toure was arrested, state troopers ground the heels of their boots into his face while he lay handcuffed on the ground.

Sekou Odinga was captured after a shoot out with police. During the shoot out, his companion, Mtayari Shabaka Sundiata, was murdered by the police while he was laying on the ground wounded and unarmed. Sekou was then arrested and tortured for hours while the police attempted to interrogate him. He was beaten so badly that he was unrecognizable and his pancreas was almost destroyed. He was hospitalized for over 3 months. As a result of the beating, his eyesight was permanently damaged. During the interrogation sessions, Sekou's head was repeatedly flushed in the toilet, his toenails and fingernails were ripped out and cigarettes were snuffed out all over his body.

James "Tarif" Haskins, a BLA member, has been the subject of psychological torture. Tactics of mind manipulation and drug experimentation resulted in him suffering from hallucinations.

Health and Medical Care

In general, the health and medical care provided to prisoners is abhorrent. Appendix E. Faced with a life and death situation, Dr. Alan Berkman has languished in the local jail for the District of Columbia and the D.C. General Hospital for the past year and a half. He is suffering from a reoccurrence of Hodgkin's Disease. BOP refused to transfer Dr. Berkman to the Rochester Medical Facility which is reputed to have state of the art equipment. On more than one occasion he has gone into medical crises because of medical neglect. Despite his medical emergency situation he has been denied parole and been threatened with returning to Marion.

The government has offered to strike a deal if Dr. Berkman would abandon his principals and answer its questions regarding other political people and activities.

Bashir Hameed suffers from acute hypertension. His medication has to be increased on a regular basis. His prison physician has determined that continued confinement in "the box" creates a substantial danger of a stroke. Despite his doctor's request that he be removed from "the box", the Shawangunk administrators refuse to move him.

Ahmed Evans was a Black nationalist leader from Cleveland, Ohio who was incarcerated in the infamous Southern Ohio Correctional Facility. He died of cancer at the facility as a result of glaring medical neglect.

Marilyn Buck had to undergo a thyroidectomy as a result of medical neglect. Similarly, Silvia Baraldini was forced to suffer a hysterectomy due to misdiagnosed cervical cancer. During his 5 years in solitary at MCU, Sundiata Acoli was heavily exposed to tuberculosis. Kuwesi Balagoon died in a New York State correctional facility from AIDS when he received little to no medical attention. Although he exhibited all the tell tale signs of AIDS, he was not transferred to a medical facility until ten days before his death.

Visitation, Censorship, Religious Freedom, Legal Access and Personal Hygiene

Extensive background checks are done on all visitors for political prisoners. This includes legal and social visitors. These visits are closely monitored by prison officials and sometimes denied for fabricated reasons. Prisoners in federal custody are only allowed to visit with their attorneys, immediate family and those individuals with whom they were friends prior to their incarceration. The obvious hardship this works on prisoners serving lengthy sentences is that with each passing year, they grow further away from developing new friendships.

Legal and social visitors are usually harassed by prison officials in an effort to discourage them from visiting. Frequently family members, friends and lawyers travel many miles to visit a prisoner only to be told that they have not followed some procedure that either does not exist or has already been complied with to the letter.

Social visiting time is reduced with no explanation. Legal visiting rooms often times are not made available to lawyers and paralegals. Frequently, without notice to the prisoner or the visitor, the visitor's name is removed from the prisoner's visiting list thereby preventing the visitor from gaining access to the prison until a new background check is done. Although the check can be completed in less than 24 hours, visitors and prisoners are usually told that it will take 6 to 8 weeks to complete a background check. Ricardo Jiminez has only been allowed 5 visitors on his list.

All social mail is read and most, if not all, is photocopied. Received as part of the discovery in the D.C. Resistance Conspiracy case were photocopies of all social mail received by Susan Rosenberg and Timothy Blunk. In addition, they received photocopies of the envelopes for all legal mail. It is widely believed that legal mail is also read and photocopied. Carlos Torres was told that all of his letters had to be written in English or they would be returned to the sender. He was also told that all of his phone conversations must be in english so they could be monitored. Ultimately he was placed on restrictive correspondence and only allowed to write to his parents, sisters and his wife. The women at Lexington HSU were only allowed to correspond with a pre-approved list of people.

Reading material is sanctioned according to the whim of the institution. Political materials come under heavy scrutiny. In some prisons, books may only come in if they are sent by the publisher or a book store.

There are many irrational rules and restrictions imposed on the exercise of religious freedom. Particular targets of this sort of harassment are Muslims, MOVE members, Native Americans and prisoners who refuse to cut their hair for religious reasons.

Generally, prisoners who are held in solitary confinement are not afforded adequate opportunities to shower. Showers are allowed at the whim of the guards. Clothing is limited and clean clothing is difficult to obtain.

It is very difficult for political prisoners and prisoners of war to remain in regular contact with lawyers if they are in solitary confinement. Phone access to lawyers is extremely limited. *All* phone calls are monitored. When an attorney calls a prison requesting that their client be allowed to call their office, the message is usually not given to the prisoner or delivered days after the call was requested.

Conclusion

The pattern of harassment and torture to which political prisoners and prisoners of war are subjected is calculated to achieve the goals of the BOP and the U.S. government. In it's campaign of repression the government has exercised every available means to silence resistance. To their credit, our political prisoners and prisoners of war have remained steadfast in their commitment to their beliefs and to their people.

Thanks and credit for assistance in preparation of this paper is given to all political prisoners and prisoners of war, friends, supporters and lawyers who have been involved in this work over the years.

ENDNOTES

[1] Oscar Gamba Johnson, also an Atmore inmate convicted of participating in the rebellion, is serving a 148 year sentence. Mark Cook was sentenced to 40 years to life. Sekou Odinga was sentenced to life plus 40 years with a recommendation of no parole. Prior to her liberation, Assata Shakur and Sundiata Acoli were both sentenced to life plus 30 years. She is now living in exile in Cuba. Kuwesi Balagoon was serving a 25 year to life sentence prior to his death in 1985. Sa'eed (Robert) Joyner and Ahmad Abdur Rahman are both serving natural life sentences. Mutulu Shakur was sentenced to 60 years. Silvia Baraldini is serving a 46 year sentence. Susan Rosenberg and Timothy Blunk were sentenced to 58 years for weapons possession. Tommy Manning is serving 53 years and his co-defendant, Ray Levasseur is serving 45 years. Alejandrina Torres and Linda Evans are each serving 35 year sentences. Eddie Hatcher was sentenced to 18 years. Jean Gump was sentenced to 8 years for her activities in the disarmament movement.

[2] Geronimo ji Jaga (Pratt) has been held for 20 years. Jalil Muntaquin, Dhoruba Bin-Wahad (prior to his release), Seth Hayes and Nuh Washington have all served 19 years already. Herman Bell has served 18 years and Sundiata Acoli, who had a bright future as a mathematician and computer analyst, has served 17 years.

[3] The following techniques were also suggested by Dr. Schein:

1. Spying on the prisoners and reporting back private material.
2. Tricking men into written statements which are then shown to others.
3. Exploitation of opportunists and informers.
4. Convincing the prisoners that they can trust no one.
5. Treating those who are willing to collaborate in far more lenient ways than those who are not.
6. Punishing those who show uncooperative attitudes.
7. Preventing contact with anyone non-sympathetic to the method of treatment and regimen of the captive populace.
8. Disorganization of all group standards among the prisoners.
9. Preventing prisoners from writing home or to friends in the community regarding the conditions of their confinement.
10. Placing individuals into new and ambiguous situations for which the standards are kept deliberately unclear and then putting pressure on them to conform to what is desired in order to win favor and a reprieve from the pressure.
11. Placing individuals whose will power has been severely weakened or eroded into a living situation with several others who are more advanced in their thought reform and whose job it is to further the undermining of the individual's emotional supports which was begun by isolating him from family and friends.
12. Meeting all insincere attempts to comply with cell mates pressures with renewed hostility.
13. Repeated pointing out to prisoner by cell mates of where he was in the past, or is in the present, not even living up to his own standards or values.
14. Rewarding of submission and subservience to the attitudes encom-

passing the brainwashing objective with a lifting of pressure and acceptance as a human being.

15. Providing social emotional supports which reinforce the new attitudes.

4 When a bogus investigation of escape charges commenced, he was snatched during the early morning hours and thrown in administrative segregation. Shortly thereafter, he was moved to a new special housing unit (SHU) built at Leavenworth on the model of Marion. Sekou remained in SHU after the investigation cleared him of escape allegations. After 9 months of being held in solitary confinement at Leavenworth, Sekou was returned to Marion. He spent a month in the control unit there, and then was moved to D Block, which is a 23 hour lock-down.

5 He finally worked his way up to the honor block which precedes a transfer to another facility. While on honor block, Oscar was framed and keys and a knife were found planted in his cell. He was sent back to one of the tight security blocks and his challenges to the frame-up were dismissed. As a result, his stay at Marion has been prolonged.

6 Judge Parker's order closing HSU was eventually reversed by the Circuit Court. However, the BOP simply readied Marianna as a substitute for Lexington.

7 Like Sekou, he was also placed in administrative segregation during an investigation of the same fabricated escape charges. He spent 6 months in SHU before being returned to general population.

8 James "Blood" Miller spent over 6 years at Marion before his release in 1989. Hugo A. Dahariki Pinell, one of the Soledad Brothers, spent 20 years in solitary confinement. Nuh Washington spent 7 years in solitary and Geronimo Pratt spent 8 years in segregation. Prior to her liberation, Assata Shakur spent 20 months in solitary confinement, often housed in men's facilities.

9 Chui Ferguson is a Moorish American and part of his religious observance includes not cutting his hair.

10 To exacerbate the feeling of isolation, the state Department of Corrections has denied him conjugal visit privileges.

Patriotic Hypocrisy
by Daphne Leroy

Patriotic hypocrisy

Buries black bodies

And welcomes white ones

On the subhuman shores of

Howard beaches and Crown Heights with

Waves of David Duke disasters and

Yusuf Hawkins horrors

Pushing Haitian hysteria sinking

With a trail of blood and betrayal

Like slave ships sent to the highest bidder.

A Major Step in

GENOCIDE

The Crime Bill by Kai Lumumba Barrow

Historical Overview

The concept of Genocide is as complex as the term is controversial. The word and definition was coined during World War II by the Polish-American scholar Raphael Lemkin who believed that Nazi persecution of Jews and other groups called for an international code on the subject.

Lemkin's formulation of genocide determined non lethal acts that undermined the liberty, dignity and personal security of a group, which included attacks on political and social institutions, culture, language, national feelings, religion and the economic existence of a group. Ethnocide (a term coined by the French to describe the disappearance of a group without killing) also qualified as genocide under Lemkin's definition.

Illustration by Ademola

In 1948, the United Nations General Assembly approved the convention on the crime and punishment of genocide. The UN definition significantly narrows Lemkin's concept, altogether eliminating ethnocide.

The definition reads as follows:

Article II: *In the present convention, genocide means any of the following acts committed with intent to destroy, in whole or in part, a national, ethnicidal, racial or religious group such as:*

(a) Killing members of the group;

(b) Causing serious bodily or mental harm to members of the group;

(c) Deliberately inflicting on the group conditions of life calculated to bring about its physical destruction in whole or in part;

(d) Imposing measures intended to prevent births within the group;

(e) Forcibly transferring children of the group to another group.

The UN Genocide Convention states that perpetrators of any one or more of the above acts will be punished as genocide, a crime. Despite the lack of economic, educational and social service resources in most Black communities, the international community does not hold the United States government accountable for the crime of genocide committed against black people.

Dissatisfied with the UN definition of genocide, many schools have redefined the concept, primarily based upon the perpetrator's motives.

One such scholar, Vahakn Dadrian, defines genocide as a social and economic problem, raising related questions of collective perception and collective denial. Dadrian offers the following definition:

Genocide is the successful attempt by a dominant group, vested with formal authority and/or with preponderant access to the overall resources of power, to reduce by coercion or lethal violence the number of a minority group whose ultimate extermination is held desirable and useful and whose respective vulnerability is a major factor contributing to the decision for genocide.

Dadrian's examines power relationships between perpetrator groups and victim groups, establishing a five-category classification of genocide including (1) *cultural genocide*, in which assimilation is the perpetrators aim; (2) *latent genocide*, in which the perpetrators actions have unintended consequences; (3) *retributive genocide*, designed to punish a segment or minority of the group that challenges the dominant group; (4) *utilitarian genocide*, using mass killing to control economic resources; and (5) *optimal genocide*, in which the chief aim of the perpetrator is the total elimination of the group.

How do blacks in America describe their present conditions and experience in this context? Do we define our experience as ethnocide, a concept that evokes even less response on an international level than does genocide? Do we point to the more recent phenomena of "Black on Black" crime as fratricide? To do so is synonymous with blaming the victim.

Historically, *criminalization* of the intended victim group is one key factor perpetrators use to begin the gradual process of genocide. To gain society's approval, perpetrators must harden their citizenry to the intended victim group. In this manner, perpetrators are able to rationalize their actions. The victim group is portrayed as the aggressor – out of control; "savage redskins," "sub-human animals." Prior to inflicting genocide, Nazis spent some twenty years convincing Germans that Jews were sub-human aggressors who must be stopped.

Criminalization of the victim group is usually a major step in the genocidal process, an overview of the criminal justice system – with specific focus on the recently proposed Crime Bill – follows.

The Crime Bill

On November 19, 1993, the Senate passed H.R. 3355, "The Violent Crime Control and Law Enforcement Act of 1993" (the "Crime Bill") by an overwhelming vote of 95-4.

The House of Representatives has yet to pass a similar bill. Recently, the House Judiciary Committee reported that a series of measures have been combined into one single package, H.R. 4092, "The Violent Control and Law Enforcement Act of 1994." The Crime Bill is now one massive bill that was expected to be passed by the House in August 1994.

The Crime Bill contains a number of repressive amendments including an *expansion of the death penalty for well over 60 crimes* including drug offenses that do not involve murder; *"three strikes" provision*, sentencing those convicted of three felonies to automatic life imprisonment without parole; *trying juveniles as adults*, allowing children as young as 13 years of age to be prosecuted for numerous federal offenses including robbery and assault; *deportation of non-permanent resident immigrants* convicted of aggravated felonies, and a *$22.68 billion "Violent Crime Reduction Trust Fund"* to finance the legislation.

The trust fund includes *$3 billion in funding for the construction and operation of regional prisons and boot camps*, touted as militaristic-styled, disciplined alternatives to incarceration for young, non-violent first time offenders. Additionally, the bill establishes a *new federal anti-gang statute with mandatory minimum penalties of five years.*

Some of the most disturbing aspects of the Crime Bill significantly impact upon our youth. In examining genocide, who better to attack than children and youth? The mass media contributes largely to our perception of Black youth as a sick, immoral, abusive and criminal bunch. Though crime and violence among young adults is as real as it is alarming, the media exploits our children – portraying them as "sub-human" aggressors who must be stopped.

Crime cannot be separated from other social and economic issues. Many studies reveal that those communities with the lowest levels of social service and economic development are also those most victimized by criminal acts.

The homicide rates for young Black men are staggering. In 1991, the rate for Black males between the ages of 15-24 was 158.9 per 100,000 compared to 16.9 per 100,000 for their white counterpart. *Every six hours a Black male teenager, 15-19 years old is murdered.* Throughout the world, young Black men in the United States are viewed as a criminal class. Whenever a (young) Black male is arrested, the collective perception assumes he is guilty. Even young brothers themselves are buying into this thought. Many view prison as a rite of passage. *The Coming of Black Genocide and Other Essays* (Vanguard Press, 1993) states, "Criminalization channels the instinctive rebellion and need for survival of Black youth back against their own people. Particularly back against themselves. It concedes the legitimacy of white authority while breaking its laws."

As options for the future become more remote, anger and criminal acts become more prevalent natural responses.

Though we are victimized by crimes within our communities, the Crime Bill proposes "solutions" which are at best, ineffective. Even liberal and grassroots proposals aimed at providing conflict resolution, education, jobs and training for young adults have been virtually ignored in favor of tougher and more costly "law and order" measures.

Programs such as Job Corps., HeadStart, teen pregnancy prevention, high school dropout prevention and guaranteed college scholarships have proven effective in reducing crime at less costs. Studies show that for every $1.00 put into the Job Corps. programs, $1.45 in future expenses for each participant is saved. HeadStart shows $4.75 reduced costs for every $1.00 spent. Further, Job Corps. has proven to be one-third effective in reducing crime. The numbers are also significantly high for HeadStart.

However, none of these programs appear as "glamorous" as the Crime Bill; the society is primed for blood. The mass media and politicians have exploited every available opportunity to present an unrelenting portrait of criminals at every stop light, in every subway, and behind every rock waiting to pounce on the next easy mark.

Three Strikes

Under the three strikes provision, the Crime Bill proposes automatic life imprisonment for those convicted of committing violent felonies, which is not only limited to the attempt, threat or actual physical force against a person, but also includes the attempt, threat or actual physical force to *property.* Further, in another version of the three strikes provision (also included in the bill), a violent felony includes the above-mentioned language as well as felony drug offenses.

The only drug which carries a felony sentence for simple possession is crack cocaine. Currently federal narcotics law mandates a minimum sentence of five years for the possession of five grams of crack cocaine. Powdered cocaine mandates sentences for a minimum of five years for the possession of 100 grams.

In 1992, the discriminatory element of this law became clear when a study conducted by the U.S. Sentencing Commission stated that Blacks comprise 91.3 percent of those sentenced for federal crack cocaine offenses, while whites comprised only 3 percent. Despite statistics revealing that whites have a much higher proportion of crack use (64.4 percent) compared to Blacks (26.6 percent) and Latinos (9.22 percent).

Statistics reveal that persons over the age of 60 commit only one percent of serious crimes. Yet under "three strikes", taxpayer money will continue to house inmates for a lifetime. Considering the average costs of $20,000 a year per inmate, under the "three strikes" provision, estimates range between $600,000 and $700,000 to keep one person in jail for life.

This does not include the costs of medical care due to aging. Critics of the bill contend that it will waste billions of taxpayer funds and will do little, if anything, to reduce crime.

Racial Disparities in the Crime Bill

The proposed Crime Bill would severely impact upon people of color in the United States. Race is often used as a significant factor in determining whom is followed, detained, searched and arrested as well as the length and type of sentence imposed. A Florida study examining the state's Habitual Criminal Law found that of the 47,000 prosecuted, *the decision to prosecute was based on race alone.*

One provision will eliminate the requirement of a hearing prior to deportation of "aliens" convicted of certain crimes. This will severely impact Africans, Carribbeans, Latinos, Arabs and Asians; the selective "aliens".

All criminal penalties will disproportionately affect Native Americans, as Native lands are subject to federal criminal jurisdiction.

Moreover, as a result of the "war on drugs" local police and federal resources are often concentrated in inner-city communities, which are overwhelmingly Black and Latino. Thus, the potential for Blacks and Latinos to be subjected to criminal convictions more so than their white counterpart is highly probable.

The composition of state prisoners is currently 48 percent Black and 14 percent Latino. Assuming that these proportions will continue, the proposed funding for new prisons will house approximately 49,000 additional Black males and 14,000 Latino men above current levels. Black men are incarcerated in prisons and jails at a rate of 3,370 per 100,000 compared to an overall population of 455 per 100,000.

This bill will not make society any safer. However, many people in our communities feel under siege. They view the Crime Bill and the "tough on crime" posturing by politicians as a solution for their day-to-day survival. In Chicago, for example, residents of housing projects will be subjected to periodic "sweeps" by police searching for illegal drugs and weapons. Though many feel the "sweeps" are a violation of their rights, they are frustrated. "I'm sick of the guns and drugs" said one resident, "better safe than sorry."

Throughout the United States, grassroots groups are staging "Take Back Our Streets" campaigns. Who are the target of these efforts? Our children. The criminalization of our youth has caused us to fear our own offspring. Our future. We are prepared to go to war against our children, without even attempting to target the system that nurtures their behaviors.

States *The Coming of Black Genocide* ... "Ya can't understand 'Black-on-Black' crime without finally accepting that genocide is a real thing...the cycles of killing and ripping each other off; of children killing themselves with dope and guns overtaking the Black community is not normal crime. It is beyond crime."

Much of the funding for the Crime Bill will divert money away from social programs, reducing funding for human rights: food, clothing, shelter, medical care and education. If the Crime Bill passes into law, we can expect an even higher percentage of poverty and depression – the primary reasons for crime.

Further, given the already "sub-human" treatment African Americans receive at the hands of the criminal justice system, which has been well documented, the bill makes generalizations that are ripe for prosecutorial misconduct.

The Crime Bill: impact on youth

•The Crime Bill authorizes *$500 million to the Bureau of Prisons to establish and operate secure facilities for violent and chronic juveniles.*

•The bill authorizes *bonus grants to states that develop "bindover" systems to prosecute violent juveniles as young as 13 in courts with jurisdiction over adults.*

•The bill mandates that *juveniles as young as age 13 can be prosecuted as adults for certain federal offenses. Their fingerprints will be filed with the FBI and other federal law enforcement agencies.*

•The bill authorizes *$3 billion in funding for the construction and operation of regional prisons for violent offenders and boot camps.* States which agree to impose the federal sentencing guidelines, mandatory minimum penalties and pre-trial detention would be eligible for this money. Juveniles most likely convicted of drug trafficking or violent crimes could be mixed with adults. Youth and adults have been separated in prison facilities since 1899, with the start of the juvenile court system. As for boot camps, a recent National Government Association study showed youth sent to boot camps commit more crimes once released, than those placed on probation.

•The bill mandates that *parents or legal guardians of juveniles charged with a federal offense must attend all court sessions.* If the court determines the parent did not exercise "reasonable" control of the child, parents will be forced to perform community service. *Parents of any juvenile convicted of a federal offense will be liable to pay up to $10,000 and/or perform community service.*

•The bill establishes a new *federal anti-gang statue with minimum mandatory penalties. Those who attempt or commit gang crimes; conspire to our participate in criminal street gangs within a 10 year period are subject to federal sentences between five and 20 years incarceration, life imprisonment or the death penalty.* The Crime Bill does not substantively define what constitutes a gang member, but gives sweeping descriptions. Groups of five or more exhibiting the following five traits:

1)Requires formal membership with required rules;

2)Has a recognized leader;

3)Has common clothing, language and/or tatoo;

4)Has a turf where the group is known, and

5)Has a group name.

It has been argued that sports team fraternities/sororities would qualify as a gang if two or more of its members committed a crime, either individually or in concert, within a 10 year period. The anti-gang provision mirrors the arbitrarily used Racketeer Influenced and Corrupt Organization (RICO) Act. *It should be flagged as potentially dangerous for revolutionary and/or activist organizations.*

Police agencies throughout the U.S. have developed computerized rosters of gang members and their "affiliates." These rosters are used to track alleged gang members and strongly indicate that race, class, neighborhood and culture, not conduct, often characterize a person as a gang member.

In Los Angeles, 47% of the county's Black men are considered gang members, though nearly half of those tracked have no arrest record. In Denver, police records of gang members list 93% as Black or Latino. Blacks, only representing 5% of the residents, account for half of the names on the list. Whites who make up 80% of the city's residents, accounted for less than 7% of the list.

Black Women on Death Row

by Rebecca Billips

Is capital punishment a fitting punishment or an unnecessary evil?

Rebecca Billips was a former prisoner in Muncey State Prison for three years. Convicted on four counts of forgery, she received a 40 year sentence. However, she escaped three times from Muncey and her sentence subsequently escalated to 52 years. On her last escape she was out in "society" and gainfully employed, for 17 years. Her original charge was vacated after capture and she received seven years probation. On her escape charges she was paroled after serving 13 months probation.

Both the female death sentencing rate and the female death row population remain very small in comparison to that for males. Actual execution of female offenders is quite rare, with only about 520 documented instances, with the first in 1632. These 520 female executions constitute less than 3% of the total of approximately 18,600 confirmed executions since 1608.

The First and the Last:

Bathsheba Spooner has the distinction of being the first female executed in America. Bored after ten years of marriage to Joshua Spooner, a squire, thirty-two year old Bathsheba took Ezra Ross, a passing soldier returning from a battle as her lover. The thought of murdering her wealthy husband occurred to Bathsheba and she tried to convince Ross to perform the deed. The young man was squeamish and Bathsheba enlisted the aid of two passing British soldiers. They bashed Mr. Spooner over the head cracking his skull and threw his body down a well. They were not clever men. All three men were found days later wearing Spooner's clothing and carrying other personal property belonging to the victim. In the first capital case of American jurisdiction in Massachusetts, the three men and Bathsheba were convicted and sentenced to death. The four murderers were hanged at Worcester, Massachusetts on July 2, 1778.

The last female executed was Velma Barfield, a 54 year old White female convicted for the poisoning death of her spouse, she was executed in North Carolina on November 2, 1984. Prior to this current era, the last female offender executed was Elizabeth Ann Duncan, executed in California on August 8, 1962 for the contract murder of her pregnant daughter-in-law.

Of the 101 death sentences imposed upon females since 1973, only 39 sentences (imposed upon 36 females) remain currently in effect. Aileen Wuornos, a 33 year old White female hooker murdered four men, she was sentenced to four death sentences in Florida in 1993. The press has listed Wuornos as America's first female serial killer. This is not true. As far back as I have researched, Sarah Jane Robinson deserves this label. Mrs. Robinson immigrated from Ireland to Boston, Massachusetts in the 1860s. She was convicted and given a life sentence for five murders. Two were her own children, five other children and her husband died of mysterious illnesses, she died in prison in 1905.

Two years after slavery was abolished in New York State, Catharine Cashiere, a Black female servant got drunk and stabbed another female to death. Her death would have gone unnoticed had she not been executed along with a young White male, who some felt wasn't quite right in the "noggin". Both were hanged on Blackwell's Island May 7, 1829.

Age is no deterrent when it comes to the death penalty. Ray and Faye Copeland, an elderly farm couple married 50 years, was sentence to death in Northern Missouri for five murders. They are the oldest couple ever sentence to death in America. Mr. Copeland at the time of his conviction was 75 years old, Mrs. Copeland was 69 years old. Now at age 74, Mrs. Copeland sits alone on death row with double grief, her husband died of natural causes, October 19, 1993.

Two highly publicized female cases in the 1950s were that of Ethel Rosenberg and Barbara Graham. Ethel and Juluis Rosenberg were found guilty of conspiracy to commit war time espionage. The Rosenbergs were executed June 19, 1953. Their co-defendant, Morton Sobell, the brother of Ethel, testified against his sister, and was given a 30 year sentence, he was released in 1969.

Barbara Graham, along with two male companions was executed in California on June 3, 1955 for the fatal pistol beating of Mrs. Monohan, an elderly woman, for the purpose of stealing her jewels. Mrs. Graham actually did the killing. The murder was in vain, there were no jewels. Susan Hayward won the 1958 academy award for best actress for her portrayal of Mrs. Graham in the movie "I Want to Live."

Of the 36 females on death rows there are 22 White, 11 Black and three Hispanics. Here I have listed the 14 women of color and a brief synopsis of their case:

• Alabama has three females on death row, two are white. Louise Harris, at the age of 34 was sentenced to death for the contract murder of her husband on March 11, 1988 in Montgomery.

• California has four females on death row, one Latino and one Black. On June 10, 1993 Catherine Thompson was sentenced to death in California for the contract murder of her husband on June 14, 1990.

• Maria Del Rosia Alfaro was only 18 years old at the time of her crime. She is now 22 years old. She was sentenced to death on July 14, 1992 in Anaheim, California. for burglary, robbery and the murder of a nine year old child.

• Florida also has four females on death row. Ana Cardona, a 30 year old Cuban woman was sentenced to death for the murder of her three year old son in Miami Beach, on April 1, 1992.

• Illinois has five females on death row, the highest of the 14 states. Geraldine Smith was 39 years old when she hired a hit man to kill her lover's 37 year old wife in Chicago in June 1987; Smith was sentenced on February 20, 1991.

• Dorothy Williams' case is like too many of the women I was incarcerated with in Pennsylvania. Like Williams, these women robbed and murdered elderly women and men, some of the murderers were employees of these unfortunate victims. Ms. Williams was 35 years old at the time she robbed and murdered a 97 year old woman in Chicago.

• The youngest female on death row in Illinois and also the last to be sentence to death as of August 1994, is now 23 years old: Latasha Pulliam was 19 years old when she murdered a six year old neighbor. She was sentenced on June 5, 1994.

• Marilyn Mulero, now 24 years old, was only 20 years old when she murdered two men in Chicago.

• Debra Denise Brown is the only female on death row in Indiana. At the age of 21, Ms. Brown was more of a follower than a murderer. Unfortunately, she chose to follow her lover; he chose to rape, rob and murder. One victim was only seven years old. Ms. Brown aided and abetted her lover by conning young women to enter her lover's car. She was convicted for the murder of the seven year old victim in Gary, Indiana on June 23, 1986. She was also sentenced to death in Ohio but that sentenced was commuted in 1991.

• In 1985, Paula Cooper, a 15 year old Black female, robbed, and fatally stabbed, 78 year old Mrs. Ruth Pelke, a White female. This vile murder also happened in Gary, Indiana. The vicious part about this circumstance is it was reported that the woman was always giving Paula and her friends money; she would feed them and let them stay at her home. Paula and another teenage friend showed their appreciation by torturing, murdering and robbing her. July 1989 the Indiana Supreme Court barred Cooper's execution. The Pope even got in on the act, writing to Governor Orr asking for mercy for Cooper.

• In Nevada, Priscilla Ford, is also a lone female on death row, she is also the oldest Black female on death row. Ms. Ford was 51 years old when she drove her car upon a crowded sidewalk in Reno and ran down 29 people on Thanksgiving Day of 1980, six people died. In an interview with Dr. Lenore Walker in 1989 Ms. Ford states "I've never been sorry about what I have done."

• There are four females on death row in Oklahoma. Wanda Jean Allen is the only Black woman. At 29 years old she was convicted for the murder of another female.

My saddest memory of prison is of a 17 year old Pittsburgh woman found guilty of murder and bank robbery in Harrisburg, Pennsylvania and sentenced to death in 1969. Being that I was (naturally) in maximum security because of my numerous escapes this young woman being on death row was housed in my unit. After the U.S. Supreme Court abolished capital punishment in 1972 her death sentence was commuted to life imprisonment. As of this writing, October 1994 she is still incarcerated.

• As of July 1993 there are three females on death row in Pennsylvania, two are black. Donnetta Hill at the age of 23, murdered a 72 year old Asian man on June 20, 1990 in Philadelphia, unfortunately she was not apprehended immediately. Less than a year later on March 24, 1991 she murdered a 21 year old man. She was finally caught and sentenced to death on July 1, 1993.

• Delores Rivers, also from Philadelphia, and like Ms. Hill is on death row in Muncy Prison. Rivers was 34 years old when she murdered Mrs. Carol (Shaky) Baker, a 74 year old female for money to buy drugs. Mrs. Baker is cousin to a very close friend of mine.

Ms. Rivers' sister-in-law is serving a life sentence at Muncy. The sister-in-law fatally stabbed a White woman sitting on her porch enjoying a warm evening. The victim was also a stranger to the murderer. The sister-in-law's brother is serving a life sentence at the Huntingdon Prison for the murder of their 18 year old nephew. The sister-in-law was also my number six cell mate in 1988.

• Frances Elaine Newton is one of four females on death row in Texas, and the only Black female. At the age of 21 she poisoned her 23 year old husband, seven year old son and her two year old daughter for insurance money. She was sentenced to death in Houston, Texas on November 11, 1988.

Five States, Arizona, Indiana, Mississippi, Nevada and Tennessee, have one female each on death rows. Of the five there are two Black females.

This is only a list. I have not attempted to analyze the repression of Black women in U. S. society.

Although women's response to violence, poverty and repression has never been as explosive as men's, with the continued implementation of supposed crime reduction apparatuses, like the new Crime Bill – which is poised to further divide the Black family – coupled with society's continued degradation of the Female Principle, we can expect an increase in our sisters arriving on Death Row.

After A Long Time

(after Ai)
by Staci Rodriguez

I've heard of women's lips
cracking to pieces
not remembering
the smell
the taste
the feel
of a man
lips deteriorating
After a Long Time
I knew a young woman
victim of idle sex
victim of a child
she avoided the birth
and destruction of her future?
she fell
victim to a botched abortion
her mind cracked to pieces
her lips cracking to pieces
no love
could
even cause
your lips
to dry and break
After a Long Time.

i Can't Promise Anything: Struggling in Puerto Rico

by **Ronald Fernandez**

The following is excerpted from Ronald Fernandez's new book *Prisoners of Colonialism: The Struggle For Justice in Puerto Rico*

The judge was Irish. So much so that instead of the stars and stripes, Judge James Bailey flew Ireland's green, white, and orange. Court watchers claimed he was a sympathizer of the Irish Republican Army, a revolutionary organization that produced support, contempt and controversy whenever anyone discussed the bloody streets of Belfast, Northern Ireland.

Luis Rosa saw the flag. He didn't know what to expect but he knew it wasn't empathy when two sheriffs began to punch and kick him right in front of the judge and his flag. The sheriffs used force because Luis Rosa and Alicia Rodriguez shouted "*Viva Puerto Rico libre*" (Long live a free Puerto Rico) when they entered Chicago's Cook County Courtroom on April 25, 1980. Their passion produced similar shouts from the many spectators who, even before the defendants appeared, had received orders to stand at attention until the judge gave them permission to sit.

Disobedience had no place in James Bailey's courtroom. As two sheriffs grabbed Ms. Rodriguez by the chin and neck, pushed her head backwards and dragged her from the room, another three sheriffs continued to punch and kick the now bloody Luis Rosa. Meanwhile, Judge Bailey, "screaming and waving his hands" ordered that spectators be removed from the courtroom and the courthouse. They could return to their neighborhoods or take a flight to Puerto Rico, but they were not staying in a Cook County judicial facility.

One of the lawyers got arrested when he pleaded with sheriffs to stop beating Mr. Rosa. They continued to kick Luis, and then, under the judge's orders, they grabbed Attorney Brian Glick. The presumed charge was contempt of court, later disregarded when Judge Bailey released the attorney without pressing formal charges.

Mr. Rosa and Ms. Rodriguez faced life in prison. Along with nine others, they were apprehended on April 4, 1980. Police spotted a stolen truck near the campus of Northeastern University and arrested Luis and Alicia when they tried to enter the vehicle. It looked like a simple car theft until anxious residents told police they spotted a number of other people walking in and out of a van parked in the vicinity. Officers rushed to the scene and immediately arrested nine people dressed in jogging suits. At the time police had no idea what was planned; later they said it was "an as yet unknown terrorist action." But, whatever the group's goal, the six men and five women were arrested with a stolen truck, several stolen vans and cars, 13 weapons, and a number of disguises and false identifications.

The specific charges filed against Luis Rosa and Alicia Rodriguez included armed robbery of the two vans, unlawful possession of weapons, transportation of a stolen vehicle across state lines and seditious conspiracy because they were allegedly members of the FALN, the Spanish acronym for the Armed Forces of National Liberation.

Sedition is a federal offense. Since the 1920s, *no one* except Puerto Rican revolutionaries went to trial for "conspiring to overthrow, put down, or destroy by force the government of the United States." In this case, all the arrested Puerto Ricans were charged with seditious conspiracy, but, in what attorneys believed was an effort to create informers, only Alicia and Luis received the special treatment offered by Judge Bailey and his assistants. For example, "while Luis and I always experienced physical and psychological abuse," Alicia recalls "that the other compañeros(as) were escorted into a deliberation room for the entire trial. While the only thing in our bullpen was a cold cement floor, the others sat in chairs around a large table and with a bathroom in the adjoining room. Even though the only one of us who had a toilet was Luis, his was in clear view of every passerby. What separated us was only a thin metal sheet."

Marrying everyday abuse and humiliation to serious federal *and* serious state charges, the government hoped to get what it wanted: reliable information about a group that had, among other things, bombed military establishments and taken over the Chicago campaign offices of President Jimmy Carter.

One initial problem with the government's approach was the attitude of the defendants: Claiming the status of prisoners of war, they refused to participate in the judicial proceedings. Indeed, one reason for the actions in Judge Bailey's courtroom was his contempt for a political position that had a long and respected history in the Caribbean. For more than eighty years, many Puerto Ricans had challenged a claim made by Senator Albert Perkins on April 2, 1900. He told his colleagues in the Senate that Puerto Rico came under the U.S. flag as "a prize of war." Perkins said this was legal; the islanders who were a battlefield reward said this was nonsense. They argued that U.S. authority was always illegitimate because, among other reasons, no Puerto Ricans had been asked if they wanted their homeland to be a piece of real estate for the Spanish or war booty for the Americans.

Luis and Alicia wanted to explain why they were prisoners of war.

Puerto Rico was a U.S. Colony, illegally invaded and maintained by force of conquest since July 25, 1898. Under international law, "anti-colonial combatants" had the right to use all legitimate forms of struggle, including armed struggle, to secure the independence of their country. The FALN took the war to the United States to help create a revolutionary conscience among the Puerto Rican people and to serve notice on Washington that colonialism was an intolerable political condition. Finally, they argued that it was absurd to believe that the colonizer could fairly judge his own crimes. To the defendants, only an international tribunal had legitimate authority to judge their revolutionary stance and their admittedly revolutionary activities.

Judge Bailey refused to let the accused speak. He removed their chosen legal advisor and imposed a public defender despite Luis Rosa's "knowing waiver and strenuous objection." When Attorney Michael Deutsch tried to explain the defendant's rights under international law, he was immediately threatened with contempt, and Judge Bailey ordered sheriffs to restrain Deutsch when the attorney tried to approach the bench. Meanwhile, Luis Rosa was sentenced to six months in jail for contempt of court. (He also later received a sentence of 30 years on the state charges to be followed by a 75 year federal prison term for seditious conspiracy and membership in the FALN.)

Alicia Rodriguez received special treatment. Perhaps it was the passion in her voice and eyes. Or her gender. Or some other factor which moved the judge to hold her over until the next day. Whatever the case, a jail employee warned Alicia she would be sentenced for contempt the following morning. That leak enabled Alicia to tell her family and legal advisors, they produced such a show of support that there was another confrontation before Alicia ever appeared in court.

When roughly forty friends tried to enter the courtroom, bailiffs not only barred their entrance, they forcibly removed them from the building. Alicia's supporters waited outside while attorneys Deutsch and Siegal tried to speak to the judge. He refused to see the attorneys; he barred Deutsch from entering the courtroom; and the judge failed to tell either attorney what he had already done with Alicia.

"They took me from my cell, walked me to a hallway, handcuffed me to a wooden chair outside the judge's chambers, and when he appeared he was foaming at the mouth; he looked like he wanted to eat me for lunch."

Judge Bailey had a question: "Are you going keep quiet today?"

Alicia had a response: "I can't make any promises."

The judge then ordered that Alicia be gagged.

"They stuffed two handkerchiefs in my mouth and then wrapped wide tape over my lips and surrounding areas. I felt violated when they muzzled me. I felt as if they were attempting to bury alive, not me – Alicia the person – but the revolutionary I had become. It goes without saying that rage and indignation accompany every *puertorriqueño* who views colonialism as unnatural and intolerable."

With tape and cloth, the judge thought he had silenced a strong-willed woman. What he didn't know (or, perhaps, care about) was that the Puerto Rican anti-colonial struggle was almost as old as the Irish; and, in both, one generation of revolutionaries learned from their predecessors.

Early in her incarceration, Alicia Rodriguez received a very significant visit from Lolita Lebron. In 1954, Ms. Lebron and three other Puerto Rican revolutionaries attacked the United States House of Representatives. As a result of an unconditional pardon, Ms. Lebron was released from prison in September of 1979. In public, President Carter suggested that humanitarian considerations motivated his actions, but in a memo stamped "secret" he had received this advice from National Security Advisor Zbigniew Brzezinski: "Lolita Lebron and three other Puerto Rican nationalists have been in federal prison for 24 years. "*No other woman in the Hemisphere has been in prison on such charges for so long a period; a fact which Communist critics of your human rights policy are fond of pointing out." Emphasis added.*

Ms. Lebron visited Alicia Rodriguez because the younger Puerto Rican had worked for years to "free the political prisoners." Chicago was the national headquarters of the effort that helped move President Carter to pardon the Puerto Ricans, and the neighborhood center where Alicia worked was proudly named after Rafael Cancel Miranda, another of the four revolutionaries who shot at U.S. congressmen in 1954.

During their visit in Chicago, Ms. Lebron offered Alicia this advice: Make use of all the educational opportunities available in prison and, in the meantime, "lotion yourself up."

Alicia did as she was told. She entered the "no spectators allowed" courtroom gagged, taped, handcuffed from behind, and accompanied by three "big" deputies. Attorney Mara Siegal explained the defendant's position: "This court does not have jurisdiction to try her. She is a prisoner of war. It is her demand and the demand of all her friends that they be transferred to an international tribunal where their case can be heard and they be adjudged as prisoners of war. This is an outrageous display of the United States' cruel and inhumane treatment..."

The judge interrupted. He ordered the attorney arrested for contempt, fined a thousand dollars, and held in the Cook Country jail until the fine was paid. The bailiffs removed the attorney. No one knew about the lotion on Alicia's face.

"I was pressed up against a table in the courtroom. I was spread-eagled, handcuffed from behind, and on either side of me a deputy was stepping on my feet. They were trying to muzzle me like a dog but, thanks to the lotion, the tape loosened. I could speak. I told the judge he was an

 imperialist and, before I could say another word, three guards punched my nose, jabbed my eyeballs, and punched me in the back." Meanwhile, Sheriff Rita Geoghegon made this remark: "Ms. Rodriguez is nothing but a Communist terrorist and should be shot."

The judge, once again outraged, ordered that Alicia be "retaped." She was removed from the courtroom, the tape (which held tight in some places) was ripped off and "this time they put three handkerchiefs in my mouth before they fastened the tape over my lips and around my head. I was taken back to court, forced to once again assume the position in front of the wooden table, and I immediately tried to talk. I couldn't do it. So I tried again. Still no words. But, there was no way they were going to keep me quiet. I had to do something." Alicia began to hum. And she continued the humming until the infuriated Judge Bailey gave up. He ordered Alicia removed from the court, and she was immediately placed in a holding cell near Attorney Mara Siegal. The two women waited while Michael Deutsch once again tried to speak to the judge.

Deutsch's first job was to get his law partner out of jail. But he had no written arrest order from which to appeal. When he went to ask Judge Bailey to put his contempt order in writing, he was met by a burly judge who, leaving his desk, told Deutsch, "I'm going to throw you out of the fucking window, motherfucker." Deutsch made a strategic retreat, and, still without an appealable order, field a complaint with the Judicial Inquiry Board and the Appellate Court of Illinois which subsequently reversed Mara Siegel's contempt citation and denounced the treatment of Alicia Rodriguez as "an affront to the dignity and decorum of judicial proceedings.

There was an affront, alright. And a crime. But it was not merely to the dignity of the court. Luis and Alicia argued that the proceedings themselves were no less an affront to the dignity of the Puerto Rican people than the hated presence of the "Black and Tans" in Belfast or the Tories quartering their troops in Boston. The crime at the core of their case was neither robbery nor sedition; it was colonialism. It had existed in Puerto Rico for over five hundred years–first under the Spanish, and, since 1898, under the United States of America–and it added (and adds) a unique dimension to the charges against the Puerto Rican political prisoners who are at the center of this book.

Gags could never silence a revolutionary like Alicia Rodriguez. Nor could tape seal up the arguments she wishes to present to any international forum that will listen. Puerto Rico is the oldest colony on earth. She and the other prisoners are incarcerated on foreign soil, and subjected to cruel and unusual punishment. Most important of all, presidents from McKinley to Clinton have refused to honestly address an undeniable fact. Imperial politics is the key to any understanding of the actions, arrests, convictions and treatment of the Puerto Rican revolutionaries.

A *fourth* generation of Puerto Rican prisoners–*e.g.*, Carmen Valentin,

Ricardo Jimenez, Lucy Rodriguez first became involved in political activities while trying to free the third generation revolutionaries who, in 1954, opened fire on the House of Rep-representatives. And, of those who fired in 1954, at least one–Rafael Cancel Miranda–places his political roots in a 1937 attack on his parents, then struggling as members of the second generation of Puerto Rican revolutionaries.

This is a story which spans one hundred years. To fairly understand the prisoners, *Prisoners of Colonialism* begins in the year that, as Senator Millard Tydings acknowledged, "we acquired Puerto Rico by conquest."

Prisoners' Addresses

Antonio Camacho-Negron
No. 03587-069
FCI Mc Ken-Unit 2
P. O. Box 8000
Bradford, PA 16701

Alberto Rodriguez
No. 92150-024
P. O. Box 1000
Lewisburg, PA 17837

Luis Colon Osorio
Under House Arrest in
Puerto Rico

Edwin Cortes
No. 92153-024
P. O. Box 1000 (A-3 #503)
Leavenworth, KS 66048-1000

Elizam Escobar
No. 88969-024
P. O. Box 1500, Colorado 2
El Reno, OK 73036

Ricardo Jimenez
No. 88967-024
P. O. Box 1000
Lewisburg, PA 17837

Alicia Rodriguez
No. NO7157
P. O. Box 5007
Dwight, IL 60420

Ida Luz Rodriguez
No. 88973-024
5701 8th Street
Camp Parks
Dublin, CA 94568

Luis Rosa
No. NO2743
Box 711
Menard, IL 62259

Juan E. Segarra-Palmer
No. 15357-077
USP Atlanta
Atlanta, GA 30315

Alejandrina Torres
No. 92152-024
5701 8th Street
Camp Parks
Dublin, CA 94568

Carlos Alberto Torres
No. 88976-024
P. O. Box 1000
Oxford, WI 53952

Oscar Lopez Rivera
No. 87651-024
P. O. Box 1000
Marion, IL 62959

Norman Ramirez Talavera
No. 03171-069
Reybrooke
Lake Placid, NY 12977

Dylcia Pagan
No. 88971-024
5701 8th Street
Dublin, CA 94558

Roberto Jose Maldonado
No. 03588-069
Federal Medical Facility
3150 Horton Road
Fort Worth, TX 76119

Adolfo Matos Antongiorgi
No. 88968-024 Unit J
3901 Klein Blvd.
Lompoc, CA 93436

Carmen Valentin
No. 88974-024
5701 8th Street
Camp Parks
Dublin, CA 94568

In the Tradition George Jackson:

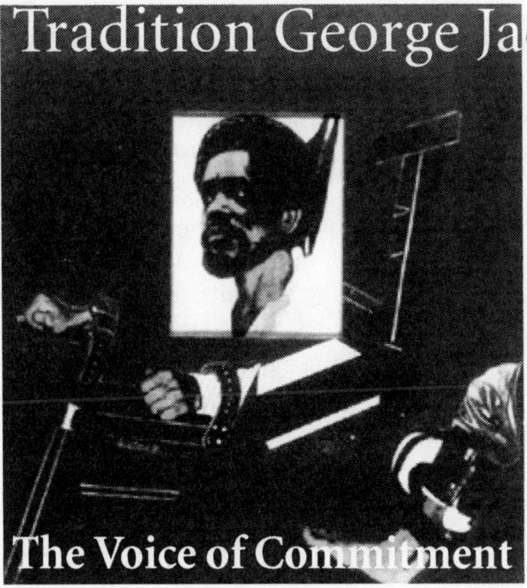

Collage by Ademola

The Voice of Commitment

The jacket flap of Monster: The Autobiography of a L.A. Gang Member *details the work by Sanyika Shakur (formerly Monster Kody Scott) as "one of the most remarkable and* important *documents "regarding the Black ghetto experience. It further compares* "Monster *to... George Jackson's* Soledad Brother *in its "power, poetry and* political resonance" [emphasis added].

The value of many written works can be considered comparable, specifically with nefarious intent by the comparee. But can the initial literate work of Sanyika Shakur be as politically resonant *as the initial literate work of George Jackson?*

Understandably, existence for Black men in the 1950s and 60s cannot be likened to the stepped up devastation of the Black male image and character in the 1980s and 90s. However, in Shakur's bodacious autobiography much more of his present day transformative ideas would have been welcomed, to give balance and thought to any young Black male who would be eagerly ingesting the bulk of his story (with is in agreement with today's pop culture): blood, dazzle and indifference. From Shakur's opus we fundamentally are apprised of gutter techniques on how to snuff Black male life. We trust Shakur will develop a book in line with, and beyond, the articles he has since written.

Jackson's education and development stemmed from being confined in prison for many years until his death, for simple, petty theft of $70 from a gas station and subsequent state machinations. In Soledad Brother, *his book of letters, Jackson reflected on his spiralling life conditions angrily and profoundly...*sharing *his observations with family members, friends and associates. While incarcerated he engendered much devotion from his younger brother, Jonathan–who later lost his young life in a serious attempt to jump-start the revolution–before Jackson was ultimately murdered in prison.*

To determine if an author's writings are truly efficacious, one revisits them after several years. Jackson in his masterwork, Blood In My Eye, *determined that "consciousness is the opposite of indifference, of blindness, blankness. Consciousness is knowledge, recognition, foresight; common experience and perception; sensibility, alertness, mindfulness."*

There cannot be a more telling prophetic quote on the divisive elements in today's Black Liberation struggle than the following from Blood In My Eye *(possibly written in reference to the battle waged between the Black cultural nationalists and revolutionaries of the 60s):*

"In the general retreat to avoid full commitment, to write the discomfort out of rev-

olution, some have raised a debate among us that has degenerated into name-calling, quoting the same authorities to validate diametrically opposed ideas, and ultimately creating a process that is dividing us into two mutually exclusive or contradictory groups, the overall effect is to reduce us to caricature."

Karen Wald, a well known activist and anti-imperialist in the 60s and 70s, interviewed George Jackson August 21, 1971, as a reporter for the Liberation News Service. *She has lived in Cuba since 1973. Below is that interview, which emphasizes Jackson's views on solidarity around prison and prison issues–inside and out. It reveals George Jackson, still, the preeminent voice of commitment to the Black Liberation struggle:*

Karen Wald: George, comment on your conception of revolution?

George Jackson: The principal contradiction between the oppressor and oppressed can be reduced to the fact that the only way the oppressor can maintain his position is by fostering, nurturing, building, contempt for the oppressed. That thing gets out of hand after a while. It leads to excesses that we see and the excesses are growing within the totalitarian state here. The excesses breed resistance; resistance is growing. The thing grows in a spiral. It can only end one way. The excesses lead to resistance, resistance leads to brutality, the brutality leads to more resistance, and finally the whole question will be resolved with either the uneconomic destruction of the oppressed, or the end of oppression. These are the workings of revolution. It grows in spirals, confrontations, and I mean on all levels. The institutions of society have buttressed the establishment, so I mean all levels have to be assaulted.

KW: How does the prison liberation movement fit into this? Is its importance overexaggerated or contrived?

GJ: We don't have to contrive any...Look, the particular thing I'm involved in right now, the prison movement was started by Huey P. Newton and the Black Panther Party. Huey and the rest of the comrades around the country. We're working with Ericka [Huggins] and Bobby [Seale, Chairman of the BPP; at the time they were co-defendants in a murder trial in New Haven, Connecticut, on charges which were subsequently dismissed], the prison movement in general, the movement to prove to the establishment that the concentration camp technique won't work on us. We don't have to contrive any importance to our particular movement. It's a real, very, very real issue and I'm of the opinion that, right along with the student movement, right along with the old, familiar workers' movement, the prison movement is central to the process of revolution as a whole.

KW: Many cadres of the revolutionary forces on the outside have been captured and imprisoned. Are you saying that even though they're in prison, these cadres can still function in a meaningful way for the revolution?

GJ: Well, we're all familiar with the function of the prison as an institution serving the needs of the totalitarian state. We've got to destroy that function; the function has to be no longer viable, in the end. It's one of the strongest institutions supporting the totalitarian state. We have to destroy its effectiveness, and that's what the the prison movement is all about.

 What I'm saying is that they put us in these concentration camps here the same as they put people in tiger cages or "strategic hamlets" in Vietnam. The idea is to isolate, eliminate, liquidate the dynamic sections of the overall movement, the protagonists of the movement. What we've got to do is prove this won't work. We've got to organize our resistance once we're inside, give them no peace, turn the prison into just another front of the struggle, tear it down from the inside. Understand?

KW: But can such a battle be won?

GJ: A good deal of this has to do with our ability to communicate to the people on the street. The nature of the function of the prison with the police state has to be continuously explained, elucidated to the people on the street because we can't fight alone in here. Oh yeah, we can fight, but if we're isolated, if the state is successful in accomplishing that, the results are usually not constructive in terms of proving our point. We fight and we die, but that's not the point, although it may be admirable from some sort of purely moral point of view. The point is, however, the face of what we confront, to fight and win. That's the real objective: not just to make statements, no matter how noble, but to destroy the system that oppresses us. By any means available to us. And to do this, we must be connected, in contact and communication with those in struggle on the outside. We must be mutually supporting because we're all in this together. It's all one struggle at base.

KW: Is the form of struggle you're talking about here different from those with which we may be more familiar with, those which are occurring in the Third World, for example?

GJ: Not really. Of course, all struggles are different, depending upon the whole range of particular factors involved. But many of them have fundamental commonalities which are more important than the differences. We are talking about a guerrilla war in this country. The guerrilla, the new type of warrior who's developed out of conflicts in the Third World countries, doesn't fight for glory necessarily. The guerrilla fights to win. The guerrilla fights the same kind of fight we do, what's sometimes called a "poor man's war." It's not a form of war fought with high-tech weaponry, or state-of-the-art gadgets. It's fought with whatever can be had–captured weapons when they can be had, but often antiquated firearms, homemade ordnance, knives, bows and arrows, even slingshots – but mostly through the sheer will of the guerrilla to fight and win, no matter what. Huey [P. Newton] says "the power of the people will overcome the power of the man's technology." and we've seen this proven true time and time after time in recent history.

You know, guerrilla war is not simply a matter of tactics and technique. It's not just questions of hit-and-run or terrorism. It's a matter of proving to the established order that it simply can't sustain itself, that there's no possible way for them to win by utilizing the means of force available to them. We have to prove that wars are won by human beings, and not by mechanical devices. We've got to show that in the end they can't resist us.

And we will! We're going to do it! There's never going to ever be a moment's peace for anyone associated with the establishment any place where I'm at, or where any of my comrades are at. But we're going to need coordination, we're going to need help. And right now, that help should come in the form of education. It's critical to teach the people out there just how important it is to destroy the function of the prison within this society. That, and to show them in concrete terms that the war is on–right now!–and that in that sense we really aren't any different than the Vietnamese, or the Cubans, or the Algerians, or any of the other revolutionary peoples of the world.

KW: In an interview with some imprisoned Tupamaros, urban guerrillas in Uruguay, the question was raised about the decimation of the ranks of Tuparmaros; comrades killed or imprisoned by the state. Those interviewed assured me that there were far more people joining the ranks than were being lost to state repression, and that the movement was continuing to grow. Do you feel the same confidence about the Black Panther Party, about the revolutionary movement as a whole in this country?

GJ: We're structured in such a way as to allow us to exist and continue to resist despite the losses we absorb. It was set up that way. We know the enemy operates under the concept of "kill the head and the body will die." They target those they see as key leaders. We know this, and we've set up safeguards to prevent the strategy from working against us. I know I could be killed tomorrow, but the struggle would continue, there would be 200 or 300 people to take my place. As Fred Hampton put it, "You can kill the revolutionary, but you can't kill the revolution." Hampton, as you know, was head of the Party in Chicago, and was murdered in his sleep by the police in Chicago, along with Mark Clark, the Party leader from Peoria, Illinois. Their loss is tremendous, but the struggle goes on. Right?

It's not just a military thing. It's also an educational thing. The two go hand-in-hand. And it's also a cyclical thing. Right now, we are in a peak cycle. There's tremendous energy out there, directed against the state. It's not all focused, but it's there, and it's building. Maybe this will be sufficient to accomplish what we must accomplish over the fairly short run. We'll see, and we can certainly hope that this is the case. But perhaps not. We must be prepared to wage a long struggle. If this is the case, then we'll probably see a different cycle, one in which the revolutionary energy of the people seems to have dispersed, run out of steam. But–and this is important–such cycles are deceptive. Things appear to be at low ebb, but actually what's happening is a period of regroupment, a period in which we step back and learn from the mistakes made during the preceding cycle. We educate ourselves and those around us from our experience. And all the while, we develop and perfect our core organization. Then the next time a peak cycle comes around, we are far readier than we were during the last time.

It's a combination of military and education, always. Ultimately, we will win.

KW: Do you see signs of progress on the inside, in prison?

GJ: Yes, I do. Progress has certainly been made in terms of raising the consciousness of at least some sectors of the prison population. In part, that's due to the limited victories we've achieved over the past few years. They're token victories perhaps, but things we can and must take advantage of. For example, we've struggled hard around the idea of being able to communicate directly with people on the outside. At this point, any person on the street can correspond with any individual inside prison. My suggestion is, now that we have the channels for education secured, at least temporarily, is that people on the outside should begin to bombard the prisons with newspapers, books, journals, clippings, anything of educational value to help politicize the comrades who are not yet relating. And we, of course, must reciprocate by consistently sending out information concerning what's really going on in here. Incidentally, interviews like this go a long way in that direction. There should be much more of this sort of thing.

KW: You disclosed a few months ago that you had been for some time a member of the Black Panther Party. Certainly, the work of the Party in this state and elsewhere, the work to free political prisoners, and of course the Party's work within the black community have been factors which influenced your decision. But has the internationalism of the Black Panther Party been one of the key aspects which attracted you to it? And, if this is so, is internationalism meaningful for people in prison, and is it therefore one reason why they'd relate to the Party?

GJ: Well, let's take it a step at a time. Huey came to the joint about a year ago because he'd heard stories about the little thing we had going on already. He talked with us, and checked it out, and he decided to absorb us. Afterwards, he sent me a message and told me that. He just told me that I was part of the Party now, and that our little group was part of the Party as well. And he told me that my present job is to build, or help build, the prison movement. Just like that. Like I said, the objective of our movement is to prove the state can't seal us off in a concentration camp, so I accepted. What else could I do? It was the correct thing.

Now, as to your second point, the people inside the joint, the convict class, have related to the ideology of the Party 100 percent. And we've moved from...well, not we, I've always been an internationalist. And a materialist. I guess I was a materialist before I was born. I'm presently studying Swahili to able to converse with comrades in Africa on their own terms, without having to rely on a colonial language. And I've been working on Spanish, which is of course a colonial language, but spoken by millions upon millions of comrades in Latin America and elsewhere. Then Chinese and possibly Arabic. When I complete this task, I will be able to speak to something like seventy-five percent of the world's people in their own tongue, or something akin to their own tongue. I think that's important.

The other brothers here are picking up on it. And there are some, especially those who are already politicized before they came inside, who are on top of it. But like I said, it's of utmost importance that people outside bombard this place with material which will help prisoners understand the importance of internationalism to their struggle. It's coming, but it's still got a way to go before the educational process is complete. Ignorance is a terrible thing and being cut off from the flow of the movement is really detrimental. We must correct the situation as a first priority.

KW: Can you receive mail and publications from other countries?

GJ: Mail can be received from anywhere on the globe. I get stuff right now from Germany and England and France as a result of the book being published in those countries. And a few copies of Tricontinental [a Cuban revolutionary journal] have gotten in. They've helped broaden the scope, and explained a few things to comrades that they didn't understand. This is something that really upsets the goons. In years past every time a black prisoner would achieve an intellectual breakthrough and begin to relate our situation to the situation of the Cubans, say, or the Vietnamese or the Chinese–or anywhere else in the Third World–well these prisoners would be quickly assassinated. Now that's become a little harder to do. So, I believe the people on the street should just start to flood the prisons with things like Tricontinental.

KW: Despite a few peaceful victories in Latin America, such as that of Salvador Allende in Chile, many people still believe that armed struggle is the only way most Latin American countries are going to be free. Also, there've been some recent victories in the courts for members of the Black Panther Party, Los Siete de la Raza, and so on. Do you believe the victories in Chile and the courts…

GJ: They were appeasement. Allende…the thing that happened with Allende…look, it was not a "peaceful revolution." That's deception. Allende is a good man, but what's going on in Chile is just a reflection of the national aspirations of the ruling class. You will never find a peaceful revolution. Nobody surrenders their power without resistance. And until the upper class in Chile is crushed, Allende could at any time be defeated. No revolution can be consolidated under the conditions that prevail in Chile. Blood will flow down there. Either Allende will shed it in liquidating the ruling class, or the ruling class will shed his whenever it decides the time is right. Either way, there's no peaceful revolution.

Much the same can be said for the court cases you're talking about. They're an illusion. Every once in a while the establishment cuts loose of a case–usually one which is so outrageous to begin with that they couldn't possibly win it without exposing their whole system of injustice anyway–and then they trot around babbling about "proof that the system works," how just and fair it is. They never mention the fact that the people who were supposed to have received the justice of the system have often already spend months and months in lockup, and have been forced to spend thousands of dollars, keeping themselves from spending years and years in prison, before being found innocent. All this to defend themselves against charges for which there was no basis to begin with, and the state knew there was no basis. Some system. You get your punishment before your trial in this country if you happen to be black or brown or political. But they use these things to say the system works – which I guess it does, from their perspective–and to build their credibility for the cases that really count, when they really want to railroad someone into a prison cell. The solution isn't to learn how to play the system for occasional "victories" of this order, although I'll admit these sometimes have a tactical advantage. Winning comes only in destroying the system itself. We should never be confused on this point.

KW: But the alternatives sometimes bear dire consequences. This raises the difficult question of the death of your brother, Jonathan, and whether his life may be a certain extent have been wasted.

GJ: Well, that's obviously a tough question for me because, emotionally, I very much wish my little brother was alive and well. But as to whether I think Jonathan's life may have been wasted? No, I don't. I think the only mistake he made was thinking that all of the 200 pigs who were there would have, you know, some sort of concern for the life of the judge. Of course, they chose to kill the judge, and to risk killing the DA and the jurors, in order to get at Jonathan and the others. It may have been a technical error. But I doubt it, because I know Jonathan was very conversant with military ideas, and I'm sure it occurred to him that there was a possibility that at least one pig would shoot, and that if one shot, they'd all shoot, and it'd be a massacre. Judge or no judge. It was all a gigantic bluff, you know? Jonathan took a calculated risk. Some people say that makes him a fool. I say his was the sort of courage that cause young men of his age to be awarded the Congressional Medal of Honor in somewhat different settings. The difference is that Jonathan understood very clearly who his real enemy was; the guy who gets the congressional medal usually doesn't. Now, who's the fool?

Personally, I bear his loss very badly. It's a great burden upon my soul. But I think it's imperative–we owe it to him–never to forget why he did what he did. And that was to stand as a symbol in front of the people–in front of me–and say in effect that we have both the capacity and the obligation to stand up, regardless of the consequences. He was saying that if we all stand up, our collective power will destroy the forces that oppose us. Jonathan lived by these principles, he was true to them, he died by them. This is the most honorable thing imaginable. He achieved a certain deserved immortality insofar as he truly had the courage to die on his feet rather than live one moment on his knees. He stood as an example, a beacon to all of us, and I am in awe of him, even though he was my younger brother.

KW: The news today said that Tom Hayden declared in front of the National Student Association Congress that there will be more actions like the one Jonathan attempted. Do you agree?

GJ: I've been thinking a lot about the situation. I'm not saying that these particular tactics–even when successfully executed–constitute the only valid revolutionary form at this time. Obviously, they don't. There must also be mass organizing activities, including large-scale nonviolent demonstrations, education of the least developed social sectors, and so on. These things are essential. The revolution must proceed at all levels. But this is precisely what makes the tactics necessary, and far too many self-proclaimed revolutionaries have missed the point on this score. Such tactics as Jonathan employed represent a whole level–an entire dimension–of struggle which has almost always been missing from the so-called American scene. And while it is true that armed struggle in-and-of-itself can never achieve revolution, neither can the various other forms of activity. The covert, armed, guerrilla dimension of the movement fits hand-in-glove with the other dimension; the two dimensions can and must be seen as inseparable aspects of the same phenomenon; neither dimension can succeed without the other.

Viewing things objectively, we can readily determine that the overt dimension of the movement is relatively well-developed at this time. Over the past dozen years, we've seem the creation of a vast mass movement in opposition to the establishment in this country. I won't go into this in any depth because I'm sure that everyone already knows what I'm talking about. It should be enough to observe that within the past two years, the movement has repeatedly shown itself able to put as many as a million people in the streets at any one time to express their opposition to the imperialist war in Indochine [this seems to be a reference to the November 1969 Moratorium to End the War in Vietnam, staged in Washington, D.C.]. The covert dimension of the movement is, by comparison, very much retarded at the present time. In part, this may be due to the very nature of the activity at issue: guerrillas always begin in terms of very small numbers of people. But, more to the point, I think the situation is due to there having been a strong resistance to the whole idea of armed struggle on the part of much of the movement's supposed leadership–particularly the white leadership–up to this point. I hear them arguing–contrary to history, logic, just plain common sense, and everything else–that armed struggle is unnecessary, even "counterproductive". I hear them arguing in the most stupidly misleading fashion imaginable that the over dimension of the movement can bring off revolution of its own. This is the sheerest nonsense, and "leaders" who engage in such babble should be discarded without hesitation.

We may advance a simple rule here: the likelihood of significance social change in the United States may be gauged by the extent to which the covert, armed, guerrilla aspect of the struggle is developed and consolidated.

If the counterrevolutionaries and fools who parade themselves as leaders while resisting the development of the movement's armed capacity are overcome–and the struggle is therefore able to proceed in a proper direction–I think we will see revolutionary change in this country rather shortly. If, on the other hand, this leadership is able to successfully do what amounts to the work of the state–that is to say, to convince most people to shy away from armed struggle, and to isolate those who do undertake to act as guerrillas from the mass of support which should rightly be theirs–then the revolution will be forestalled. We will have a situation here much the same as that in Chile, where the establishment allows a certain quality of apparent social gains to be achieved, but stands ready to strip these "gains" away whenever it's convenient. You can mark my words on this: unless a real revolution is attained, all that's been gained during the struggles of the past decade will be lost during the next ten years. It might not even take that long.

At the present time, I see a number of very hopeful signs–very positive indications–that a true revolutionary force is emerging. Most notably, of course, the direction taken by the Black Panther Party is correct. But there are many other examples I could name. Even in the white community, we have been the development, or at least the beginnings of the development, of what is necessary with the establishment of the Weatherman organization. We clearly have a long way to go, but it's happening, and that's what's important at the moment. The very fact that Tom Hayden, who is of course a white radical himself, was willing to make the statement he made, and before the audience to which he made it, indicates the truth of this. So, yes, I tend to agree with him and hope we are both correct. Clear enough?

KW: Yes. Do you see a relationship between what happened at the Marin County Civic Center, what Jonathan and the other brothers did, and the kinds of things that happen in the Third World, say, in Latin America?

GJ: Well, of course. Jonathan was a student of...he was a military-minded brother. He was a student of Che Guevarra and Ho, and Giap and Mao, and many others. Tupamaros, Carolos Marighella. He paid close attention to other established guerrillas, other established revolutionary societies, revolutionary cultures around the world. He was very conscious of what was going on in South America and, well, let's just say that about ninety-nine percent of our conversation was centered on military things. I knew him well. He understood.

KW: I was going to ask if the Cuban revolution had significance for you and Jonathan in any concrete ways.

GJ: Hmmmm...I don't think it did for Jonathan. But it did for me, because I was in prison. I was just starting my time on this beat right here when Castro, Che and the rest carried the revolution there to a successful conclusion. And the alarm that spread throughout the nation, especially, you know, within the establishment and the police...well, let's just say that as a newly-made prisoner I enjoyed that a lot. Someone else's liberation at the establishment's expense, it was a vicarious boost at a time when I most needed it. And I've always felt very tenderly toward the Cuban revolution as a result.

KW: So you weren't an anti-communist when you came into prison?

GJ: Oh, I've never been an anti-communist. I suppose you could say I didn't have much understanding of communism when I came in, and so I wasn't pro-communist in any meaningful way. But I was never "anti."

KW: But didn't you initially find it terrible that Cuba had "gone communist"?

GJ: No-no-no! That's what I'm trying to tell you. I'm trying to get across that I've always been fundamentally anti-authoritarian. Communism came later. And when the Cuban revolution happened, the very fact that it upset the authorities here so bad made me favor it right off and made me want to investigate it much further. The idea was that if they don't like it, it must be good. You see? And that's what led me to seriously study socialism. I owe much of my own consciousness to the Cuban revolution. But that's me. It doesn't necessarily pertain to Jonathan. Okay?

KW: Did the fact that such a tiny country so close to Florida pulled off a successful revolution tell you that, "If they can do it, we can do it"?

GJ: Yes, both then and now. It caused me to consider the myth of invincibility. You know, the idea of U.S. military invincibility was just completely destroyed by the Cuban revolution. The U.S. supported Batista with rockets and planes, everything he needed, and he still lost. He was destroyed by guerrilla warfare, the same thing that's taking place in Vietnam right now. And the U.S. is losing again. The Viet Cong, I mean they take these gadgets–the best things the best military minds in the western world can produce–they take them and they ball them up and they throw them right back in the face of these imperialist fools. Cuba and now Vietnam; these things catch my attention. I try to learn the lessons from other peoples' success. Now, in that sense I'm sure the Cuban revolution had significance for Jonathan, too.

KW: I see our time is almost up. Do you have any last remarks?

GJ: Yes. I'd like to say Power to the People! And I'd like to say that by that I mean all power, not just the token sort of power the establishment is prepared to give us for its own purposes. I'd like to say that the only way we're ever going to have change is to have the real power necessary to bring the changes we want into being. I'd like to say that the establishment is never going to be persuaded into giving us real power, it's never going to be tricked into, it's never going to feel guilty and change its ways. The only way we're ever going to get the power we need to change things is by taking it, over the open, brutal, physical opposition of the establishment. I'd like to say we must use, as Malcolm X puts it, any means necessary to take power. I'd like to say that we really have no alternatives in the matter, and that it's ridiculous or worse to think that we do. That's what I'd like to say.

This is for 82B2034 & 77A4283

by Yvette Love Davila

Ghetto version
of the
Fresh Air Fund
Operation Prison Gap Style

5:30 in the A.M.
I'm at Columbus Circle
asking myself
"why am I here?"

Why am I standing
at Columbus Circle
at 5:30 in the morning
in sub-zero degree weather
waiting for a bus,
which will cost me $25
I don't have,
a bus that will probably be late/
break down/
and be over crowded
with women...
Mothers/ Sisters/ Lovers/ Cousins/ and Friends.
And every single woman
on that bus
is going to visit
an innocent man.

Dona Margot
cannot be told
her baby is not innocent.
She would be the first
to call him a
"hijo de puta",
but
"bendito, mi hijo no hizo nada mal",
follows it immediately.
She doesn't think twice
about the fact that
he was almost killed
while robbing a store
right around the corner
from her house.

All those women
have an innocent tale to tell

about their loved ones...
even though
their loved ones
were caught with a smoking gun
in their hands

CHARGED GUILTY
by a jury of their peers
and sentenced to
the PEE-NAL upstate.
All those brothas were/ are GUILTY!
GUILTY of being Black men
in racist Ameri**kkk**a.
GUILTY of living under
such oppressive conditions
that they lash out at
their neighbors, families and friends.
ALL GUILTY!
ALL GUILTY!
ALL GUILTY!

And
as I sit on the bus,
still asking myself,
"why am I here?"...
they're all
AFRIKANA & LATINA.

Sistas who are,
once again, are left
HUSBAND**LESS/**
FATHER**LESS/**
SIBLING**LESS/**
FRIEND**LESS**?
by an institution
whose sole mission
is to do just that.

THE 13TH AMENDMENT DIDN'T FREE THE SLAVE
IT JUST CHANGED THEIR NAMES TO INMATE...
THEREFORE, JUSTIFYING THE INSTITUTION OF SLAVERY!!!
How else can we explain,
The Black Codes--Ameri**kkk**a's apartheid system...
&
The Convict Leasing Program!!!!

So, once again
my sistas are left

with no other choice,
but to embrace
DADDY WELFARE CHECK
for better or for worse--usually for worse
for richer or for poorer--usually for poorer
till death do they part--death usually comes early.

As the roar
of the bus' engine
signals our departure
from Columbus Circle,
I still ask myself
"why am I here?",
but I settle in my seat
and anticipate
the 2 hour ride ahead of me.

I am suddenly transported
to the status of tourist
as I
OOOH & AHHHH
at the sight of
trees & farms
animals & streams
mountains & Main Street, U.S.A.

Just then,
my sight seeing exhibition
comes abruptly to a halt
with an announcement
from the bus driver
telling us we have
reached our destination.
I am overwhelmed by
the reality of
PLANTATION LIFE.

I see
Bob wired fences/
neighboring THE BIG HOUSE
I see
Gun towers
and overseers w/ guns (ooops...correction officers)
ensuring that
the slaves (excuse me...inmates)
don't escape
and endanger the welfare of
the plantation owners (my bad...residents)

As us heifers
are corralled into the stables
they call "the processing room"
I still wonder
"why am I here?"
I start to trip
at the activity surrounding me.
The sistas who
boarded that bus with me,
the ones with
rollers in their hair/
whit shit around their mouths/
eye boogas/
jeans/
sneakers/
and sweatshirts,
were suddenly transformed to
Cinderellas on their way to the ball.
Myself,
and my Cinderella sistas
proceed to be
INTERROGATED/
HUMILIATED/
and DEGRADED
by CRACKAS
whose salaries I pay every two weeks.
We are
searched/
probed/
and prodded.
After all,
we ain't nothing more than
slave bitches...
according to them.
The saddest,
I must admit,
is going through this process
at the hands
of an eager HOUSE NIGGA.

Once again I ask myself
"why am I here?"

In the visiting room...
displaced families reunite/
distant lovers are finally within reach.
Making love is reduced to
an occasional jerk-off and finger-pop.

If you're lucky,
It'll be a festival day
which means he
actually gets to penetrate,
so that he doesn't have to
go back to his cell
to masturbate and dream...
at least for one day...
if you're lucky.

After sharing and enjoying,
5 hours of love and happiness
with my loved one
it's time to depart the plantation.
I could never help but cry
when I leave and leave them behind.
I always wish I could ball them up
and put them in my pocket.

As I turn to leave...
82B2034
kisses me/
hugs me/
and tells me he loves me.
77A4283
puts his right hand in a fist
and touches his heart
as a sign of his
revolutionary love.
And I,
stop asking myself
"why am I here?"

Published by Africa World Press
Volume II Number I
ISSN: 1056-683X

- *A Journal of salient political essays, artistic presentations and research from African Americans and people of African descent globally*

- *A timely Journal tackling the critical issues facing the freedom struggles of African-Americans and the African Diaspora*

- *A consistent Journal encouraging dialogue, debate and activist resolutions*

- *A Journal of high quality design with an eyegrabbing artistic flair featuring Black Artists from throughout the Black World*

NOBO means...

- *Helping to rebuild the Black Liberation Movement*

- *Analyzing fundamental social change in the US within the global context*

- *Continuing the tradition of progressive Black creativity*

Advisors and Contributors

◆*Muhammad Ahmad*
Activist/Scholar-Ohio

◆*Gisela Arrandia*
Activist Journalist-Cuba

◆*Mohammed Babu*
Editor-Africa World Review-London

◆*Asha Bandele*
Youth Activist/Writer-New York

◆*Amiri Baraka*
Activist/Writer-New Jersey

◆*Ashaki Binta*
Journalist/Activist-North Carolina

◆*St. Clair Bourne*
Activist Film Producer-New York

◆*Elombe Brath*
Patrice Lumumba Coalition-Harlem

◆*Linda Burnham*
Editor-Crossroads Journal-California

◆*Horace Campbell*
Activist Scholar-New York; Zimbalbwe

◆*Ron Daniels*
Activist/Writer-New York

◆*Angela Gilliam*
Activist Scholar-Washington

◆*Gerald Horne*
Activist Scholar-New York; California

◆*Ben Jones*
Activist/Artist-New Jersey; Cuba

◆*Howard "Stretch" Johnson*
Activist/Scholar-New York

◆*Keropetse Kgositsile*
Activist/Writer-South Africa

◆*Kathleen Cleaver*
Activist/Lawyer– Boston/New York

◆*Manning Marable*
Activist Scholar-New York

◆*Basir Mchawi*
Educator/Activist/Journalist-New York

◆*Rosemari Mealy*
Activist/Writer-Harlem

◆*Segundo Modibo*
Community Organizer-Georgia

◆*Modibo*
Community Organizer-New York

◆*Eric Perkins*
Activist/Scholar-Philadelphia

◆*Eugene Redmond*
Writer/Editor/Producer-Missouri

◆*A. Wanjiku Reynolds*
Activist/Writer-New York

◆*Louis Reyes Rivera*
Activist/Writer/Publisher-New York

◆*Sonia Sanchez*
Activist/Writer/Educator-Pennsylvania

◆*Tyree Scott*
Labor Activist-Washington; Mozambique

◆*Assata Shakur*
Activist/Scholar-Cuba

◆*Askia M. Toure*
Activist/Writer-Georgia

◆*Asiba Tupahache*
Activist/Writer-New York

◆*Tony Vandermeer*
Activist/Publisher-Massachusetts

◆*Patrice Wagner*
Educator/Journalist-New York

◆*Kalamu Ya Salaam*
Activist/Writer/Producer-Louisiana

nobonumbers

– with a serious nod to Harper's Index –

Average life expectancy of Africanamerican men: 65.6 years

Average life expectancy of white men: 73 years

Chances that a Black male under 35 is
within the criminal justice system: 1 in 4

Number of Africanamerican males jailed per 100,000: 3,109

Number of Black South African males jailed per 100,000: 729

Average number of days Blacks serve
longer than whites per year sentence: 72

Percentage of women prisoners who are Black or Latina: 60

Percentage of male prisoners who are Africanamerican: 50

Number of political prisoners in the US: 150

Chances that a prisoner on death row is Africanamerican: 2 in 5

Entry level hourly wage earned by a federal prisoner: 23¢

Percentage increase in California prisoner population
from 1983 to 1993: 400